The Negro
in Virginia Politics
1902-1965

The Negro

The University Press of Virginia
Charlottesville

in Virginia Politics

1902-1965

Andrew Buni

For A. Barr ''Whoops'' Snively

Preface

UNTIL recently the political role of the Negro in Virginia during the twentieth century has received little notice. Doubtless the major reason for this neglect has been the minimal participation of the colored race in politics. After the adoption of the state constitution of 1902, Negroes were deliberately disfranchised, mainly by the Democratic party "organization," using such means as the white primary, literacy tests, blank paper registration forms, and the poll tax. Colored citizens have also disfranchised themselves through their apathy, resignedly believing that politics is "white man's business." This feeling of indifference remained unchanged until after World War II.

Negroes, however, did have a prominent role in Virginia politics, though mainly in a negative sense, through the injection of the race issue by white politicians into campaigns. The Democrats employed this tactic with success against the Republicans for almost sixty years, from 1902 through 1961. On one occasion, however, the presidential contest of 1928, the G.O.P., not to be outdone by the Democracy, successfully accused the latter of attempting to build a Negro following for the Democratic nominee, Al Smith.

In the 1960's the elimination of the poll tax, the enactment of strong federal voting rights bills, and the growing miltancy of the Negro greatly increased his political importance. It is now recognized that his vote, as in the victories of President Lyndon B. Johnson in Virginia in 1964 and of Governor Mills E. Godwin in 1965, may be a significant element in future elections.

This volume is intended to be a political history. Detailed socio-economic factors influencing the politics have not been stressed. The author believes that such factors require a separate study, similar to *Race Relations in Virginia, 1865–1902,* by Charles E. Wynes, or to the more recent works dealing with the overall Southern political scene, *Negro Political Leadership in the South* by Everett C. Ladd, Jr., and *Negroes and the New Southern Politics* by Donald R. Matthews and James W. Prothro. This book also attempts to depict chiefly through their own eyes the role of the Negroes in Virginia politics. Primary sources have been difficult to obtain since few Negroes have kept extensive collections of personal papers. Much of the information, therefore, has been extracted from the two major Negro weeklies in Virginia, the Richmond *Planet,* which subsequently amalgamated with the Baltimore *Afro-American,* and the Norfolk *Journal and Guide.* Other data and views have been obtained from white daily newspapers, personal interviews with both Negro and white politicians, collections from private papers, official election returns, census reports, and other state and local collections.

For aid in gathering this material, I wish to express my thanks to the members of the staff of the Virginia State Library at Richmond, to those at the libraries at Virginia State College, Hampton Institute, and Howard University, but especially to Miss Helena C. Koiner of the Alderman Library, University of Virginia. I am further indebted to the tireless efforts of Miss Barbara Alden and Miss Marguerite L. Carder, reference librarians at Mary Washington College Library, and to its librarian and my colleague, Dr. Carrol H. Quenzel. Without the help and encouragement of Dr. Quenzel, it is doubtful that the manuscript would have been published. To Chancellor Grellet C. Simpson I am grateful for the financial support which secured for me the secretarial assistance of my typist, Mrs. Barbara Powell. While in the dissertation stage this study came under the critical analysis and close scrutiny of Professors Edward Younger and John Hammond Moore. For many helpful personal interviews I thank W. Lester Banks, Roscoe C. Jackson, Jr., Victor H. Ashe, Oliver W. Hill, Dr. William S.

Thornton, Benjamin Muse, and Moses Riddick, Jr., as well as numerous others not mentioned.

Finally, to my wife, Kelly, who maintained peace on the homefront throughout this effort, go my love and deep appreciation.

ANDREW BUNI

Fredericksburg, Virginia
December 1966

Contents

The Negro
in Virginia Politics
1902–1965

Prelude to Disfranchisement
1865-1902

VIRGINIA escaped some of the harshest aspects of radical Reconstruction in the South by accepting the provisions of the 1868 Underwood constitution. In a compromise engineered primarily by a former Whig congressman from western Virginia, Alexander H. H. Stuart, the state reconciled itself temporarily to Negro suffrage in return for the right to vote upon and defeat two other provisions of the proposed state constitution. One of these denied the suffrage to all persons who had held public office in the United States government and had then rebelled against that government during the Civil War. The other barred from public office anyone unable to take an oath that he had never held office in the Confederacy.[1] Through this compromise Negroes allied to the Republican party gained the vote, but few white Virginians lost theirs.

The Underwood constitution appeared to provide Negroes with a voice in the politics of the state. In 1867 their voting potential of 105,837 compared favorably with that of the whites at 120,-101.[2] In the General Assembly elected on July 6, 1869, 27 of the

[1] On the Underwood constitution see David L. Pulliam, *The Constitutional Conventions of Virginia from the Foundation of the Commonwealth to the Present Time* (Richmond, 1901), *passim;* Hamilton J. Eckenrode, "A History of Virginia since 1865; A Political History" (MS, Alderman Library, University of Virginia, n.d.), 50 ff.; Richard L. Morton, *The Negro in Virginia Politics, 1865–1902* (Charlottesville, Va., 1919).

[2] Morton, *Negro in Virginia Politics,* Appendix C. In 1870, there were 120,103 male Negroes eligible to vote. Doubtless this aided the Republican presidential victory in 1872, as Grant edged Greeley in Virginia by a 93,486 to 91,754 vote.

180 new members were Negroes: 6 in the senate and 21 in the house. In 1870 Negroes outnumbered whites in 40 of the 99 Virginia counties.[3]

Despite the Negro voting strength, representation in the legislature, and an appearance of moderation and amiability between whites and Negroes in the General Assembly, Conservative members attempted to curb the Negro politically. A law passed in 1870 required lists of qualified voters to be kept according to race, thus providing opportunities for voting officials to misplace or "lose" Negro voter lists at election time. Also, under the guise of reapportionment the gerrymander was employed by both the Conservatives and the Democrats who followed them in 1874–76, 1883, and 1891.[4] In 1876, in still another attempt to curb the Negro vote, an amendment to the constitution was passed making a poll tax a voting prerequisite and adding conviction of the crime of petty larceny as a disqualification for voting. It was expected that these two provisions would disfranchise many Negroes; however, the poll tax became such a source of fraud and corruption through its payment by dishonest politicians that it was eliminated by another constitutional amendment in 1882.[5]

The race issue also loomed large in Virginia political campaigns. Since the Negro allied himself with the party of emancipation, the Republicans came under attack by the Conservatives as being "the party of the Negro" and as endangering white supremacy in the Old Dominion. In the 1869 and 1871 campaigns the race issue played a minor role, but in the 1873 gubernatorial

[3] Luther P. Jackson, *Negro Officeholders in Virginia, 1865–1895* (Norfolk, Va., 1945), 5; Charles E. Wynes, *Race Relations in Virginia, 1865–1902* (Charlottesville, Va., 1961), 6–7.

[4] Wynes, *Race Relations in Virginia,* 7–8; Paul Lewinson, *Race, Class, and Party: A History of Negro Suffrage and White Politics in the South* (N.Y., 1932), 65; Richard B. Doss, "John Warwick Daniel: A Study in the Virginia Democracy" (Ph.D. dissertation, University of Virginia, 1955), 260–64.

[5] Ralph C. McDanel, *The Virginia Constitutional Convention of 1901–1902* (*Johns Hopkins University Studies in Historical and Political Science,* Series XLVI, No. 3; Baltimore, 1928), 6; C. Vann Woodward, *Origins of the New South, 1877–1913* (*A History of the South,* ed. by Wendell H. Stephenson and E. Merton Coulter, IX; Baton Rouge, La., 1951), 54–55.

election, when they believed they possessed the necessary political strength, the Conservatives clearly drew the color line. Amid the cries of "Shall the whites rule and take care of the Negroes, or shall the Negroes rule and take care of the whites?" the Conservatives elected ex-Confederate hero General James L. Kemper over Republican Robert W. Hughes. That year, with the aid of a three-to-one margin in both houses of the General Assembly, they also passed the poll tax amendment.[6]

By the time of the gubernatorial election of 1877 the Conservatives had become so firmly entrenched that the Republicans offered no candidate, and in 1878 both the G.O.P. and the Negro appeared to have been eliminated from Virginia politics. One historian claims that the Negroes had passed through "their first phase of political activity" and that, with the possible exception of the "black belt" Fourth Congressional District, as a class they had been reduced "to a position of impotence in the political life of the state." [7]

The "second phase" of political life for the Negro resulted, as had the first, from the need of his vote by white factions in a controversy among Conservatives over funding the state debt. The debt had been incurred by the state prior to the Civil War, primarily for internal improvements, and by 1869 amounted to $46,000,000. Conservative legislators who believed that the honor of the Commonwealth was at stake and who were sympathetic with bondholding creditors in 1871 passed the Funding Act, providing for payment in full. Other legislators considered payment of the entire debt to be unnecessary as well as highly burdensome. The state was divided among the partial-payment "Readjusters" and the full-payment "Funders." [8] The former claimed the alle-

[6] Edgar E. Noel, "John Lawson Kemper and the Virginia Gubernatorial Election of 1873," in University of Virginia, *Essays in History*, V (1958–59), 33–45 *passim;* Robert R. Jones, "James Lawson Kemper, 1823–1895" (Ph.D. dissertation, University of Virginia, 1964), *passim.*

[7] Wynes, *Race Relations in Virginia,* 14; McDanel, *Virginia Constitutional Convention,* 7.

[8] Charles C. Pearson, *The Readjuster Movement in Virginia* (New Haven and London, 1917); Nelson M. Blake, *William Mahone of Virginia: Soldier and Political Insurgent* (Richmond, 1935).

giance of white farmers, mainly from the western part of the state, "who opposed the debt-paying conservative-lawyer legislators" in their attempts to gain repayment for their clients, while the latter "represented the existing order, and their officeholders [consisted] largely of men from eastern and central Virginia." [9]

Initially, the Negro remained in the background, with both sides cautiously seeking his favor. Since the debt had been contracted during the antebellum slave days when they had no voice in the matter and payment in full meant higher taxes, along with curtailment of public school funds, the Negroes understandably favored the Readjusters. Aware of the danger of arousing the race issue, both the Readjusters and the Funders played down their search for Negro votes in the 1879 general elections. The result, a vote of approximately 82,000 to 61,000 in favor of the Readjusters, gave them control of the state legislature.[10] The Negro vote contributed to the Readjuster victory, which might have been even more decisive but for the poll tax prerequisite to voting. Two years later Negroes again sided with the Readjusters, and Governor William E. Cameron was elected over Funder John W. Daniel.[11]

Negroes were rewarded for their aid with minor offices and positions, such as the appointment of two of them to the Richmond School Board.[12] But nowhere did these favors amount to Negro rule, as the Readjusters were cautious in their use of the Negro as a political asset. In 1882 legislation pleasing to the Negro was easily pushed through a Readjuster-controlled legislature. The poll tax was abolished, as was punishment at the whipping post,

[9] Wynes, *Race Relations in Virginia,* 17–18; George McFarland, "Growth of Political Democracy in Virginia, 1865–1900" (Ph.D. dissertation, Princeton University, 1935), 136; William Larsen, *Montague of Virginia: The Making of a Southern Progressive* (Baton Rouge, La., 1965), 1–69 *passim.*

[10] Eckenrode, "Virginia since 1865," 124–40 *passim;* William M. Mabry, "The Disfranchisement of the Negro in the South" (Ph.D. dissertation, Duke University, 1933), 341–90 *passim;* Harry S. Ferguson, "The Participation of the Lynchburg, Virginia Negro in Politics, 1865–1900" (Master's thesis, Virginia State College, 1960), 32. There were three Negro senators and thirteen House members in the 1880 Assembly.

[11] Herman Lionel Horn, "The Growth and Development of the Democratic Party in Virginia since 1890" (Ph.D. dissertation, Duke University, 1949), 19–22.   [12] Eckenrode, "Virginia since 1865," 165.

which had been regularly inflicted upon Negroes. Virginia Normal and Collegiate Institute and a Negro asylum for the insane were established; closed schools were reopened; and teachers received back pay.[13]

Readjuster control lasted only until 1883. Its collapse has been attributed partially to internal corruption under the political machine dominated by General William Mahone. Moreover, by the time of the election of 1883 "the Readjuster party had largely fulfilled its destiny. Lacking a continued, liberal program, it fell apart from within while wrangling over the division of the spoils and future leadership." [14] Equally harmful were charges by the Funders of Negro domination and of recognition of the Mahone faction as a part of the national Republican party.[15]

In the 1883 general election the Funders, adopting the Democratic banner for the first time, drew the color line and made it the predominant issue. They were aided on November 4, just a few days prior to the election, by a major race riot in Danville. The melee apparently began after a Negro jostled a white man in the streets. It ended in a pistol and straight-razor fight killing one white man and four Negroes. The Democrats capitalized on the riot by attributing it to the fact that "the local government of a sizeable and populous area" was under Negro rule. A historian observed, however, that although Negroes had a majority of the city councilmen, four of the nine policemen, and the superintendent of the public market, this was hardly Negro domination when the mayor, judge, Commonwealth's attorney, city sergeant, constable, commissioner of revenue, and chief of police were white.[16]

[13] Wynes, *Race Relations in Virginia,* 22–23; James H. Johnston, Jr., "A History of Virginia State College" (MS, Virginia State College, June, 1963), 1–100 *passim.*

[14] McFarland, "Democracy in Virginia," 141–44; Blake, *William Mahone,* 225–30.   [15] Eckenrode, "Virginia since 1865," 171.

[16] *Ibid.,* 182–85; Charmion Woody Higgenbotham, "The Danville Riot of 1883" (Master's thesis, Virginia State College, 1955), 1–45 *passim;* John T. S. Melzer, "The Danville Riot, November 3, 1883" (Master's thesis, University of Virginia, 1963). For the viewpoint that Negroes did indeed control much of Petersburg's government, see Allen W. Moger, "The Growth of the Democratic Machine in Virginia," *Journal of Southern History,* VIII (May 1942), 190.

The news of the riot spread rapidly throughout the state and doubtless aided the Democrats in winning two-thirds of the seats in the state legislature. According to one source, this sweeping victory marked the end of the Readjuster party. A number of its white members returned to the Democratic party, but the majority became Republicans, thus forming battle lines for the future.[17]

Fearful of intimidation, the Negro stayed away from the polls. One witness described the situation in Halifax Court House as follows:

They [the Funders] have carried the election here by fraud, intimidation, shooting and cutting the negroes. The funders went to the election . . . swearing they would kill the negroes. The negroes have no protection here. They are scared now and I think most of them would leave the country if they could.[18]

Voting fraud was common during these years, nor did it diminish throughout the period to the 1900's. Both parties practiced it and dishonesty became a major reason for the calling of the constitutional convention in 1901. J. D. Clay wrote his political ally Mahone:

We have lost at least 160 negro votes by the committee striking off names from the Registration books . . . and at least 60 votes by the funders paying them from $2 to $5 to stay home and not vote . . . the funders had their whiskey by the five gallons and made a number of negroes drunk and led them to the polls like sheep to the slaughter . . . we have no one to prosecute the offenders.[19]

With the decline of the Readjuster party, the second phase of the Negro in Virginia politics ended. Male Negroes over 21 years of age approximated 128,000,[20] however, and the Democrats were determined that another era like that from 1879 to 1883 should

---

[17] Horn, "Democratic Party in Virginia," 26–27.

[18] J. D. Clay to William Mahone, Nov. 12, 1883, Mahone Papers, Duke University, cited in Wynes, *Race Relations in Virginia,* 33.

[19] *Ibid.;* William Francis Cheek III, "The Forgotten Prophet, The Life of John Mercer Langston" (Ph.D. dissertation, University of Virginia, 1961), 295–328 *passim.*

[20] *The Warrock-Richardson Almanack for the Year 1890* (Richmond, 1891), 37.

not reoccur. In its attempts to curb the Negro politically, the Democratic majority reapportioned congressional districts and enacted the Anderson-McCormick election law over the veto of Readjuster Governor William Cameron. This act provided that in 1884 and every four years thereafter three "freeholders" would be elected for each city and county to appoint local election officials. The law was invalidated by the Virginia Supreme Court of Appeals for violating the state constitution and establishing a freehold or landholding qualification. Undeterred, the legislature forced Governor Cameron to call a special session and in December 1884 enacted a bill similar to the original one except for the deletion of the freehold requirement.[21] This measure enabled the Democrats to control city and county electoral boards as well as the registrars and election judges. But, though it denied the vote to most Negroes, it also led to wholesale fraud among factions of the Democratic party. In an attempt to remedy that situation, another election law was passed in 1894.

Despite the 1883 setback and the 1884 election restrictions, it was estimated that the Republicans could muster between 63,000 and 87,000 Negro votes in 1885,[22] potentially enough to elect their gubernatorial candidate John S. Wise over Democrat Fitzhugh Lee. In a close election, in which both sides were accused of fraudulent practices, Lee, the popular ex-Confederate general and nephew of Robert E. Lee, won by the narrow margin of 8,000 votes.[23] In assessing the degree of corruption and fraud, perhaps it is safest to conclude that, though both parties were guilty, Democratic control of the election machinery tipped the balance toward

[21] Most of the work was that of a white supremacist, Delegate William A. Anderson of Rockbridge County, who was State Attorney General from 1902 to 1910 and played a key role in Negro disfranchisement cases. Lois G. Moore, "William Alexander Anderson: Attorney-General of Virginia, 1902–1910" (Master's thesis, University of Virginia, 1959), 22–23.

[22] "A Statement on Behalf of the Delegation of Which General Mahone is Chairman to the Republican National Convention at Chicago, June 3, 1884," in James D. Brady Scrapbook, 2 vols., University of Virginia; undated Richmond *Whig,* cited in Eckenrode, "Virginia since 1865," 200.

[23] Eckenrode, "Virginia since 1865," 195–203; Wynes, *Race Relations in Virginia,* 41–42.

Lee. The Democrats gained a more impressive victory in the state legislature, capturing 29 of the 40 senate seats and 72 of the 100 house seats. Negro representation plummeted to one senator and one delegate.[24]

After 1885 the Democrats had the governor, a majority of state legislators, and a predominance of election officials and thus were able virtually to exclude the Negro and his party from Virginia politics. Surprisingly, though, in the heavily Negro-populated Fourth Congressional District, Negroes displayed temporary strength in the 1888 congressional election. There colored leaders had attempted earlier to nominate a candidate for Congress and in 1884 ran Joseph D. Evans of Petersburg as an independent. He was badly defeated.[25] Four years later John Mercer Langston sought the regular Republican nomination. Born in Louisa County, reared in the North, and educated at Oberlin College, this illegitimate son of a white planter and a freed slave had served in the Civil War as a Negro recruiter. After the war he was professor and dean of the Howard University Law School, United States Minister to Haiti, and subsequently the President of Virginia State College.[26]

General Mahone blocked Langston's nomination and forced the latter to run as an independent Republican against Democrat Edward C. Venable and regular Republican Judge R. W. Arnold. Amid frantic pleas by the Democrats that Langston must be defeated to save Southern civilization, the Negro was ruled second to Venable in an election rife with fraud and vote buying. Langston demanded a recount, and after a lengthy investigation by the United States House of Representatives was declared the winner by the narrow margin of 209 ballots out of the 29,174 cast.[27]

---

[24] William Edward Larsen, "Andrew Jackson Montague" (Ph.D. dissertation, University of Virginia, 1961), I, 75–76; Jackson, *Negro Officeholders in Virginia,* 81.

[25] Jackson, *Negro Officeholders in Virginia,* 46; Cheek, "John Mercer Langston," 246.

[26] Cheek, "John Mercer Langston," 122–244; George Washington Crawford, "John Mercer Langston, a Study in Virginia Politics, 1880–1890" (Master's thesis, Virginia State College, 1940), 109.

[27] Cheek, "John Mercer Langston," 244–328 *passim.*

Because of the lengthy investigation Langston served only from the last week of the regular 1890 congressional session through March 3, 1891, of the lame-duck session. In November 1890 the Democrats elected J. F. Epes by a vote of 13,325 to 9,991 in a congressional district with 13,770 whites and 19,855 Negroes eligible to vote.[28] The Democrats insisted it was no longer a question of party politics "but rather whether intelligence or ignorance should rule, whether civilization should be preserved, in short, whether the white man or the negro should rule the Commonwealth of Virginia." [29] They accused the Langston faction of fraudulent practices in the 1888 election and of favoring the Force Bill pending in Congress in 1890. This bill provided for supervision of congressional elections by federal officers to check increasing restrictions on Negroes' political rights in Southern states.[30]

In 1891, for the first time since the adoption of the Underwood constitution, no Negroes served in the General Assembly. Only three Republicans remained.[31] Two years earlier Mahone had made the last major G.O.P. bid for the governorship, but neither white Republicans nor the Negroes gave him solid backing. The General had alienated such lieutenants as John S. Wise and former Readjuster Governor William E. Cameron. Moreover, his opposition to Langston's candidacy in 1888 and his insistence that Negroes be "made to understand that they must take a back seat and let their white bosses and political masters run the machine and have all the offices" lost him most of the colored vote.[32] Thus, it was not surprising that the Democratic candidate, Philip W. McKinney, defeated the Republican by about 42,000 in a total vote of 284,-000. After this drubbing the Republicans offered no candidate for governor in 1893. "Gone was not only the Mahone era, but

[28] *Ibid.,* 337–47; *Warrock-Richardson Almanack for the Year 1889,* 36.
[29] Richmond *Dispatch,* Nov. 2, 1890, cited in Cheek, "John Mercer Langston," 343.
[30] Allen W. Moger, *The Rebuilding of the Old Dominion: A Study in Economic, Social, and Political Transition from 1880 to 1902* (Ann Arbor, Mich., 1940), 29.
[31] *Warrock-Richardson Almanack for the Year 1892,* 38.
[32] Wynes, *Race Relations in Virginia,* 45; Eckenrode, "History of Virginia since 1865," 228.

two-party government as well. The Democratic party was in complete control." [33]

During the 1890's, however, with the flurry of Populism in the Old Dominion, the Negro temporarily regained a modicum of political influence. Populism, the grass-roots revolt of farmers, attracted not only the small white farmer but also men of means and distinction who opposed the low prices of crops, scarcity of cash and credit, and railroad monopolies. But this reform movement did not extend to the recognition of Virginia Negroes as political equals. Populists who may have coveted their votes were also aware of the stigma of being branded as the "party of the Negro." Even the poor white farmers, discontented with the Democrats, reluctantly remained with the latter when the race issue was injected into the political campaigns of the 1890's. One source asserts that the Populists did not seek a Negro alliance in order to dispel the charges of befriending Negroes. As proof of this, not even one Negro attended the 1892 Virginia People's Party Convention.[34] Another authority on race relations maintains that, though the Populists offered the only serious threat to the Democrats during the 1890's, much of their strength came from white Republicans who believed they could defeat the Democrats through the People's movement. He supports his position by pointing out that in 1893, when the Populist candidate Edmund R. Cocke received 81,239 votes to Democrat Charles T. O'Ferrall's 127,940, only one-third of the 132,697 male Negroes over 21 years old voted, and it was the white Republicans who swelled the Populist total.[35] Also, since the Populists were so wary of seeking Negro support, many colored

[33] *Warrock-Richardson Almanack for the Year 1895*, 65–66; Horn, "Democratic Party in Virginia," 30, 33.

[34] William D. Sheldon, *Populism in the Old Dominion: Virginia Farm Politics, 1885–1900* (Princeton, N.J., 1935), 87–88, 101; Helen M. Blackburn, "The Populist Party in the South," (Master's thesis, Howard University, 1941), 45.

[35] Charles E. Wynes, "Charles T. O'Ferrall and the Virginia Gubernatorial Election of 1893," *Virginia Magazine of History and Biography*, LXIV (Oct. 1956), 451; *Warrock-Richardson Almanack for the Year 1890*, 37; *ibid., 1897*, 76–81.

voters turned to the Democratic party. One group, the Negro Democratic League, asserted it was to their best interest to follow "that class of white people that own and control everything." It was hardly surprising "that with the Republican party a virtual nullity and Negroes' support unsolicited and discouraged by the Populists, large numbers of Negroes turned to the Democrats in furtherance of what appears to be their best interests." [36]

Thus, during the early 1890's, if not welcomed within the Populist fold, Negro voters sought renewed allegiance with the G.O.P. and also with the Democrats. [37] And despite attempts of election laws such as the Anderson-McCormick Act to exclude that vote as well as to end political corruption, both persisted. Even after the passage of the Walton Act of 1894, the situation was unaltered. Though that law provided for secrecy in the polling booths and assistance by the constable for any who could not read or who had other difficulties with the ballot, it also had its defects. Ballots, regardless of their length or complexity, had to be polled within two and a half minutes. Moreover, if a prospective voter in the secrecy of a voting booth sought aid, what was to prevent the constable from giving him misleading information? This occurred frequently until the act was amended in 1896 and the special constable was replaced by an election judge. Even this did not convince the skeptical of the judge's honesty. Rather than face the embarrassment of admitting their lack of education, illiterate Negroes often marked the wrong candidates' names, or so filled in the ballot as to have it rejected as defaced. Segregated voting lines were also employed, and the Negro line frequently was slowed down by constant challenges or the restricted number of polling booths in the colored areas. [38]

In addition there were numerous flagrant incidents of the purchase or miscounting of votes. In southeastern Virginia in 1889

[36] Lynchburg *Daily Advance,* Oct. 10, 1893, cited in Wynes, *Race Relations in Virginia,* 49.

[37] *Warrock-Richardson Almanack for the Year 1890,* 37; *ibid., 1902,* 31.

[38] Woodward, *Origins of the New South,* 275; McDanel, *Virginia Constitutional Convention,* 29–30; Wynes, *Race Relations in Virginia,* 51–52.

it was charged that Negro ministers received as much as $100 from the Democrats for the 137 votes cast in their district.[39] Bullock Precinct of Amherst County contained an estimated total vote of 750; yet in the 1894 state election a Democratic candidate received 2,601 votes.[40] In the Norfolk district election for United States Representative in 1898 deceased persons and those no longer resident in the district allegedly voted.[41] As late as 1901, 115 votes were cast for governor in McGruder Precinct, Amherst County, though the precinct contained only 45 registered voters.[42] Equally striking was the fact that from 1874 to 1900 fraud was involved in 16 of the 20 contested elections in Virginia for the United States House of Representatives.[43]

Concern over the situation was evidenced by frequent editorial comment during the 1890's. The consensus was that whether or not the Negro was to blame for the dishonesty in the elections, his vote had become the pretext for all sorts of political corruption and only by purging the ballot could it be eliminated. The Richmond *Times,* a leader in the Negro disfranchisement move, commented:

I had rather see the Democrats take shot guns and drive the negroes from the polls than to see our young men cheat. If they have once learned that lesson they will not stop at cheating negroes. It is more courageous to come out boldly and honorably for public morals and good government . . . and disfranchise the negro than to make a pretense of letting him vote and then cheat him at the polls.[44]

Though the Negro was no real threat to white rule nor the vil-

[39] Moger, *Rebuilding of the Old Dominion,* 27, n. 74.

[40] Victor Duvall Weathers, "The Political Life of Allen Caperton Braxton" (Master's thesis, University of Virginia, 1956), 13; Joseph Manning, *The Fadeout of Populism* (N.Y., 1940), 52.

[41] McDanel, *Virginia Constitutional Convention,* 31.

[42] Richmond *Dispatch,* June 11, 1901, cited in Weathers, "Allen Caperton Braxton," 13.

[43] Woodward, *Origins of the New South,* 326–27; William C. Pendleton, *A Political History of Appalachian Virginia: 1776–1927* (Dayton, Va., 1927), 424–28.

[44] Undated Richmond *Times,* 1893 election, cited in Moger, *Rebuilding of the Old Dominion,* 85; Richmond *Times,* Jan. 27, 1900, cited in McDanel, *Virginia Constitutional Convention,* 33.

lain in fraudulent electioneering, he remained "an irritant and a sign all was not well with the body politic." Whites of both parties agreed that with the irritant removed, fraud would also end and Virginia could return to an honest two-party system based on legitimate issues, unmarred by the race question. In a fresh interpretation stressing Virginia's participation in the Progressive movement, William Larsen portrays Andrew Jackson Montague as a "Southern Progressive" who felt the purification of the electorate was as much of a reform as improved schools, the direct primary, or stronger state control over railroads. According to Montague, after a period of education, qualified Negroes would subsequently be reassimilated into Virginia politics.[45]

The attempt to eliminate the Negro politically by constitutional means was made initially in 1888, the year provided for in the Underwood constitution for a reevaluation of the document. Despite the need for election reform, interest was minimal. Neither party supported a proposal to call a constitutional convention, and the vote was overwhelmingly against it, 63,125 to 3,698. The Republicans opposed revision since they had nothing to gain from a constitution framed by Democrats. The Democrats dissented because they feared a return to "Mahoneism" if serious attempts were made to alter Virginia's laws. Negroes logically voted in opposition as voting rights gained through the Underwood constitution were endangered.[46]

Despite this defeat another attempt was made in 1896, when Senator Eugene Withers managed to get a bill through the General Assembly calling for a vote in 1897. The measure was rejected again 83,435 to 38,326. Since the Democrats disagreed among themselves on the changes desirable in the constitution, the party deliberately omitted a proconvention plank from their party platform. The Republicans and the Negroes remained

[45] Larsen, *Montague of Virginia,* 108–9, 151–56; Woodward, *Origins of the New South,* Chapter XIV, "Progressivism for Whites Only"; Dewey W. Grantham, Jr., "The Progressive Movement and the Negro," *South Atlantic Quarterly,* LIV (Oct. 1955), 461–77.

[46] McDanel, *Virginia Constitutional Convention,* 10; Wynes, *Race Relations in Virginia,* 44. To illustrate the lack of interest, in the same year the vote cast for the presidency was 301,519.

strongly opposed. Furthermore, since the state was still recovering from the depression triggered by the Panic of 1893, it was deemed too expensive. Finally, the threat of Populism frightened conservative Democrats who feared that "Kansas ideas would be introduced into the organic law of Virginia." [47]

By 1900 the Populist threat was over, the Republicans offered little active resistance on the state level, and federal interference was not feared, especially since the United States Supreme Court in the *Williams* v. *Mississippi* case found the disfranchising clause in the Mississippi constitution of 1895 to be constitutional and not a violation of Negro rights.[48] In the North, Republicans busied themselves "taking up the white man's burden," directing the annexation of Hawaii in 1898 and the acquisition of the Philippines, Guam, and Puerto Rico as fruits of the Spanish-American War. They could hardly condemn the South for depriving the Negro of his constitutional rights when the nation acted similarly abroad.[49] Negroes themselves also appeared to realize they were not ready for an active role in Southern politics. President Booker T. Washington of Tuskegee Institute, generally recognized to be the spokesman for the Negro, in effect renounced political aspirations in his 1895 "Atlanta Compromise." Instead he advised a policy of education and economic advancement.[50]

A constitutional convention had not been convened in the late eighties and nineties because the Democratic party had withheld its official sanction of the movement. But in 1900, despite intra-

[47] Doss, "John Warwick Daniel," 264–66; Wynes, *Race Relations in Virginia,* 55; Horn, "Democratic Party in Virginia," 41.

[48] Woodward, *Origins of the New South,* 322–23; Mabry, "Disfranchisement of Negro in South," 482–88. Undated notes in the papers of William A. Anderson and John W. Daniel, University of Virginia, indicate a thorough investigation had been made by these men into the constitutionality of disfranchisement.

[49] John G. Van Deusen, "The Negro in Politics," *Journal of Negro History,* XXI (July 1936), 256–74; I. A. Newby, *Jim Crow's Defense: Anti-Negro Thought in America, 1900–1930* (Baton Rouge, La., 1965), 15; Woodward, *Origins of the New South,* 324–26.

[50] Woodward, *Origins of the New South,* 323, 337–38, and Chapter XIII, "The Atlanta Compromise"; Rayford W. Logan, *The Betrayal of the Negro: From Rutherford B. Hayes to Woodrow Wilson* (N.Y., 1954, 1965), 276–312.

party disagreement, the third attempt received party backing. The boss of the state machine, United States Senator Thomas Staples Martin, remained noncommittal on the matter, and his silence was interpreted as disapproval. The machine feared that efforts might be made to streamline the state government by the elimination of unneeded and excessive county, city, and state positions, depriving the organization of patronage. Nevertheless, independent Democrats, including Carter Glass, William A. Anderson, and Andrew Jackson Montague, favored a convention not only for election reforms but for a general reorganization of the state government as well.[51]

The Virginia General Assembly on March 5, 1900, enacted legislation providing for a popular referendum on the question of calling a convention. On May 2, the State Democratic Convention in Norfolk accepted a constitutional convention as party policy. The Democrats also pledged that any revisions made in the Underwood constitution would be submitted to the people for approval, that no white man who had the right to vote as of 1861 would be disfranchised, and that no descendant of any such person would be disfranchised.[52] The Republicans, with the exception of those who wished to eliminate the Negro vote in hopes of a return to an honest two-party system, opposed the convention proposal.

Despite attempts by the Richmond *Times* and other newspapers to whoop up interest in the referendum, little more enthusiasm could be mustered than had been manifested earlier. On May 24, 1900, by only 77,362 to 60,375, the issue carried.[53] The vote was a sectional one, with most cities and "black belt" counties, which favored Negro disfranchisement, voting heavily for a convention. Counties heavily populated by white Republicans opposed the

[51] Larsen, *Montague of Virginia,* 40–121 *passim;* Doss, "John Warwick Daniel," 266–69; Jacob N. Brenaman, *A History of Virginia Conventions* (Richmond, 1902), 82.

[52] Horn, "Democratic Party in Virginia," 55–59; "Suffrage Clause of the Norfolk Democratic Platform of 1900," John W. Daniel Papers, University of Virginia.

[53] Rondle E. Edwards, "A Study of the Virginia Constitutional Convention as Seen through the Richmond *Times*" (Master's thesis, Virginia State College, 1960), *passim; Warrock-Richardson Almanack for the Year 1903,* 50.

convention for fear their inhabitants might be disfranchised by new constitutional amendments.[54] In the balloting the proconvention faction held a decided advantage because the only marking on the ballot was "For Constitutional Convention." Those favoring the measure dropped their unmarked ballots into the box without entering the polling booths. Opponents of the convention had to enter the booths, perhaps seek aid from Democratic election officials, and then delete all the words on the ballot. If any words remained unmarked, the vote was cast out as mutilated.[55]

With the approval of the people, the General Assembly in special session on February 16, 1901, passed the necessary legislation for the convention. Selection of the one hundred delegates was based on representation in the House of Delegates. The legislature also renewed the pledge made by the Democratic State Convention in May 1900 that the work of the convention would be submitted to the people for approval.[56]

Despite the overwhelming majority of Democrats over Republicans in the convention (88 to 12), almost a year dragged by before an acceptable document could be drafted. From the outset the delegates were beset by argument. When M. R. Thom of Norfolk moved that the convention members take an oath required by the Underwood constitution, Allen Caperton Braxton objected that since the delegates were members of a convention and not officers in the purview of the constitution, they were not so obligated. By a vote of 57 to 37 the motion was tabled, thus effectively sidestepping the oath-taking ceremony.[57]

The major question and dilemma before the convention was how to disfranchise the Negro. Fears arose that their exclusion would also exclude poor white illiterates. What methods should be

[54] For an analysis of the voting by counties and cities, see Morton, *Negro in Virginia Politics*, 148–49; V. O. Key, *Southern Politics in State and Nation* (N.Y., 1949), 546–47.

[55] Pendleton, *Appalachian Virginia*, 440–41. Editor of the Tazewell *Republican*, Pendleton was one of the most severe critics of these tactics, as well as of the convention and of the Democratic party.

[56] Complete convention proceedings are in *Report of the Proceedings and Debates of the Constitutional Convention, State of Virginia, 1901–1902*, 2 vols. (Richmond, 1906).

[57] McDanel, *Virginia Constitutional Convention*, 21–22.

employed, therefore, to avert such a possibility? Should there be a poll tax, a grandfather clause, a literacy test, or a combination of the three? Some delegates objected that such proposals would be invalidated by the courts as discriminatory against the Negroes. To this Delegate Carter Glass of Lynchburg bluntly retorted:

Discrimination! Why that is exactly what we propose; that exactly, is why this Convention was elected—to discriminate to the very extremity of permissible action under the limitations of the Federal Constitution with the view to the elimination of every Negro who can be gotten rid of, legally, without materially impairing the strength of the white electorate.[58]

The debate continued. Almost in despair, after earlier apologetic editorials for the convention's seeming inaction, the Richmond *Dispatch* candidly pleaded, "Wanted, A Plan." [59]

From October 8, 1901, to March 28, 1902, the convention adjourned daily after roll call, and the Democratic delegates met in conference to labor on an acceptable suffrage proposal. Finally, a measure was presented to the convention and subsequently passed on April 4, 1902, 67 to 28.[60] The suffrage provisions stipulated that prior to January 1904 any male might register to vote who had met the age and residence requirements and could read and explain any provision of the state constitution. If unable to read, the individual should be able to explain any section of the constitution read to him. After January 1904, this literacy test, or temporary "understanding clause," was to be replaced by a yearly capitation tax of $1.50 as a voting prerequisite. Those exempted from poll tax payment included veterans on either side during the Civil War, sons of veterans, and owners of property who had paid taxes of at least one dollar in the preceding year.[61] It was unlikely that many Negroes would have served during the Civil War or that

[58] *Virginia Constitutional Convention, 1901–1902*, II, 3076; Woodward, *Origins of the New South*, 332–34.

[59] McDanel, *Virginia Constitutional Convention*, 38.

[60] *Virginia Constitutional Convention, 1901–1902*, II, 3079.

[61] Payment was made on a yearly basis but three consecutive payments had to be paid in order to continue voting. For example, if a person had paid the capitation tax in 1905, 1906, and 1908, but not in 1907, he was ineligible to vote. *Virginia State Constitution of 1902*, Article II, Sections 18–21. See also p. 131 of this work for capitation time requirement.

they would be taxpayers to any extent since few owned property. And of those Negroes who did, most would undoubtedly disfranchise themselves as they were generally delinquent about paying their taxes.

Finally, the temporary "understanding clause," which went into effect at the first registration under the new constitution and which expired on January 1, 1904, was replaced on that date by a requirement stipulating that every prospective voter had to answer under oath to the satisfaction of local registrars any questions pertaining to his qualifications as an elector.[62]

With the disfranchising measures accepted by the convention, the remaining obstacle to overcome was ratification. The Democratic party at the Norfolk Convention in 1900 and the General Assembly in February 1901 had pledged a referendum by the people to accept or reject. Though ethically bound by such promises, a majority of the delegates, led by Carter Glass (who had originally been in favor of "restricted submission")[63] and backed by an extensive newspaper campaign, successfully proclaimed the constitution.[64] This was accomplished on May 29, 1902, 48 to 38. Those who favored proclamation argued that the constitution might be defeated in a popular referendum by a combination of white Republicans and poor white Democrats who feared being discriminated against. And since voter interest had been so slight in the convention attempts of 1888 and 1897, only a small opposition vote would be necessary to defeat the constitution.[65]

Over the protests of a handful of Republicans after the proclamation, the constitution became the law of Virginia on July 10, 1902, by resolution as adopted by the convention. Led by Governor Andrew Jackson Montague, all executive and judicial officers promptly took an oath to support it. All members of the General

[62] Wynes, *Race Relations in Virginia,* 64–65.

[63] Richmond *Dispatch,* May 30, 1902. "Restricted submission" provided that only those who could qualify under the new constitution could vote, thus eliminating virtually all the Negroes.

[64] Richmond *Dispatch,* April 25, 27, May 27, 1902; McDanel, *Virginia Constitutional Convention,* Chapter V, "Proclamation or Submission?" *passim.*

[65] McDanel, *Virginia Constitutional Convention,* 125.

Assembly did likewise in special session on July 15, except for one dissident Republican, Delegate E. P. McLean. His case was referred to the Committee on Privileges and Elections on January 28, 1903, which concluded that the seat in question was vacant unless McLean took the oath within three days. When he did not, the committee passed a resolution on February 6, 1903, declaring the seat vacant.[66]

On July 10, 1902, old voter registration books were purged and the provisions for new registrations went into effect. The Richmond *Times* declared triumphantly, "At the hour of noon today the dark cloud will be lifted, and peace and sunshine will come to regenerated Anglo-Saxon people as a result of the organic law made with its own hands." [67] Whether the "dark cloud" would remain lifted, however, was a matter for the courts to decide.

[66] *Ibid.,* 130–31.
[67] Richmond *Times,* July 10, 1902; Lynchburg *News,* Aug. 30, 1902.

II

Closing the Door

1902–1907

THE constitutional convention had formulated the necessary provisions for Negro disfranchisement. Their implementation during the 1902–7 period, especially of the temporary "understanding clause" and of the more permanent poll tax, made exclusion a reality. As a result what little political strength the Negro possessed in preconvention days disappeared almost entirely after 1902.

The first major disfranchisement step was taken prior to the adjournment of the constitutional convention, when registration ordinances and lists of registration boards were adopted by the convention. Each ward in the cities was allotted one registrar and each magisterial district in the counties three, their terms to run until January 1, 1904. As selected by the convention, the vast majority of officials were Democrats, who by means of the understanding clause would almost completely curtail Negro suffrage.[1] As no state agency supervised the local registrars, they were a law unto themselves and the type of questions asked Negroes depended upon the officials' attitude concerning disfranchisement. If, in some instances, the Negro was able to answer difficult questions, "the registrar could always fall back on the demand for explana-

---

[1] *Virginia State Constitution of 1902*, Section 31; Key, *Southern Politics*, 562; Horn, "Democratic Party in Virginia," 148. After the first election of officials, selections were subsequently by county electoral boards chosen by the circuit or corporation court. Since the latter had originally been selected by the predominantly Democratic legislature, there was little doubt concerning their party affiliation.

tion of an ex-post facto law." [2] That extralegal methods were employed during the September–October 1902 registration seems to be evidenced in letters from two registrars to United States Representative Henry D. Flood. The spelling and grammar of one of the letters expose the writer's own educational limitations.

All right will sirtainly do my best to get the Democratic voters to register & vica versa I am one of the registrars their seems to be verry little interest taken in the registrations but I think they are awakening to the necesity prety fast There wont be no negro registered that aint entitled to You bet.[3]

We hope to get most of our men registered. We have knowed [knocked] out some white reps [Republicans] and paralyzed the negroes. I do not think that we knocked any democrats but we will lose one or two. They may not aplly.[4]

The letters to Flood abounded with such statements as "there were only three negro applicants and all were turned down. I think every democrat was present and registered all O.K." [5]

On one occasion Republican Robert W. Blair of Wythe County charged that three "worthy citizens" were deprived of their registration rights in Wytheville Precinct, and that in Crockett Precinct thirty-four white Republicans and two Negroes were refused while no Democrats were rejected. He added that election board meetings were closed to the public and that applicants were not allowed to be accompanied by anyone when appearing before the board. Two years later in an unsuccessful attempt to prevent exclusion, the Republicans in the General Assembly offered a resolution to require in each precinct the appointment of one registrar, judge, and clerk from the minority party. After its defeat, some Democrats openly admitted that they had voted against the measure in

[2] McDanel, *Virginia Constitutional Convention,* 48; Robert E. Martin, *Negro Disfranchisement in Virginia* (*The Howard University Studies in the Social Services,* ed. by Abram L. Harris, Vol. I; Washington, D.C., 1938), 148.

[3] W. Rudsill to "Hon HD Floot [*sic*]," Sept. 20, 1902, in Henry D. Flood Papers, Library of Congress.

[4] Ernest H. McClintic, Sept. 20, 1902, *ibid.*

[5] C. W. Manger, Sept. 29, 1902, *ibid.*

the interest of "one party regardless of the rights of others." [6] William Pendleton, Republican editor of the Tazewell *Republican,* protested that the registrars had disfranchised 90 per cent of the Negroes and 50 per cent of the whites. Republicans who attempted the " 'understanding clause' had to submit to the humiliation of having their educational qualifications passed upon by ignorant and bitterly partisan boards of registration." [7]

Nevertheless, from the outset about one-half of the Negroes disfranchised themselves. Of the approximately 147,000 Negroes of voting age in 1900, 76,764 were illiterate and thus had to register as ex-soldiers, sons of ex-soldiers, or as property holders who had paid at least $1.00 in taxes. Few Negroes could do this. At the time of the constitutional convention only 8,144 male Negroes owned real estate valued at $300, which was slightly in excess of the amount of property on which the state tax would be one dollar.[8] The only alternative for most Negroes was to pass the "understanding clause," over which the local registrar had control.

Doubtless registrars disfranchised the Negro through devious means, but in all fairness to the officials it should be admitted that the poorly educated Negroes in many instances were unable to answer the most simple questions. According to the Richmond *Times,* an old Negro, Henry Scruggs of New Canton Precinct, Buckingham County, when asked what a representative body was, answered that it was a body of baptized believers.[9] The same paper reported that in Dendrow a Negro could not decide who the President of the United States was. He told the registrar that "he was not exactly certain whether it was Mr. Edward Rogers or Mr. Ernest Rogers, but he believed it to be Mr. Edward Rogers." [10]

[6] *House Journal and Documents, 1904,* 113; Horn, "Democratic Party in Virginia," 98, 152.

[7] Pendleton, *Appalachian Virginia,* 457–59.

[8] *Documents of the Virginia Constitutional Convention of 1901–1902,* Document VIII, cited in McDanel, *Virginia Constitutional Convention,* 48–49; Martin, *Negro Disfranchisement in Virginia,* 147.

[9] Richmond *Times,* Sept. 17, 1902. The *Times* had by far the most extensive coverage of the 1902 registration.

[10] *Ibid.,* Sept. 24, 1902.

Mr. Edward Rogers was general superintendent of the Surry Lumber Company.

The newspapers seemed to vie with each other in publicizing the most ridiculous answers. And they were ridiculous. For instance, "Twelve months in jail," was the reply of a Blackstone Negro to a query, "What would be an appropriate punishment for a man who had committed suicide?" [11] In the Newport News–Hampton area most Negroes defined the Virginia General Assembly as a place of religious worship.[12]

Random samples of voter registration lists illustrate the inability of the Negro to get on the rolls via the "understanding clause." At Ballsville in Powhatan County no whites failed the test, but only 14 Negroes of 140 were registered, and 13 of those were property owners. In King William Court House Precinct none of the 95 white applicants were rejected while 76 of the 106 Negroes were. On the first day of registration at Booker, Sussex County, all 75 whites who applied were accepted, but only 12 of the 150 Negroes attempting were declared eligible. In Ware District of Gloucester County 42 of the 69 registered Negroes qualified under the property clause. The district had formerly registered 771 Negroes. Salem District, Roanoke County, while rejecting but 10 whites, rejected 90 colored, and of the 46 Negroes who registered most did so by meeting the property qualification.[13]

Another reason for the few registered Negroes in 1902 was that many, convinced that white registrars would reject them, did not even attempt to register. Said Democratic politician Claude A. Swanson concerning their disfranchisement, "The colored people are accepting the new condition stoically. They seem to regard it pretty much as what might have been expected." [14] A Richmond paper summed up the situation by saying, "The negroes manifested but little interest." [15] This statement, written in 1902, was to prove

[11] *Ibid.,* Sept. 18, 1902.   [12] Richmond *Dispatch,* Sept. 14, 1902.
[13] Richmond *Times,* Sept. 12—Oct. 8, 1902, *passim.*
[14] *Ibid.,* Sept. 19, 1902.
[15] Richmond *Planet,* Nov. 5, 1902. See also Newby, *Jim Crow's Defense,* 149, 151.

true during most of the next half-century. Even after voting restrictions were lifted by the mid-1930's, apathy, produced by disfranchisement thirty years earlier, appeared to be the Negroes' worst enemy.

Whether intentionally or not, Virginia's registrars, with the aid of the "understanding clause," almost totally excluded the Negro from the electorate. Of the estimated 147,000 Negroes of voting age prior to the adoption of the 1902 constitution, only 21,000 remained on the registration lists by October 15, 1902.[16] By 1905, after the capitation tax had become a voting requirement, it was estimated that less than one-half of that 21,000 had met both poll tax and registration requirements.[17]

Striking examples of disfranchisement were especially evident in the major cities. In 1900 Richmond had 6,427 registered Negroes, but by the 1902 registration the number was reduced to 760.[18] During the same period Norfolk's colored vote was reduced from 1,826 to 504, Petersburg's from 2,400 to 620, Staunton's from 443 to 84, and Culpeper's from 1,075 to 153.[19] One of the most conspicuous reductions occurred in the predominantly Negro-populated Jackson Ward of Richmond. Since Reconstruction that area had elected 20 Negroes to the city's common council and others to the board of aldermen,[20] and in 1900 had 15,592 Negro

[16] *Warrock-Richardson Almanack for the Year 1902,* 30–33; Moon, *Balance of Power,* 74. Moon credits this figure to a survey, undated, made by the Lynchburg *News.*

[17] Richmond *Times,* April 5, 1905. Attempts to find more complete figures met with almost total failure. A written questionnaire to 50 county and 15 city registrars, in addition to personal visits to the registration offices of Richmond, Norfolk, Petersburg, Charlottesville, and Fredericksburg, did not uncover adequate figures for this period. A resolution in the 1903 legislative session was adopted in the senate requiring the recording of the total number of registered voters according to race. The measure was killed, however, in the house. It was not until 1938 that the State Board of Elections compiled a listing by race on the county and city level. Richmond *News Leader,* Nov. 25, 1903, hereafter cited as *News Leader.*

[18] Richmond *Dispatch,* Oct. 2, 1902. For a more complete tabulation on the county and city level, see below, Appendix A.

[19] Richmond *Times,* Sept. 28—Oct. 16, 1902.

[20] James H. Brewer, "The Futile Trumpet: The Wars of the Richmond *Planet* against Disfranchisement and Jim Crow, 1900–1904" (MS, Virginia State College, 1959), 16.

and 3,121 white residents. Four years earlier the ward included 2,983 colored and 789 white voters. With the adoption of the constitution in 1902, the colored voting majority was lost to the whites, 468 to 347.[21] By September 29, 1903, registration of Negroes stood at a lowly 33.[22] In July 1903, upon the recommendation of a subcommittee, the Council Committee on Ordinances, the city's wards were reapportioned. This resulted in the elimination by gerrymander of Jackson Ward.[23] Parceled out among neighboring wards, Jackson's Negro population lost the remainder of its already diminished voting strength.

While the whites, especially the Democrats, were elated over the removal of most Negro voters, they themselves were plagued by the problem of voter apathy. With the Negro disfranchised and the Democratic party in control of the political situation, there appeared little incentive for whites to register. The continued weakness of the Republican party was a further reason for lack of voter interest. What strength the G.O.P. retained appeared mainly in the Ninth Congressional District under the leadership of Colonel Campbell Slemp, and this the Democrats hoped to end in the 1902 congressional elections.

The small number of those bothering to register in 1902 and the light vote that November was a clear indication of the grip of apathy. One registrar in Chesterfield County summed up the situation as one of "pitiful indifference to a sacred duty and trust," while a second in Clarksville wrote, "I have never seen so little apparent interest, nor heard as little talk of registration and election before. Nobody seems to know much about it, nor do they seem to care." [24] Still another registrar from Fort Lewis stated that "we have a class of Democrats to deal with that are right hard to get at." He recommended that the registration board "sit at each man's door [and] we might get them to register. But we have some I fear we won't get on the books." [25] Finally, from Warm

21 Richmond *Dispatch,* Oct. 2, 1902.
22 *News Leader,* Sept. 29, 1903.
23 *Ibid.,* July 15, Sept. 20, 1903.
24 Richmond *Times,* Sept. 4, 7, 1902.
25 Robert McClintic to Flood, Sept. 30, 1902, Flood Papers.

Springs came the comment that the Democrats might suffer defeat there unless

we can get out people to turn out and register though there has been no stir & our people have the idea that the opposition does not amount to anything, and that disfranchisement of the negroes will do the work without the effort on their part, so this apathy may hurt us all over the state.[26]

As the campaign for the ten congressional seats dragged along, it became obvious that interest in the election was slight. Despite almost daily pleas by Virginia newspapers for Democratic voters to participate actively in the contest, the Richmond *Times* saw "little prospect of any heavy 'scrapping' at the stump" and added that never "since Reconstruction has one been conducted so quietly or so little interest shown in it." On election eve it could only comment, "END OF A DULL CAMPAIGN." [27]

On November 6 the Democrats swept nine of ten congressional seats, 82,526 to 37,878, losing only in the Ninth District in a close contest to Republican Campbell Slemp. The 1902 total vote of 123,112 was less than half the 269,112 cast for congressmen two years earlier,[28] a clear indication of disfranchisement and voter apathy. No figures are available for the total number of Negro voters in the 1902 election, but at best it was small. Newspaper reports indicate that the Negroes realized the futility of casting lone ballots and that many did not wish to risk the embarrassment they undoubtedly would have faced at polling places. Dinwiddie County reported that "the Negroes manifested little interest," and in Amherst County only "about" 15 of the 47 registered Negroes bothered to vote.[29] In Prince Edward County a Negro candidate for Congress, James C. Jones, running as a Republican against Democrat R. C. Southall, received four votes. Twelve persons had voted for Jones but eight ballots had been defaced and were disqualified.[30]

[26] William McAllister to Flood, Sept. 19, 1902, *ibid.*
[27] Richmond *Times,* Oct. 21, 26, Nov. 2, 1902.
[28] *Warrock-Richardson Almanack for the Year 1903,* 68.
[29] *News Leader,* Nov. 5, 1902.
[30] *Warrock-Richardson Almanack for the Year 1903,* 66; Farmville *Herald,* Nov. 7, 1902.

The two-year understanding clause "temporarily" reduced the Negro eligibility to 21,000. The poll tax, effective on December 14, 1903, and other requirements placed disfranchisement on a permanent basis by 1904. In the first place payment of $1.50 was a problem in itself to the Negro. He also was required to face local registrars and make application without assistance in his own handwriting on a blank white piece of paper. On that blank application he was to write *in proper order* his name, age, date, place of birth, residence, and occupation at the present time and the two years next preceding, whether he had previously voted and, if so, where.[31] If these hurdles were topped, the final provision, that the registrant answer any and all questions affecting his qualification as an elector, was enough to stump the best of would-be applicants.

The Richmond *News Leader* estimated that no more than 15,-000 Negroes in the state voted in the 1904 presidential election, and that number "was so distributed as not to threaten white supremacy in the control of local affairs anywhere and not to be a serious threat in any congressional district."[32] In the same year only 253,870 of the 400,220 citizens assessed the poll tax met payment—a delinquency rate of 36.5 per cent. Over the next four decades delinquencies increased until by 1942 the percentage stood at 50.5 per cent.[33] Although no state agency to date has analyzed the number of delinquents by race, in 1941, the newly formed Virginia Voters' League, organized by Professor Luther Porter Jackson of Virginia State College, compiled by counties Negro poll tax payments and delinquencies. This compilation set the number of Negroes meeting all voting requirements in 1941 at approximately 25,000—a total little higher than that of the 1904–5 period. The number of Negroes in Virginia who met the three-year poll tax requirement for voting was 25,441, an increase of about four and a half thousand since 1904; and this despite

[31] McDanel, *Virginia Constitutional Convention,* 51; Key, *Southern Politics,* 564.

[32] Nov. 28, 1904; Larsen, *Montague of Virginia,* 140.

[33] Horn, "Democratic Party in Virginia," 223, Appendix I; *Annual Report of Auditor of Public Accounts* (Richmond, 1925), 236, cited in McDanel, *Virginia Constitutional Convention,* 50.

the fact that Negroes over twenty-one years of age had increased from 146,122 in 1900 to 364,144 in 1940. Even the advent of women's suffrage in 1920 did little to raise the figure appreciably over the 21,000 figure.[34]

The continuing decline in registration resulting from the poll tax was apparent especially in the cities, where Negroes had previously polled sizable votes. Petersburg, which in 1900 had a voter potential of 2,400 Negroes and 4,600 whites, showed a count of only 1,542 qualified whites and 299 Negroes for the 1904 presidential election.[35] By 1906, the combined total of white-Negro tax payees stood at a lowly 1,300.[36] Richmond in 1900 had a voter registration of 12,338 whites and 6,427 Negroes, but by December 14, 1903, only 6,264 of those had paid the capitation tax for the June 1904 elections.[37] Three years later 10,127 whites were qualified, but only 228 Negroes were.[38] The Lynchburg *News* estimated that 1,200 voters there had disfranchised themselves for the 1905 elections, as only 2,200 of the 3,400 assessed paid the capitation tax.[39] When the city treasurer's office closed on May 4, 1907, 2,295 whites and 447 Negroes of the 5,240 assessed had met tax requirements.[40] The number paying in Norfolk in December 1903 was small, 6,140 whites and 150 Negroes. Owing to nonpayment in Portsmouth, it was estimated that 3,700 voters had been disqualified.[41] Alexandria, which had cast 3,152 votes in the 1900 presidential election, registered only 1,112 whites and 49 Negroes by December 14, 1903.[42] In Danville, the heart of the Virginia black belt, 24 Negroes paid the capitation tax.[43]

[34] *Third Annual Report, The Voting Status of Negroes in Virginia, 1942* (Petersburg, Va., April 1943), 3; *Twelfth Census of the United States, 1900: Population* (Washington, D.C., 1902), lxxvi; *Sixteenth Census, 1940* (Washington, D.C., 1943), 144.

[35] *News Leader*, Nov. 1, 9, Dec. 15, 1903; Roanoke *Times*, Jan. 16, 1904.

[36] Richmond *Times-Dispatch*, Dec. 19, 1905, hereafter cited as *Times-Dispatch*.   [37] *News Leader*, Jan. 18, 1904.

[38] *Times-Dispatch*, Jan. 17, 1907; Petersburg *Daily-Index Appeal*, Oct. 27, 1907.

[39] May 3, 1905.   [40] *Times-Dispatch*, May 5, 1907.

[41] Fredericksburg *Daily Star*, Dec. 16, 1903.

[42] Alexandria *Gazette and Virginia Advertiser*, Dec. 15, 1903.

[43] Roanoke *Times*, Jan. 16, 1904.

A basic aim of the constitutional convention of 1901–2 had been to eradicate fraud and corruption from Virginia elections. Nevertheless, the poll tax, instituted to play a basic part in the disfranchisement of the Negro, was considered the cause of the perpetuation of such dishonesty. Though most of the Negro voters had been eliminated, it did not prevent white politicians from manipulating tax payments, a violation of the constitutional provision stipulating that the capitation tax be paid personally by the taxed individual. Democrats and Republicans alike resorted to "block payment," or "payment of the faithful," the use of large amounts of campaign funds to pay taxes owed by loyal members of their parties who either neglected to pay or who could not afford to. One source asserts that politicians generally deposited funds with the county treasurer, who had access to the poll tax records and thus knew who had not paid. He would furnish party workers with the names of delinquents and, if the latter could not pay the tax, the county treasurer would do so from the funds given him. He then delivered the receipts to the party workers, who gave them to prospective voters. Another common practice was for treasurers to hold out tax bills for the "faithful" and certify that they had been paid. So widespread did this practice become that upon investigation by the General Assembly in 1932 it was found that forty county treasurers had a payment shortage totaling $1,119,-300.56.[44]

One of the first publicized accounts of block payment occurred in Russell County in May 1905. On the day after the expiration date for tax payments, two Democrats allegedly went to the treasurer's office and paid the tax for 107 loyal party members. Though the Commonwealth's attorney, a Republican, threatened to prosecute the alleged offenders, nothing is known to have come of the threat.[45]

That block payment was standard practice seems borne out in the Flood correspondence. A resident of Indian Rock, Botetourt County, concerned over the party's prospects in the 1906 elections,

[44] Horn, "Democratic Party in Virginia," 223–24.
[45] *Ibid.,* 224.

wrote Flood, "I think that about 90% or possibly 95% of the voters in this precinct have paid the capitation tax, and that the largest loss will be on the Democratic side, the Republicans having been active in this respect, aided by the Republican Treasurer and his Deputies." [46] Another correspondent during the same campaign informed Flood, "Now about capitation taxes, quite a number of Democrats around here failed to pay. I urged all I saw to pay before May 7th and *assisted* a few, but I think every Republican voter in the district has paid. We neglected this matter. . . . This is confidential, of course." [47]

When Flood was informed that one R. M. Anderson was paying the poll tax for prospective Republican voters, he inquired into the situation, and Anderson replied, "I have not paid as many taxes for people this year as I generally have. I paid more capitation taxes for your friends than I did for your foes." [48]

By no means did the Democrats have a monopoly on payment of the poll tax for the "faithful." By the admission of the Republican congressman of the Ninth Congressional District, C. Bascom Slemp, payments were made under his direction for approximately twenty years. It was reported that a Republican county chairman might handle as much as $2,500 yearly for that purpose. [49] During the 1906 congressional campaign, Democrat R. P. Bruce, running against Colonel Campbell Slemp, complained, "We had about 2,700 Democrats who did not pay their poll tax and had at least $30,000.00 money to run against. If our democratic friends had voted, I would have won, all right, not withstanding the odds." [50] With the death of the elder Slemp in 1907, his son C. Bascom succeeded him as United States Representative in the "fighting

[46] L. P. Dillon, Sept. 23, 1904, Flood Papers.

[47] P. M. Jones, Sept. 23, 1904, *ibid.*

[48] R. M. Anderson to Flood, Oct. 27, 1904, *ibid.*

[49] Guy Hathorn, "Political Life of C. Bascom Slemp" (Ph.D. dissertation, Duke University, 1953), 44.

[50] R. P. Bruce to J. Taylor Ellyson, Nov. 12, 1906, J. Taylor Ellyson Papers, University of Virginia. The Roanoke *Times,* May 3, 1906, on information from a "friend" also charged that Ninth District Republicans paid poll taxes and then issued $1.50 I.O.U.'s to the "faithful."

Ninth" until 1922. Presumably the reason the latter was unbeatable was because he kept his supporters paid up in advance "on the assumption that he might want to run for Congress again. The Democrats in the Ninth District were at a disadvantage since they did not begin paying until they had decided upon a candidate." [51]

Though block payment for Negroes was not as common as it was for whites, it was practiced by some, especially in the struggle for political supremacy in the Norfolk area. Led by Norfolk County Clerk Alvah H. Martin, a faction of the Democratic party known as the "Fusionists" (those who sought the aid of Republicans, renegade Democrats, and Negroes) made a concerted effort to pay the tax for Negroes.[52] In 1911 the "Straightouts" (those Democrats loyal to party and opposing outside alliances) accused the Fusionists of manipulating the remnants of the Negro vote and a group of dissident Republicans, thereby controlling political activity in the Norfolk area. Charges of block buying and fraud were common at election time, and it was also alleged that while the Fusionists solicited Negro votes, they prevented the Straightout Democrats from paying poll taxes before registration deadlines by closing collection offices early.[53]

Amid party charges and countercharges, block payment continued. Warnings from the attorney general's office, especially aimed at the Republican Ninth District, were ineffective. Both in 1904 and 1907 Attorney General William A. Anderson announced that all capitation taxes were to be paid "personally." [54] This prohibition against the payment of poll taxes for others was

[51] Hathorn, "C. Bascom Slemp," 45–46; Larsen, *Montague of Virginia*, 141.

[52] Norfolk *Virginian-Pilot*, Dec. 2, 1903, hereafter cited as *Virginian-Pilot;* Fredericksburg *Daily Star,* Dec. 3, 1903; Larsen, "Andrew Jackson Montague," II, 477–82.

[53] Harold G. Wheatley, "The Political Career of William Atkinson Jones" (Master's thesis, University of Virginia, 1953), 114–16; *Virginian-Pilot,* Dec. 2, 1903.

[54] Roanoke *Times,* Nov. 5, 1904; Anderson to R. S. Parks, May 5, 1907, in *Annual Report of the Attorney General to the Governor of Virginia for the Year 1907,* 27.

not enforced or even effectively curbed until the state comptroller's office began to clamp down on this violation in 1930.[55]

Owing to the many questionable practices involved in poll tax payment, cries were raised, especially by the Republicans, that this tax, though successful in disfranchising the Negro, had not eliminated dishonesty in Virginia politics. Mounting complaints resulted in the introduction of a resolution in 1906 before the General Assembly requesting an amendment to the constitution for the abolition of the poll tax as a voting prerequisite. The measure was killed, for, as one in favor of the tax argued:

We have purged the suffrage by requiring the poll tax to be paid six months in advance and we have eliminated a large number of objectionable voters in both races. The negro is no longer a factor and the shiftless whites, who used the vote for what they could get out of it, no longer hang around the polls for bids. . . . The man who is unwilling to pay such a tax for the privilege of voting is not a desirable voter and the state is better off without his vote than with it.[56]

The same source added that to end the poll tax would mean to throw down "the bars to negroes and bummers, and [to] demoralize the suffrage." [57] Future attempts at amending the constitution for the purposes of voter reform would meet similar arguments through the year 1965.

By 1907 the voting barriers had been employed successfully in eliminating the Negro vote and influence from Virginia politics. For those few Negroes who attempted to defy disfranchisement, immediate attention centered around the unsuccessful court cases challenging the constitutionality of the voting provisions of the 1902 constitution. As will be seen presently, the Republicans offered little consolation or aid to their former allies. Instead the G.O.P. began reshaping itself into a party of whites. In 1907 Governor Claude A. Swanson summed up the white man's con-

[55] Key, *Southern Politics,* 594.

[56] *Times-Dispatch,* Jan. 24, 25, 1906; Horn, "Democratic Party in Virginia," 277; Pendleton, *Appalachian Virginia,* 466–67.

[57] *Times-Dispatch,* Jan. 25, 1906. This newspaper in the 1930's and 1940's, along with the *News Leader* and the *Virginian-Pilot,* reversed itself and crusaded for the elimination of the poll tax.

ception of Negroes' place in the Old Dominion as follows: "We have no Negro problem here. . . . The suffrage question has been determined with justice and fairness and has ceased to be a subject of discussion or agitation. . . . With firmness and fairness Virginia has for the present settled the matter, and is now in an era of unexampled prosperity." [58]

[58] Henry C. Ferrell, Jr., "Claude A. Swanson of Virginia" (Ph.D. dissertation, University of Virginia, 1964), 240–41; *Manufacturers Record,* XLI (Feb. 28, 1907), 180.

III

The Negro Legal Counterattack
to Regain Suffrage, 1902–1912

DISFRANCHISEMENT of the Negro led inevitably to a prolonged court fight over the constitutionality of Virginia's new organic law. Even before the adoption of the constitution of 1902 white and Negro Republicans who were determined to combat their exclusion prepared for the first court cases. A series of cases during the next six years, 1902–8, were decided in favor of the Commonwealth. Thereafter, one last half-hearted effort was made in 1912 to contest disfranchisement, but apparently no court decision was reached. Not until 1928 in the white primary cases did the Negroes again make a serious effort to contest election laws in Virginia through the courts.

To elaborate, legal action was quickly taken by Republicans of both races. As early as October 1901 the Negro Industrial and Agricultural League, a leader in the fight to maintain suffrage for Negroes, had started formulating plans to challenge the new laws.[1] Another body, the Virginia Educational and Industrial Association, formed in 1900 primarily for the promotion of business and education, declared that henceforth all of its energies would be devoted to politics, the raising of funds to employ attorneys, and the Negro's political education.[2] The *Negro Advocate,* a Richmond newspaper, was also established to protest the constitutionality of the 1902 document.[3]

Reports came from within and outside the state that the fight

[1] Richmond *Dispatch,* Aug. 16, 1902; Rayford Logan, *The Negro in the United States: A Brief History* (N.Y., 1957), 62.

[2] Richmond *Dispatch,* Aug. 16, 1902.

[3] *Ibid.,* Sept. 14, 1902. Unfortunately, as is true of many earlier Negro sources, no copies of the *Advocate* are available today.

would be waged aggressively against suffrage limitations. According to the president of the Negro Industrial and Agricultural League, "some whites and Democrats" also agreed to aid.[4] Specific names, however, were not mentioned. From Petersburg came the news that Negro leaders had begun a drive for funds to defray legal expenses. James Hayes, a Negro lawyer and a key figure in the ensuing court cases, returned from a tour of New Jersey, New York, Massachusetts, and Washington with glowing reports that the Negro Franchise Association of Newark, New Jersey, had pledged $1,000 to the cause and that members of the Union League in New York had also raised funds to test the validity of the constitution of 1902.[5] Publicity was provided by Negro editors of six Virginia cities, who, under the auspices of the Negro Press Association of Richmond, met in convention and condemned disfranchisement in the Southern states.[6]

Through the efforts of Hayes and the Negro Industrial and Agricultural League, John S. Wise of New York was retained as counsel for the Negroes in the disfranchisement cases. A member of one of the most prominent families in the state and the son of Henry A. Wise, who had been governor just prior to the Civil War, he appeared to be an unusual choice to crusade for the Negroes. Wise had been a Conservative in 1869 but broke with that group during the Readjuster crisis and joined the Mahone camp. After an unsuccessful attempt to win the Republican gubernatorial nomination in 1881, he was nominated in 1885 only to lose the election in a close race against Democrat Fitzhugh Lee. Realizing that political advancement thereafter in predominantly Democratic Virginia was unlikely, Wise moved to New York, where he established a successful law practice. Within a short time, having been active in Republican politics, he was admitted to the "citadel of conservatism," the Union League Club, allegedly the first Confederate so honored.[7] The opportunity afforded by the Negroes in 1902 to return to the Virginia political

[4] Jordon Thompson as quoted in the *Virginian-Pilot*, Oct. 23, 1902.
[5] Richmond *Dispatch*, Sept. 16, 1902.
[6] *News Leader*, Feb. 5, 1904.
[7] Curtis Carroll Davis, "Very Well-Rounded Republican: The Several Lives of John S. Wise," *Virginia Magazine of History and Biography*, LXXI (Oct. 1963), 461–62, 472–81.

scene and battle the Democrats was perhaps too tempting for Wise to refuse.

Further hope for the Negroes rested with the Republican party in the state. Initially the outlook was encouraging, as the G.O.P. State Committee on June 17, 1902, passed a resolution condemning the adoption of the constitution by proclamation and denouncing it as illegal and contrary to the republican form of government. State Chairman Park Agnew also intimated that if lawyers deemed it advisable, the ablest attorneys would be employed to test its constitutionality.[8]

On the eve of the first court case, it appeared that the Negro fight would be waged vigorously. Unfortunately, the battle lines were not complete or unified. Though many Negroes protested disfranchisement, other Negroes accepted the status quo, believing that their race was not yet sufficiently educated or ready to participate in Virginia politics. Moreover, what appeared to be a promise of Republican support became instead a repudiation by the G.O.P. of its Negro ally. In a period of "white man's" politics, a faction of Republicans hoped to restore two-party politics in Virginia by becoming an all-white ("lily-white") party, a process that enfranchised Negroes would hamper.[9]

For the less militant Negroes, including those resigned to disfranchisement, the adoption of the constitution of 1902 had settled the issue. To resist would only cause hard feelings between the races. Before delving into politics, Negroes must first lift themselves up by their own bootstraps economically and educationally. A striking example of this attitude could be found in the person of John T. Mitchell, Jr.[10] Mitchell had been editor since 1884 of the Richmond *Planet,* the largest Negro weekly in Virginia, and

[8] Richmond *Dispatch,* June 18, 1902.

[9] Consult Stanley P. Hirshson, *Farewell to the Bloody Shirt: Northern Republicans and the Southern Negro, 1877–1893* (Bloomington, Ind., 1962); Vincent P. DeSantis, *Republicans Face the Southern Question: The New Departure Years, 1877–1897* (Baltimore, 1959).

[10] Despite his long career no Mitchell papers are available today. The best sources are Brewer, "The Futile Trumpet"; Joseph E. Boris, ed., *Who's Who in Colored America* (N.Y., 1927), I, 143; Roscoe Lewis, *The Negro in Virginia* (N.Y., 1940), 284–85; August Meier, *Negro Thought in America, 1880–1915* (Ann Arbor, Mich., 1963), 79–80, 233–99.

as president of the Mechanics Savings Bank he was the first Negro to be elected a member of the American Bankers' Association. In civic affairs he had been a member of the Richmond city council and board of aldermen. During the late 1880's the "Stormy Petrel," as Mitchell liked to call himself, had conducted a strong fight among his fellow Republicans for the retention of Negro political rights. In 1896, when the G.O.P. denied Negroes any voice in local and state policy or a just share of what Mitchell referred to as the financial "Hanna Barr'l," the *Planet's* editor refused to publish the Republican slate in his newspaper.[11]

Editorially, the paper denounced the constitutional convention of 1901–02 and all its works. While whites complained of Negro domination, Mitchell retorted that the Negro had been deprived of the vote "for more than ten years. . . . If this illegal body can do any more disfranchising . . . or make a dead man any 'deader' after he is dead then the country will look with interest upon the experiment." [12] If there must be disfranchisement, argued Mitchell, let it be against the uneducated and unqualified whites as well as Negroes.[13]

Until disfranchisement became a reality, Mitchell continued the fight against discrimination at the polls, even recommending Negro boycotts of white businesses and products. Thereafter, he became resigned to the hopelessness of the situation and eschewed politics.[14] His editorial mood became more conciliatory and appeared to echo the practical vocational education approach of Booker T. Washington. Typical of his brief weekly "Words of Advice," concerned mainly with the Negroes' progress economically and industrially, is the following:

Colored men, continue to save money and buy property. . . .
Any colored man who opposes race enterprises among the colored people is his own worst enemy. . . .

[11] John Latané Lewis III, "The Election in 1896 of William Jennings Bryan in Virginia," (MS term paper for Edward Younger, American History 103–104, University of Virginia, Jan. 1959).
[12] Brewer, "Futile Trumpet," 38; Richmond *Planet,* Aug. 10, 1901, hereafter cited as *Planet.*   [13] Brewer, "Futile Trumpet," 27.
[14] One searches almost in vain for political comment in the *Planet* from June 1902 through December 1904. Though now unavailable, a second Negro weekly, the Newport News *Star,* was circulated widely in the lower

Colored men should make friends with the better element of white men in the Southland. . . .

It should not be forgotten that colored men themselves are directly responsible for many of the ills from which they suffer.[15]

In an apparent attempt to assure the white citizenry that the Negro accepted his proper station in Virginia and that such men as lawyer James Hayes were unrepresentative of the race, Mitchell wrote that "the Negro is devoting himself now to business and industrial pursuits [rather than politics]. . . . Then, why not permit them to rest or rather to work in peace?" [16]

This same point of view was voiced, following the Negro attorney's first defeat in the disfranchisement cases, by a Washington weekly, which stated that Hayes "had returned to his Richmond home, a sadder and we hope a wiser man. . . . Mr. Hayes should beware the fate of the 'versatile' man. Do one thing well and continue to do that, venturing not upon the unknown seas where shipwreck and disaster alone await the untried mariner." [17]

Equally effective in dampening the antidisfranchisement movement was the comment, or lack of it, by the president of Tuskegee Institute, Booker T. Washington. As president of the newly founded Negro Business League, while presiding over the second annual meeting in Richmond in August 1902, Washington made no mention in his keynote address of the Virginia political situation. Before an estimated crowd of five hundred he instead urged the League to stimulate industry and business development.[18] When he was asked later by a newspaper reporter whether or not

---

Tidewater area from 1901 to 1940. The *Colored American* of Washington sheds little light on the political picture and was primarily business-education oriented. The weekly Norfolk *Journal and Guide,* originally the official organ of the Knights of Gideon under the name *The Lodge Journal and Guide,* is also not available before 1916, owing to a fire in the plant which destroyed all back issues. Letters to the author from Mrs. Maurice N. Derbigny, Hampton, Va., June 24, 27, 1964, and from Thomas W. Young, publisher of the Norfolk paper, June 3, 1964.

[15] *Planet,* March 14, 1903.

[16] *Ibid.,* Feb. 7, 1903.

[17] *Colored American,* Feb. 7, 1903.

[18] Richmond *Dispatch,* Aug. 26, 1902; *Planet,* Aug. 30, 1902; Scrapbook, May–Dec., 1902, Booker T. Washington Papers, Library of Congress.

the suffrage question would be discussed at the meeting, the Tuskegee educator declared the object of the gathering was business and industry. He had no idea that anything smacking of politics would arise.[19]

Again on November 27, 1902, when asked by the Norfolk *Virginian-Pilot* to clarify his political position, Washington replied by telegram:

My life work is the promotion of the education of my race. It is well known that I have always advised my people, that it is of supreme importance at this period of their development that they should concentrate their thought and energy on the securing of homes, the cultivation of habits of thrift, economy, intelligence, high moral character and the gaining of respect and confidence of their neighbors, black and white both in the south and the north. . . .

At every proper opportunity I say to the youth of my people that they will make a mistake if they seek to succeed in life by mere political activity or the hope of holding political office.[20]

In contrast to the conciliatory attitude of John Mitchell, Jr.,[21] and Booker T. Washington, a bolder confrontation of the Hayes faction was made by a Negro lawyer from Richmond, Giles B. Jackson. A conservative Republican, popular among whites as

[19] Richmond *Times,* Aug. 26, 1902. See also telegram from Washington's secretary, E. J. Scott, to Richmond *Times,* Aug. 21, 1902, Washington Papers.

[20] *Virginian-Pilot,* Nov. 27, 1902. August Meier, in a reappraisal of Washington politically, contends that many Negroes and whites mistakenly thought Washington's short-range objectives were also his long-range goals. Meier holds that the Negro leader quietly worked behind the scenes for Negro political rights, especially in the disfranchisement cases in Georgia, Alabama, and Virginia. "Toward a Reinterpretation of Booker T. Washington," *Journal of Southern History,* XXIII (May 1957), 220–27; Meier, *Negro Thought in America,* 121–256 *passim;* also Samuel R. Spencer, *Booker T. Washington and the Negro's Place in American Biography,* ed. by Oscar Handlin (N.Y., 1955), 125–28.

[21] At the National Bankers' Association meeting in 1904, Mitchell declared, "I came to this convention after I had consulted with white men. I would not have come, if you please, unless they had advised it. I love the white man. There is no quarrel between me and him." New York *Times,* Sept. 17, 1904, in John Mitchell, Jr., Scrapbook, Hampton Institute, Hampton, Va.

well as Negroes, Jackson was "ever an ardent spokesman for Negro business and certainly its best publicist."[22] In 1904, after a caucus of the Negro Development and Exposition Company, he denounced Hayes for feeling

> he can devour the white Republicans along with the men who framed the constitution. . . . Hayes is a failure at almost everything. Take, for instance, the National Suffrage Convention, which broke up in general discord. I fail to see how he expects to succeed in this constitutional fight by *fighting an enterprise which is endorsed by the very elements of both parties.*[23]

To Giles Jackson and his followers, disfranchisement was a reality to be accepted. He insisted that

> good moral character and industrial efficiency, resulting in ownership of property, are the pressing needs and the sure and speedy path to recognition and enfranchisement. A few able Negroes are disposed to press for the free and unrestricted vote immediately. We cannot but hope that the wiser policy will prevail.[24]

As the pros and cons of Negro disfranchisement were argued, a third Negro faction stood by apathetically, voicing no opinion. Typical of this apathy were the words of "an old colored brother":

Dey don't bother me none, I can't vote no how.
Now dey wanta violate de constitution without violating de constitution
In other words
Dey want water to run down the hill, without water running down the hill,
Dey want the man to shoot the turkey, without the man shooting the turkey

---

[22] Giles Jackson, born a slave in Goochland County in 1852, was aided by whites to become one of Richmond's most successful Negro citizens. He was the grand attorney for the Knights of the True Reformers, a member of the board of directors of the True Reformer Bank, first vice president of the Negro National Business League, and owner of a profitable bakery. Lewis, *Negro in Virginia,* 297–98; interview with Giles Jackson's son, Roscoe C. Jackson, June 14, 1964, Richmond.

[23] *News Leader,* Feb. 9, 1904.

[24] *Ibid.;* Giles B. Jackson and D. Webster Davis, *The Industrial History of the Negro Race in the United States* (Richmond, 1908), 376–78.

Dey want an act done without the act,
Well, if the white folks can stand it, I can, too.[25]

The *Planet,* apparently little concerned with voter registration in 1902, commented simply, "The Negroes are indifferent," and in the weeks prior to the November election the newspaper omitted politics almost completely.[26]

Involved in their own political hassle, on the eve of the disfranchisement cases the Negroes faced the even greater problem of the desertion of their white allies in the Republican party. As early as March 1900, during the debate over the merits of a constitutional convention, many Republicans had favored Negro exclusion in the hopes of ending fraud and voter manipulation. Equally important, they hoped for the reestablishment of a genuine two-party system in the Old Dominion. With disfranchisement in 1902, the G.O.P. grasped the opportunity to shake itself loose from the "party of the Negro" label it had borne since Reconstruction. Virginia Republicans watched with interest the successful establishment of a "lily-white" party in North Carolina and were quick to follow suit.[27]

Negroes protested that the G.O.P. had not come to their defense during voter registration in 1902. To these complaints, Park Agnew, chairman of the Republican State Central Committee, denied that colored registrants had been discriminated against. Though they had been rigidly examined, Agnew concluded, "It is my belief that whenever a negro measures up to the requirements he is promptly allowed to register." [28] It should be recalled that earlier, at the executive committee meeting on June 17, 1902, the Republican State Committee had adopted a resolution condemning the proclamation of the constitution as illegal. Agnew had also implied that court action would be forthcoming if G.O.P.

---

[25] Brewer, "Futile Trumpet," 38–39.

[26] *Planet,* Oct. 25–Nov. 8, 1902, *passim.* As was typical of *Planet* reporting during that period, the newspaper instead carried an extended serialized account of the wooing and kidnapping by a white farmer of a fourteen-year-old Negro girl.

[27] Horn, "Democratic Party in Virginia," 100–101; "Southern Republican Elimination of the Negro," *World's Work,* IV (Oct. 1902), 2491.

[28] Richmond *Times,* Sept. 12, 1902.

State Committee attorneys requested it. The Washington weekly, *Colored American,* one of the first to view this resolution as a façade, also predicted little future aid from the G.O.P.; "in fact, it seems that the Republicans rather enjoy the condition in which the Negroes find themselves." [29]

Meanwhile, in several areas of the state Negroes found themselves excluded from Republican meetings and conventions. On September 13, 1902, only seven Negro members attended a nominating convention for a subsequent meeting to be held in Cape Charles. They made no objections to the full slate of whites nominated as delegates, and the whites appeared to be "greatly relieved that they did not have to put up with the usual interruptions and objections from that quarter." [30] In New Kent County, for the first time in its Republican political history, the delegates chosen to its congressional district convention were all white.[31] When the G.O.P. met at West Point to nominate a candidate for the House of Representatives for the Third Congressional District, the consensus on Negro disfranchisement was that "the negro is a dead letter in politics and some expressed the view that disfranchisement had done the Republican party more good than harm." [32] At the Second Congressional District's nominating convention, from which Negroes were conspicuously absent, resolutions were passed in opposition to the new constitution. They were carefully worded, though, to avoid seeming to promise an aggressive campaign in defense of the Negro. One of the district's candidates, Captain C. H. Caussey, voicing his "lily-white" opinion, declared, "I am opposed to the Republicans making any attempt to contest the franchise clause of the new Constitution. A white man's country for me. A white man's country." [33]

On October 11, 1902, 50 Negroes at a Pulaski County Court House rally were "Jim Crowed" in a separate corner of the meeting hall while Republican party candidates busied themselves de-

---

[29] Oct. 11, 1902.   [30] Richmond *Dispatch,* Sept. 14, 1902.
[31] Richmond *Times,* Sept. 12, 1902.
[32] Richmond *Dispatch,* Sept. 18, 1902.
[33] Petersburg *Daily Index-Appeal,* Oct. 8, 1902.

nouncing Democrats and the constitution.[34] Shortly thereafter, according to an "unqualified statement" in Colonel Campbell Slemp's hometown newspaper, the Big Stone Gap *Post,* Slemp openly lauded the disfranchisement provisions of the new constitution as an aid to both parties. He charged that John S. Wise had committed a serious error in stirring up a fight against it. Adding to Slemp's words, the *Post* continued:

The majority of white men, if not all of them agree with the Colonel. . . . It is refreshing to know that prominent and leading Republicans in Virginia . . . [are] willing publicly to make known their condemnation of [Wise's] course. There can be no doubt that Colonel Slemp is right in saying that the new Constitution has benefited the Republican party. . . . It has insured to the Republican Party fair elections with the guarantee that in a contest between white men, decided by the suffrage of white men, the man who will poll the most votes for an office in Virginia will win.[35]

Finally, in the heavily Negro-populated Fourth Congressional District, where Negro John Mercer Langston had won a seat in the House of Representatives in 1888, for the first time in many years the Republicans did not offer a candidate for Congress. Instead, the party backed an independent Democrat, R. T. Vaughan. In protest of Vaughan, whom they considered to be a "lily white," Negroes stayed away from the polls on election day. Earlier, Petersburg Negroes had sent a delegation to President Theodore Roosevelt to oppose the rising lily-white spirit in the Fourth District, but apparently nothing came from this protest.[36]

As a sidelight to the Republican exclusions, Negroes asserted that the G.O.P. also deprived them of patronage, most of which originated on the federal level. The *Colored American* charged that of the sixty-five appointments to the census office in Virginia, only Julia H. Hayes was a Negro, and she had not received the recommendation of the Republican dispenser of spoils, Park

[34] Richmond *Dispatch,* Oct. 11, 1902.
[35] Big Stone Gap *Post,* Nov. 27, 1902, cited in Horn, "Democratic Party in Virginia," 101–2.
[36] Richmond *Times,* Oct. 12, 30, 1902.

Agnew.[37] In 1904 Negro leaders in Richmond and Henrico County petitioned the Republican State Committee against the removal of a colored bailiff, Wilson Nash, from the United States Circuit Court of Appeals in favor of a white man. The appeal pointed out that, except for the Post Office, Negroes held but one position in the internal revenue service, two or three in the United States courts, and several as janitors in federal buildings.[38]

This was the situation as the Negroes attempted to regain the suffrage in the Old Dominion. On November 14, 1902, two suits testing the validity of the new constitution were filed in the United States Circuit Court at Richmond. The first, *Jones et al.* v. *Montague et al.*, charged that Governor Montague, members of the registration boards of election, and about fifty members of the constitutional convention had deprived Negroes of the right to vote by favoring proclamation of the constitution. A writ of prohibition was sought by the plaintiff to prevent the State Board of Canvassers from delivering certificates of election to Virginia members of the House of Representatives in November 1902, on the basis that the state constitution had denied Negroes their legal rights.[39] The second suit, *Selden et al.* v. *Montague et al.*, sought the same relief by applying for a writ of injunction. The prosecution charged discrimination by registrars against colored citizens. For example, William Selden, an undertaker who could read and write and paid property taxes on $1,500 worth of real estate, was denied voting rights because he failed the "understanding clause." William H. Anderson, a lieutenant in the Spanish-American War, now a manufacturers' agent, was rejected because he registered as W. "A." Anderson. A third applicant, Charles Gilpin, a Virginia school teacher for over ten years, failed to answer the registrar's question to that official's satisfaction.[40]

Attorneys John S. Wise and James Hayes, representing the

[37] March 29, 1902.

[38] *News Leader,* May 19, 1904.

[39] Moore, "William A. Anderson," 87; McDanel, *Virginia Constitutional Convention,* 132–33; Richmond *Dispatch,* Nov. 29, Dec. 2, 1902. Among the Representatives-elect awaiting the outcome of the case was Carter Glass, then serving the unexpired term of Peter J. Otey.

[40] Richmond *Times,* Nov. 26, 1902.

plaintiffs, attacked the election laws as unconstitutional, maintaining that according to the Underwood constitution of 1869 and a federal statute of 1870 Virginia could return to the Union only under certain conditions. One of these stipulated that the constitution of Virginia should never be changed to deprive any citizen of the United States of the right to vote who had been entitled to vote by the Underwood constitution, except as a punishment for felonies.[41]

In what appeared to be an attempt to sidestep the constitutional issue, Chief Justice of the Supreme Court Melville W. Fuller, hearing the cases in circuit, dismissed both suits on the grounds of lack of jurisdiction. The cases against the Commonwealth, argued Fuller, were against "an indispensable party, and cannot be made such," as it then took on a political nature and "cannot be disposed of at such a hearing." With the decision, the State Board of Canvassers issued certificates of election to the awaiting officeholders.[42] Wise and Hayes appealed the decision on a writ of error to the United States Supreme Court, an appeal not to be judged until 1904. During the interim two other cases dealing with the constitutionality of state law established a trend toward upholding the constitution of 1902.

In a disfranchisement case similar to those being heard in the Old Dominion, the Supreme Court decided in April 1903 against Jackson W. Giles, a Negro of Montgomery County, Alabama. Giles claimed to have been deprived of his right to vote under the new Alabama constitution by the board of registrars. The Court, however, in upholding the constitution declared that the question of voting rights was a political one in which the Court lacked jurisdiction to interfere.[43]

The case of *Taylor* v. *Commonwealth,* decided by the Virginia Supreme Court of Appeals, strengthened the apparent

[41] *Ibid.,* Nov. 21, 1902; *Virginian-Pilot,* Nov. 26, 1902.

[42] Richmond *Times,* Nov. 30, 1902; McDanel, *Virginia Constitutional Convention,* 132–33.

[43] *Jackson W. Giles* v. *Board of Registrars of Montgomery County, Alabama,* 189 U.S., 475; Carter G. Woodson, "Fifty Years of Negro Citizenship as Qualified by the United States Supreme Court," *Journal of Negro History,* IV (Jan. 1921), 38–41.

validity of the state constitution. John Taylor, a Negro who had been charged with housebreaking in Augusta County, pleaded guilty and, without his consent but with the consent of the attorney for the Commonwealth, was found guilty without a jury trial and sentenced to one year in the penitentiary. On a writ of error to the Supreme Court of Appeals, Taylor's attorney contended that the court had no authority to judge him guilty without benefit of jury. The "supposed" authority relied on by the Augusta court appeared in Article I, Section 8, of the constitution of 1902. According to Taylor's lawyer, however, since that document had not been submitted to the people for approval, the provision was unconstitutional. In sustaining the previous decision, the Appeals Court left little doubt as to the constitutionality of Virginia's new organic law. It held that the work of the convention of 1901–2 had been accepted and implemented by branches of the state government and by the people. There being no other government in the Commonwealth opposing it as the only rightful constitution in the state, it deserved, therefore, the loyal allegiance of its citizenry.[44]

A year later the United States Supreme Court arrived at similar decisions in the previously mentioned cases of *Jones* v. *Montague* and *Selden* v. *Montague*. The high court dismissed both suits on the grounds that they involved moot questions and "the thing sought to be prohibited [the seating of United States Representatives] has been done and cannot be undone by any order of this court."[45]

Any disfranchisement cases decided subsequently would be anticlimactic. According to a Lynchburg citizen, the decisions were welcomed as thrilling "the hearts of many an Anglo-Saxon."[46]

[44] *Taylor* v. *Commonwealth*, 101 Virginia, 892, 44 S.E., 754; Martin, *Negro Disfranchisement in Virginia*, 142–43.

[45] Wise's argument was basically the same as in 1902. For the state's case, see *Supreme Court of the United States, October Term, 1903. Jones and Others* v. *Virginia State Board of Canvassers No. 189–In Prohibition, Selden and Others* v. *Virginia No. 190–In Equity,* in William A. Anderson Papers, University of Virginia; Robert Julius Steamer, "The Supreme Court and Negro Suffrage" (Master's thesis, University of Virginia, 1951), 34–35.

[46] Tipton D. Jennings to W. A. Anderson, April 26, 1904, in Anderson Papers, University of Virginia.

To the Negroes, though Hayes promised to continue the struggle, future prospects were discouraging. The office of the Suffrage League in Richmond suspended publication of the *Negro Advocate*. Though it appeared that the League still maintained a large following in Richmond, it did not issue a call for district or state conventions to elect delegates to the forthcoming National Suffrage Convention.[47]

In defeat, John S. Wise, conceding that the Negro was a "friendless institution politically and has no sympathy in the North or South," admitted that

Congress doesn't want to do anything, the Supreme Court doesn't want to do anything, and so it goes. The Supreme Court passes the question along to Congress, and Congress politely passes it along to the Supreme Court. It is a game of "After you, my dear Alphonse," and it is amusing to everybody, except the Negro.[48]

Oddly enough, Wise, who like his father had opposed slavery, had also opposed unrestricted Negro suffrage after the Civil War. However, once the Republican party had declared itself in favor of enfranchising the Negro, he insisted that the G.O.P. honor its pledge. By following any other course, the party would be guilty "of an outrage against both the whites and the blacks." To him

The time has come when we must either enforce these laws or repeal them.
As they stand, they are a delusion and fraud to the negro. . . .
So I say to the Republican party, be worthy of your great record of the past; deal frankly and boldly with the negro problem before it destroys you.[49]

His plea fell upon deaf ears and, according to Wise, Negro suffrage failed because the G.O.P., "which enacted it, dares not call upon the country to support it in the enforcement of the laws." [50]

---

[47] *News Leader*, June 8, 1904.   [48] *Ibid.*, Dec. 16, 1904.

[49] John S. Wise, "The History of Negro Citizenship and Suffrage in the Past—The Outlook for It in the Future" (undated speech, 1902 or 1903), in John S. Wise Papers, Farmington, Va.; C. C. Davis, "John S. Wise," 468–71.

[50] "The Republican Party and the Suffrage: What It Can Do, What It Cannot Do, What It Ought to Do," speech delivered on Lincoln's Birthday, Feb. 12, 1904, at Grand Rapids, Mich., in Wise Papers; John S. Wise, *The Lion's Skin: A Historical Novel and a Novel History* (N.Y., 1905), 401–2.

The Southerners had disfranchised the Negro, but the Northerners had no intention of interfering. Evidence of this could be found in the remarks of such men as Lyman Abbott, editor of *Outlook* magazine. While addressing an anniversary audience at Hampton Institute, he declared Negro suffrage to have been a mistake and repeated "what I said in RICHMOND: Manhood first, and then suffrage." [51]

With so many factions against the Negroes they stood little chance of a victory in the courts. Following these Supreme Court decisions there was little mention of the suffrage cases for the next few years. Three other suits were pending, but they dragged on through 1907 without final settlement.[52] Furthermore, Attorney General William A. Anderson commented that of these only *Brickhouse* v. *Brooks* was being considered, and even this case had lost any significance because of the lapse of time and changed conditions under the constitution. The Attorney General virtually dismissed the *Lee* v. *Montague* and *Pinner* v. *Montague* cases with the comment that "the plaintiffs seem disposed to let them sleep. It may be well perhaps to let them die a natural death." [53]

The *Brickhouse* v. *Brooks* suit finally appeared on the docket of the United States District Court for the Eastern District of Virginia in February 1907. Once again John S. Wise and James Hayes opposed Attorney General Anderson. As in previous cases, Wise argued that the constitution was invalid because it had not been framed by duly authorized delegates. He also stressed its unconstitutionality since the law had been proclaimed rather than submitted. Anderson retorted that the constitution of 1902 had gained *de facto* recognition in November of that year when all public officials of the state pledged their allegiance to it.[54]

After the decision by Judge Nathan Goff upholding the con-

[51] *News Leader*, April 30, 1903. See also C. Vann Woodward, *The Strange Career of Jim Crow* (2nd ed., N.Y., 1966), 73–74, 113.

[52] *Edgar Poe Lee* v. *A. J. Montague and Others; Arthur S. Pinner* v. *A. J. Montague and Others; Brickhouse* v. *Brooks et al.*

[53] *Annual Report of the Attorney General to the Governor of Virginia for the Year 1905*, 4; *ibid., 1907*, 7.

[54] Moore, "William A. Anderson," 89; Anderson Papers, University of Virginia, have extensive newspaper coverage of the 1907 decision.

stitution, the plaintiffs appealed to the United States Circuit Court of Appeals. On November 7, 1908, the higher court upheld Judge Goff. Employing the *Taylor* v. *Commonwealth* case as precedent, the court held that the constitution had been accepted as law in 1902 by all departments in the state. It added that whether or not certain of its sections were in conflict with the requirements of the federal Constitution was strictly a "political" question to be determined by the legislative and executive departments of the United States. In the absence of such action the presumption should be that the necessity for it did not exist.[55]

Any remaining cases apparently were dropped. A final effort was reported on March 12, 1912, when counsel for both parties in the *Lee* v. *Montague* suit were informed that the case would be called up on April 1 and that if both were not present then it would be dismissed. To this announcement, John S. Wise allegedly replied in resignation, "Let her go—Dead horse." [56]

Though the Negroes were successfully disfranchised, none of the cases answered the real question at issue. According to one source this was whether or not the constitutional convention had the right to proclaim the organic law of 1902 contrary to the provisions of the Underwood Constitution.[57] In all of the suits the decisions came after the law of 1902 had become a *fait accompli*. Time proved to be on the side of the state, and prolonged inactivity inevitably meant victory for Virginia. Despite the efforts of men such as Wise and Hayes, therefore, the struggle for Negro suffrage in the courts was bound to end with "Let her go—Dead horse."

[55] *Brickhouse* v. *Brooks et al.*, 165 *Federal Reporter* 545; Moore, "William A. Anderson," 90; Richmond *Evening Journal*, Nov. 8, 1908, in Anderson Papers.

[56] McDanel, *Virginia Constitutional Convention*, 134–35; C. C. Davis, "John S. Wise," 471. Papers for this case are at the office of clerk of the United States District Court, Richmond, File 1762. Several of the defendants recalled that the case came to trial, but neither the records nor the Court Order Book indicate this.

[57] McDanel, *Virginia Constitutional Convention*, 145.

IV

Exclusion from the Republican Party, 1905-1916

DURING the first decade of the 1900's Negroes had been either eliminated as voters in the South or subordinated to a secondary position by a rising lily-white Republican party. Nevertheless, they continued to play a major but negative role in Southern politics. After disfranchisement, Negroes furnished "for politicians with their backs to the wall a bogus issue with which to becloud the real issues at stake, . . . an ever-present scapegoat upon which the southern white masses might vent their frustrated emotions." [1] In Virginia, despite the insistence of G.O.P. leaders such as Colonel Campbell Slemp that politically the Negro "never interested us much at all" and that "the negro is completely out of politics and that settles that," [2] the Democratic party persisted in using the "issue." It charged that from the beginning the G.O.P. was the enemy of most Southerners, a party whose very name was "an offense to most of the white people of the South, and in our opinion it will be many a day before the party will have respectable standing south of Mason and Dixon's line." [3]

An early example of the race bogey being employed in a Virginia election occurred in the Ninth District congressional election of 1904 between Campbell Slemp, Republican, and J. C. Wysor, Democrat. Early in the campaign Slemp charged Democratic

[1] Arthur S. Link, "The Negro as a Factor in the Campaign of 1912," *Journal of Southern History,* XXXII (Jan. 1947), 82; Key, *Southern Politics,* 5, 9. See also Newby, *Jim Crow's Defense,* Chapter V, "The Issue of Political Equality." [2] Roanoke *Times,* March 18, 1903.
[3] Richmond *Times,* Nov. 6, 1902.

State Chairman J. Taylor Ellyson with playing "the race issue for all it is worth." [4] He added that the opposition, in its accusation that President Roosevelt befriended Negroes in Washington, attempted to condemn Virginia Republicans for national policy. Such allegations led one to believe that the election of either Roosevelt or Slemp would be attributed largely to the Negro vote and that, thereafter, the victors would most certainly work for political and social equality for the Negro.[5] Whatever emphasis the Democrats may have placed on the issue in the Ninth District, it was not enough to defeat Slemp.[6]

The gubernatorial race of 1905 proved a different story and illustrates the potency of the race issue in Virginia politics. Led by Colonel Slemp, the newly appointed state chairman, the Republican State Convention in Roanoke on August 9 nominated Judge L. L. Lewis for governor.[7] The party platform included a denunciation of the Democratic party "for the manner in which the new Constitution was forced upon the people of Virginia by proclamation, after the pledge that the same should be submitted to the people for ratification or rejection." It did not, however, recommend provisions for testing the constitutionality of the election laws in the courts. It was a convention from which "the colored element [was] practically excluded." [8] Delegate W. H. C. Brown, "the only negro that has shown up in the convention outside the peanut gallery," set the tone for the meeting when he declared in a seconding speech that his race only wished to help

[4] Big Stone Gap *Post,* Aug. 25, 1904; Pendleton, *Appalachian Virginia,* 509.

[5] Slemp was alluding to Roosevelt's appointment of a Negro, Dr. W. D. Crum of Charleston, S.C., as collector of that port and his entertaining Booker T. Washington at the White House. Roosevelt was thereafter accused by Southern newspapers of being a "CARPETBAGGER." Governor Andrew J. Montague chastised the Republican party for treating the Negro better than the white man. To Montague, the white race was "by divine right . . . entitled to supremacy. . . . One race must guide . . . and one must be guided. . . . Do we want negroes dining in our executive mansion?" Larsen, *Montague of Virginia,* 111; *Virginian-Pilot,* Nov. 12, 1902.

[6] *Times-Dispatch,* Nov. 10, 1904.

[7] Hathorn, "C. Bascom Slemp," 30–33; Pendleton, *Appalachian Virginia,* 513–14.

[8] Roanoke *Times,* Aug. 8, 10, 1905; *Planet,* Aug. 12, 1905.

out in the material development of the state, enjoying the blessings of Republican prosperity. Brown assured the white audience that it need not fear the Negro as a menace to its social institutions or that the Negro would strive for social equality. Rather, the colored man wished to copy "the civilization of the whites and [follow] at a respectable distance." [9]

Shortly after the Lewis nomination, the Republican candidate came under heavy Democratic fire. In a speech at Fredericksburg, Congressman William A. Jones charged that Lewis in a discussion with General George J. Hundley at Chesterfield Court House either in 1877 or 1878 had advocated miscegenation. This accusation arose over a bill then before the state legislature prohibiting intermarriage of the races. Lewis opposed the legislation while Hundley supported it. In reply to Jones' charge, Judge Lewis declared that he had not advocated miscegenation; rather he had believed that if a prohibitory law passed, the courts might declare it unconstitutional. He had reasoned that since marriage was founded upon a contract, a law forbidding intermarriage might be a violation of that contract. [10]

When asked for his version of the incident, Hundley confirmed Jones' accusation. He also recollected that Lewis had remarked that people should marry whom they pleased. [11] The Republican candidate then flatly denied the allegation and charged the Democrats with stirring up racial animosity. [12] He singled out Democratic State Committee Chairman J. Taylor Ellyson, accusing him of spreading the miscegenation story and of flooding the state with such race-baiting leaflets as the following:

SERIOUS CHARGE AGAINST LEWIS
CONGRESSMAN JONES SPRINGS SENSATION BEFORE AN AUDIENCE
AN ADVOCATE OF INTER-MARRIAGE
THE REPUBLICAN CANDIDATE ALLEGED TO HAVE SPOKEN
IN OPPOSITION
TO A BILL IN THE LEGISLATURE PROHIBITING MISCEGENATION. [13]

[9] Roanoke *Times*, Aug. 10, 1905.   [10] *Times-Dispatch*, Oct. 17, 1905.
[11] *Ibid.*, Sept. 3, 1905.   [12] Roanoke *Times*, Oct. 19, 26, 1905.
[13] *Times-Dispatch*, Oct. 25, 1905; Pendleton, *Appalachian Virginia*, 516; Scrapbook for 1905, C. Bascom Slemp Papers, Southwest Virginia Museum, Big Stone Gap, Va.

This circular, which offered a detailed account of the miscegenation case, prophetically concluded, "That it will cause Judge Lewis to lose thousands of votes, if allowed to stand uncontradicted, goes without saying." So damaging were these leaflets that one Republican campaign manager, Edward deBordenave of Southampton County, ended a letter to one of his party's leaders with the plea, "Can't you send literature to contradict the statement?" [14]

Additional accusations of befriending the Negro were lodged against Lewis. He was condemned for his defense of Edmund McKinney, who in 1878–79 had been sentenced to a five-year prison term for having married a white woman.[15] The Farmville *Herald* charged that Lewis favored increasing the taxes on whites $30,000 to furnish free textbooks to Negroes.[16] Democratic gubernatorial candidate Claude A. Swanson warned the whites of Virginia that "the return of the Republican party to power in this State would be followed unquestionably by a repeal of those constitutional and other provisions which have destroyed the negro as a voter in Virginia, and would witness his return as a dangerous factor in our politics." [17]

The capstone of the campaign, however, was furnished by Carter Glass, who ridiculed Lewis' attempt to depict the G.O.P. as the "New Republican party" or "white man's party." Quipped Glass:

I answer, we have the same sort of Republican party in Virginia which existed before the negro was eliminated. We whipped them then and will whip them worse without their negro allies. Oh, but they say it is a new party. My friends, it is the same old Republican party minus the dehorned darkey.[18]

The effect of Democratic campaigning on the racial issue against Lewis cannot be numerically gauged, but his defeat on election

[14] Scrapbook for 1905, Slemp Papers.

[15] *Times-Dispatch,* Oct. 28, 1905, in George Jefferson Hundley Scrapbook, Hundley Papers, University of Virginia; Roanoke *Times,* Oct. 25, 1905.

[16] Nov. 3, 1905.

[17] *Times-Dispatch,* Sept. 19, 1905.

[18] *Ibid.,* Nov. 3, 1905.

day was resounding, 83,544 votes to 45,795.[19] There is little evidence that the Negro participated actively in the campaign. Leading newspapers such as the Richmond *Times-Dispatch* and the Norfolk *Virginian-Pilot* made no mention of the Negro in their election reports. The Roanoke *Times* commented that "the returns of every section indicate that the negroes are completely alienated or are cunningly biding their time until they can dictate their own terms." [20] That the Negroes of Roanoke were "biding their time" hardly seems likely with voter registration down from 2,456 in 1900 to 127 in 1902.[21]

The poor showing of Lewis in 1905 doubtless further convinced white Republicans that they must rid themselves of the Negroes. One of the first steps in that direction was taken in the following year at the congressional nominating convention for the Third District in Manchester. In no uncertain terms nominee George A. Hanson announced to the "pitifully few" Negroes in attendance:

If you come into the Republican party seeking to exalt your race, we do not want you. If you come as a Republican seeking to bide by the decisions of its councils you are welcome. The time has come for the negro as a leader to take a back seat. He must be content to follow, not to lead, and if he cannot lead he must get behind the party and shove.[22]

Though he considered the constitution of 1902 to be one of the greatest thefts ever perpetrated upon the state, Hanson admitted that the Democrats had benefited the Commonwealth by disfranchising the Negro, who was incapable of voting intelligently.[23]

Rather than accept Hanson's ultimatum of subordination to white leadership, Negroes at Richmond on October 11 selected an independent candidate, J. B. Johnson of Manchester, for the Third District race. This nomination was a slap against the lily

[19] The Republican total was about 35,000 less than the 81,366 the party had cast for its gubernatorial candidate in 1901. The over-all total of 129,782 votes for governor in 1905 also showed a decline of nearly 70,000 compared to the 198,048 cast in 1901. Eckenrode, "Virginia since 1865," 309. [20] Nov. 9, 1905. [21] *Ibid.,* Oct. 2, 1902.
[22] *Times-Dispatch,* Sept. 26, 1906.
[23] *Ibid.*

whites, whom the Negroes no longer considered to be the true representatives of the party of Lincoln.[24] They realized their candidates could not win, but they hoped to impress upon the lily whites that by forsaking the colored vote the G.O.P. could not win either.

It was rumored that some Negroes were seriously considering shifting to the Democratic party. Such stories persisted until 1928, when sizable numbers actually did so.[25] Regardless of whether or not Negroes voted Democratic, Republican, or independent, the Democrats had little difficulty in sweeping all but the perennially Republican Ninth District in the 1906 election. In a contest "in which the great mass of people seemed to display . . . little interest," the victors polled 55,259 votes to the G.O.P.'s 30,558 for a 85,157 total—well below the 1902 total of 123,100, let alone that of the preconstitution days of 1900 when 269,112 votes were tallied.[26] The decline is more vividly seen when one recollects that there were 447,815 male adults of voting age in 1906.[27] In the Third Congressional District, which in 1900 had a voting potential of 27,896 whites and 18,443 Negroes, the Democrat won easily with a vote of 3,908 to 639 for regular Republican Hanson and 196 for the independent Johnson.[28]

Despite the maltreatment Negroes received from the state Republican leadership, they still considered themselves loyal and active members of the national party led by President Theodore Roosevelt. Along with Roosevelt's willingness to appoint Negroes to federal positions, the Negroes believed that their own leader,

[24] *Ibid.*, Oct. 12, 1906; *Planet*, Nov. 10, 1906.

[25] W. J. Snodgrass to J. Taylor Ellyson, Oct. 26, 1906, Ellyson Papers, University of Virginia. Snodgrass, a county chairman, wrote, "The negroes in Richmond were going to write all the voters not to vote the Republican ticket on account of their treatment by the Republican party. If this is a fact, I can furnish you a list of the negroes in this county."

[26] *Times-Dispatch*, Nov. 4, 1906; *Warrock-Richardson Almanack for the Year 1908*, 71; *ibid.*, *1902*, 31; *ibid.*, *1903*, 68.

[27] Of the 447,815, 301,379 were white and 146,122 were Negroes. *Abstract of the Twelfth Census of the United States, 1900* (Washington, D.C., 1902), 77.

[28] *Warrock-Richardson Almanack for the Year 1908*, 68.

Booker T. Washington, had the President's ear.[29] But even on the national level their faith was shaken when Roosevelt in 1906 had three Negro companies dishonorably discharged from the United States Army. The discharge resulted from a shooting fray in Brownsville, Texas. On the night of August 13, after earlier incidents allegedly involving Negro soldiers from Fort Brown, unknown assailants shot and killed one citizen and wounded another. Though the camp commander insisted no Negroes had been allowed off the post that day, townspeople testified that Negroes had been seen in Brownsville that evening. Their testimony, coupled with other circumstantial evidence, induced Roosevelt to make the dismissals.[30] Because Roosevelt did not act until after the November elections, however, many Negroes were convinced that he purposely waited until the Northern Negro vote was safe in the fold before intervening.

In Virginia the *Planet* denounced the discharges as "the monumental blunder of his administration" and accused Roosevelt of doing an "about face" against the colored race.[31] Secretary of War William Howard Taft, a prospective Republican nominee for the presidency in 1908, was also criticized for backing Roosevelt's decision.[32] "Yes," editorialized the *Planet,* "we would like to see Secretary Taft president—of some Negro-hating society. . . . A colored man who now endorses Secretary of War Taft for the presidency may next be expected to endorse Senator Tillman for the same position." [33] The situation became even more sensitive

[29] Meier, *Negro Thought in America,* 112–13; Woodward, *Origins of the New South,* 462–68; Spencer, *Booker T. Washington,* 133–40, 167–69; Seth M. Scheiner, "President Theodore Roosevelt and the Negro, 1901–1908, "*Journal of Negro History,* XLVII (July 1962), 169–82. Woodward and Scheiner discuss fully the change in Roosevelt's policy toward the Negro from one of friendship and patronage to that of his "revised Southern policy" which sidestepped the Negro issue.

[30] Henry Pringle, *Theodore Roosevelt* (N.Y., 1931), 323–27; Meier, *Negro Thought* in America, 164–65; Emma Lou Thornbrough, "The Brownsville Episode and the Negro Vote," *Mississippi Valley Historical Review,* XLIV (Dec. 1957), 469–83.

[31] Nov. 10, 1906. See also *Planet,* Nov. 10, 1906—Nov. 7, 1908, *passim,* for continuous fight against the Brownsville dismissals.

[32] Henry Pringle, *Life and Times of William Howard Taft* (N.Y., 1939), I, 326.   [33] *Planet,* Dec. 22, 1906.

when by presidential order in June 1907, as executed by Secretary Taft, all remaining Negro troops in the United States were transferred to the Philippine Islands.[34] Protests went unheeded and the Negro had little choice but to accept the situation and cling to the Republican party. Occasionally thereafter the Negro press lashed out against the Roosevelt and Taft administrations, but their tirades were mainly ineffective.

Political exclusion of the Negro continued in the Republican State Convention at Lynchburg on April 8, 1908. During the nominations of delegates to the national convention that summer in Chicago, the Richmond *Times-Dispatch* reported, "Some of the speeches made in opposition to allowing negroes to be seated would have aroused applause in the Virginia Democratic convention in the days of Reconstruction." [35] Among the 921 delegates present, only a dozen were Negroes. When Delegate Morgan Treat attempted to speak in opposition to Republican State Chairman C. Bascom Slemp [36] and in favor of seating colored delegates, "he was greeted by such a volley of howls, hisses, and demands that he sat down." Another delegate quickly rose, shouting, "If any man look upon this convention today and say the Republican party of Virginia is not a respectable white man's party, that man is a liar." [37]

C. Bascom Slemp, a leading lily white in the eyes of most Negroes, was easily reelected state chairman, and Taft was nominated for the presidency. Negroes contested the seating of the delegation chosen to attend the national convention on the grounds that the Slemp organization had controlled the convention illegally by previously holding closed city, county, and district conventions. Meeting in Richmond on May 14, the Independent Republicans, composed mainly of Negroes and old-line white Republicans,

[34] *Ibid.*, June 15, 1907.

[35] April 9, 1908; *Planet,* April 11, 18, 1908; Hathorn, "C. Bascom Slemp," 74.

[36] Congressman Campbell Slemp died in 1907, and by special election his son was elected for the remainder of the term. C. Bascom was elected in his own right in 1908, defeating Democrat J. Cloy Byars by over 4,000 votes. Hathorn, "C. Bascom Slemp," 36–40; *Annual Report of the Secretary of the Commonwealth for 1908,* 321.

[37] *Times-Dispatch,* April 9, 1908; *Planet,* April 11, 1908.

selected their own delegation to represent them.[38] In Chicago, however, their protest challenge failed and all twenty-four of the lily-white Slemp delegates were seated. Twenty-one of them voted for Taft's nomination on the first ballot.[39]

Although Booker T. Washington urged the 10,000 remaining Negro voters in Virginia to vote for Taft, the Richmond *Planet* editorialized that "we are confronted by Rooseveltism on the one hand and Bryanism on the other. The voter can choose between the two. Republicanism and Democracy are treated as strangers in both camps." The newspaper recommended that Negroes "practice individualism" and vote for the candidate who would aid them most.[40] There is little evidence, though, to indicate that the handful of Negro voters bolted from the Republican banner. Almost gleefully on election day the *Planet* chided the Democrats, who, though able to carry Virginia for William Jennings Bryan by approximately 30,000 votes, had suffered defeat nationally.

In the Capitol Square, thousands had gathered to see the display of the *Times-Dispatch*. Hundreds of colored people, silent and inexpressive, watched the returns with grim satisfaction. They had not been permitted to vote, but they looked at the anguish of the Bryanites with grim satisfaction.[41]

If the Negroes looked on "with grim satisfaction" at the Democratic defeat in the 1908 presidential race, they still received little satisfaction from the Republicans. At the Republican State Nominating Convention in Newport News on July 28, 1909, only six Negroes occupied convention seats.[42] Just prior to the meeting it had been rumored that State Chairman Slemp favored the adoption of a resolution that no Negroes be appointed to federal positions in Virginia who would be objectionable to the whites in the communities in which they were to serve.[43]

---

[38] *Ibid.*, May 23, 1908.

[39] *Official Report of the Proceedings of the Fourteenth Republican National Convention* (Columbus, Ohio, 1908), 317–18; Hathorn, "C. Bascom Slemp," 77.   [40] *Planet*, July 4, Oct. 17, 1908.   [41] *Ibid.*, Nov. 7, 1908.

[42] Petersburg *Daily Index-Appeal*, July 29, 30, 1909; *Planet*, July 31, 1909.

[43] *Planet*, May 8, 1909. In his inaugural address, President Taft essentially agreed with regard to Negro appointments. Pringle, *Taft*, I, 390, and Woodward, *Origins of the New South*, 468.

Despite such rejections by the Slemp-led Republicans and the attempt to win back white voters to the G.O.P., the race bogey was again employed by the Democrats in 1910 against Slemp in the Ninth District congressional election. Campaigning under the slogan "Redeem the District," the Democrats nominated Henry C. Stuart for the House. He had served in the constitutional convention of 1901–2 and voted for franchise restriction "in the interest of white supremacy in Virginia, necessary for our civilization." During the 1910 campaign Stuart attacked the one remaining "barrier" in the franchise question, the Fifteenth Amendment. If elected he pledged to work for its repeal, "so that Virginia may impose no condition on white suffrage. . . . I ask my opponent to say if he would so vote." [44]

This challenge placed Slemp in a predicament. If he endorsed repeal, it amounted to repudiating a cherished Republican principle. If he opposed repeal, Slemp would be accused of not supporting white supremacy. In an attempt to avert this political trap, the Republican candidate insisted that the Negro suffrage question was settled in the South and a challenge of the Fifteenth Amendment would only make the issue a national one, something the South did not desire.[45]

Slemp was further castigated because he had not favored separate street cars for Negroes and whites while in the Virginia legislature. To the Democrats, here was a man who regarded the Negro's vote "as counting for as much as a white man's vote." [46]

Both sides conducted an intensive campaign in the "Fighting Ninth." The Democrats flooded the district with political leaders such as Senators Martin and Swanson, Congressmen Flood and Glass, former Governors Montague and Tyler, and future Governor Trinkle. Slemp attempted to go them one better by having

[44] Harrisonburg *Daily News,* March 3, 1910, cited in Hathorn, "C. Bascom Slemp," 48; Guy B. Hathorn, "The Congressional Campaign in the Fighting Ninth: The Contest between C. Bascom Slemp and Henry C. Stuart," *Virginia Magazine of History and Biography,* LXVI (July 1958), 340.

[45] Hathorn, "C. Bascom Slemp," 56–57; J. F. Essary, ed. *Selected Addresses of C. Bascom Slemp* (Washington, D.C., 1938), 60–61; Hathorn, "Congressional Campaign in the Fighting Ninth," 341.

[46] *Times-Dispatch,* Oct. 15, 1910, cited in Hathorn, "C. Bascom Slemp," 63.

ex-President Theodore Roosevelt speak in the district on his behalf. The campaign was also marked by poll tax payment "for the faithful" and vote buying. Estimated expenses by each side for the campaign ranged from $100,000 to $500,000. One Slemp campaigner admitted paying $86 for a key vote, though the average price was $15. The Democrats, in turn, reportedly purchased the services of Republican election officials and even "imported" voters from the Kentucky and Tennessee border areas.[47]

Though Stuart cried fraud at the election results, Slemp was declared winner by the narrow margin of 16,958 votes to 16,731.[48] No recount was requested as undoubtedly both parties would have had explaining to do about their campaign practices. This election provided evidence of Virginia's inability to rid itself of election practices which had existed prior to the adoption of the constitution of 1902. Eliminating the Negro politically retained the race issue and did not curb corruption and votebuying.

For approximately the next eight-year period, 1911–18, political activity by the Negroes in the Old Dominion was at a standstill. Even those few remaining registered Negroes who may have wished to bolt from the G.O.P. were unwanted in the Democratic party. To further stress this point the Democrats in 1912 successfully excluded Negroes from their party primaries. To understand just how the white primary developed, let us return to the early years of this century. In 1903 the debate over a direct primary resulted in an intraparty struggle between the machine faction, led by Senator Thomas Staples Martin, Charles A. Swanson, and Henry D. Flood, who opposed it, and those "independents" favoring it, headed by Congressmen William A. Jones and Carter Glass and Governor Andrew Jackson Montague.[49] Its proponents hoped to eliminate nomination of candidates by a select few in caucus or convention and place nominations squarely before the people. After the "independent" Democrats won, the

---

[47] Horn, "Democratic Party in Virginia," 192; Hathorn, "C. Bascom Slemp," 67–71; Bristol *Herald-Courier*, Nov. 16, 1910.

[48] *Warrock-Richardson Almanack for the Year 1911*, 73; Scrapbook for 1910, Slemp Papers.

[49] Eckenrode, "Virginia since 1865," 314–15; Larsen, "Andrew Jackson Montague," II, 455–75; Horn, "Democratic Party in Virginia," 244, 245–58.

primary became highly significant, especially since Republicans no longer competed successfully for public office. Success in the primary was tantamount to victory since Democratic nominees were frequently unopposed and seldom defeated by Republicans.

Despite attempts to exclude Negroes, there was nothing in the state primary law barring them from the primaries until 1912. A typical exclusion attempt was made at the State Democratic Convention in May 1905 at Richmond. The State Committee proposed that the primary law be amended so that, like the wording in its own party rules, only white Democrats could vote in any primary election to nominate party candidates.[50] The danger of such a proposal, however, lay in the fact that the amendment specifically admitted that race was the basis for exclusion. Conflicting with the Fifteenth Amendment, this would invite a legal test in the courts. Effective disfranchisement of the Negro "had to be accomplished by methods appearing to comply with the Federal Constitution." Since the Democratic party was recognized as a private organization, it could legally discriminate along whatever lines it so desired.[51] Party rules were less likely to be scrutinized by the courts than were the actions of the state government.

In the Primary Law of 1912 the General Assembly therefore placed the formulation of rules and the calling of conventions in the hands of the party. One of the rules adopted restricted voting in the primary to Democrats who had voted in the last general election for the Democratic nominees.[52] Since most Negroes voted Republican, they had already disqualified themselves. Other Negroes hesitated to join the Democratic party because it involved an open declaration of intentions to a registrar who would undoubtedly reject their application. Furthermore, fellow Negroes frequently looked askance at members of their race who became Democrats.[53] Section 21 of the Primary Law of 1912 seemed harmless enough, but its acceptance of the state's financial

[50] O. Douglas Weeks, "The White Primary," *Mississippi Law Journal,* VIII (Dec. 1935), 135–36; Roanoke *Times,* May 17, 1905.

[51] Key, *Southern Politics,* 619–20.

[52] *Acts and Joint Resolutions . . . of the General Assembly, 1912,* 613–14; *ibid., 1914,* 516–24, *passim; Planet,* Aug. 1, 1914.

[53] Personal interview with Roscoe C. Jackson, Aug. 14, 1964, Richmond.

responsibility for an election was destined to be construed by the courts as recognition that holding a primary election was a governmental function.[54]

Previously a few of the "better sort" of Negroes had been permitted to vote in the primaries, but the 1912 legislation excluded even these. The *Planet* condemned this exclusion of Negroes in Richmond and Petersburg from the 1912 primary. Negroes had not expected this treatment, for they originally believed the law had been designed to exclude white Republicans. According to the Richmond weekly, this development was so unexpected that Negro voters did not have time to contest its validity in the courts.[55]

Negro Democrats received unfavorable publicity for alleged misconduct in the 1912 Fourth Congressional District primary. About fifty Negroes voted in the election; and, because of the closeness of the contest and charges of vote buying, a recount was taken. Both candidates, Congressman Robert Turnbull and Judge Walter A. Watson, disclaimed any knowledge of illegal practices or of any "worthy Negroes" voting for them. As a result of the State Democratic Committee decision that Negro votes not be counted, Turnbull triumphed, 4,447 to 4,443.[56] As in 1902, the Negro was linked to political corruption, and the moral drawn was that the way to end fraud was to exclude him from the polls.

On February 13, 1913, the Democratic party reaffirmed its white primary policy. Negro exclusion was further strengthened by an opinion of State Attorney General John Garland Pollard. In upholding the law, Pollard asserted that the General Assembly had the right to prescribe qualifications for party primaries.[57] An act in the General Assembly in 1920 also tightened the grip of the white Democrats on the primary.[58]

[54] *Acts and Joint Resolutions, 1912,* 618; *ibid., 1914,* 524; *Annual Report of the Attorney General to the Governor for the Year 1912,* 53–54.

[55] *Planet,* Aug. 17, Sept. 21, Oct. 12, 1912.

[56] Petersburg *Daily Index-Appeal,* Oct. 15, 1912.

[57] *Planet,* Aug. 1, 1914. Periodically thereafter the Democratic State Committee renewed its pledge that only "white persons who are qualified to vote in the next ensuing general election" were to be declared members of the Democratic party. Weeks, "White Primary," 140; Martin, *Negro Disfranchisement in Virginia,* 153.

[58] *Virginia Code, 1924* (Charlottesville, Va., 1924), 155, Section 228; Lewinson, *Race, Class, and Party,* 155.

The little political activity still maintained by the Negro was on the national level, largely in a defensive effort to curb lily-whitism within the Republican party. Owing to the lack of source material during these particular years, one can only surmise that state and local political activity was minimal. Nationally, from the time of the presidential campaign of William Howard Taft in 1908 the G.O.P. moved away from the Southern Negro. Declaring that he "would not be president of half of the country," [59] Taft broke precedent by touring the white Democratic South in the hope of winning votes. The Republican candidate maintained that "the way for the colored race to make a path for themselves to success is to show how useful they are in the community of which they are a part, not only how useful they are but how indispensable they are." [60]

After his election Taft initially was cautious and declared he would avoid haste in making Negro appointments in the South. He would not go "into places of such prominence as the South, where the feeling is strong," as it "will only tend to increase the race feeling," but he did promise to "look about and make appointments in the North and recognize the Negro as often as I can." [61] Shortly after he took office, however, the Collector of Customs for Charleston, W. D. Crum, appointed by Roosevelt in 1902, resigned. Negroes accused Taft of applying pressure on Crum to bow out.[62] They charged further that Taft had not kept his campaign promise to appoint J. C. Napier as Register of the Treasury of the United States. Napier was relegated to a lower position and the expected appointment went to a white man. Negroes were also dismayed because the President took no action to curb lynching, a crime committed mainly against the colored race.[63]

As a result of the Taft administration's lily-whitism many Virginia Negroes who had always been loyal Republicans deserted

[59] Woodward, *Origins of the New South,* 467; E. Merton Coulter, "The Attempt of William Howard Taft to Break the Solid South," *Georgia Quarterly Review,* XIX (June 1935), 134–44.
[60] Address to Fisk University, Nashville, Tenn., May 22, 1908, in Booker T. Washington Papers.
[61] Woodward, *Origins of the New South,* 468; Pringle, *William Howard Taft,* I, 390.   [62] Pringle, *William Howard Taft,* I, 390.
[63] Elbert L. Tatum, *The Changed Political Status of the Negro, 1915–1940* (N.Y., 1951), 92–93.

him in the presidential election of 1912. Some supported the Progressive candidate, Theodore Roosevelt, apparently having forgiven him for the Brownsville dismissals in 1906. Others even voted for the Democratic nominee, Woodrow Wilson.

The political turnabout began at the Republican State Convention in Roanoke on March 12, 1912. Under the watchful eye of State Chairman C. Bascom Slemp, twenty of the twenty-four delegates selected for the national convention at Chicago pledged themselves for Taft.[64] In protest, Negro leaders met in Petersburg on May 15 and selected a pro-Roosevelt delegation.[65] Attempts to generate enthusiasm for the protest movement, though, were unrewarding. In one instance, a political rally in Richmond on May 17, which anticipated a capacity crowd of one thousand, drew only seventy Negroes.[66] On the eve of the Republican convention, the bolting Negroes had little to cheer about.

In Chicago, despite protests by the Negro delegation led by lawyer James A. Hayes, the National Committee recognized the delegates selected at Roanoke.[67] The Negroes countered with a convention of their own in Richmond on July 30. Its purpose was to sponsor Roosevelt through a Negro-white alliance. Apathy prevailed, however, and only eighteen Negroes responded to the call.[68]

Roosevelt, who had been out of the political spotlight for the past four years, had not yet expressed his views on the Southern Negroes' grievances or lily-white Republicanism. He had been warned by John M. Parker, his chief adviser in New Orleans, that he could hope for little Southern support if any Negro delegations were seated at the Progressive party convention.[69] On the other hand, he did not wish to forfeit Negro support in such key states as Rhode Island, Maryland, New York, Illinois, and New Jersey.

In an obvious political maneuver to maintain Northern Negro

[64] *Planet,* March 16, 1912; Hathorn, "C. Bascom Slemp," 87–92.
[65] *Times-Dispatch,* May 16, 1912.   [66] *Ibid.,* May 18, 1912.
[67] *Ibid.,* June 16, 1912; Hathorn, "C. Bascom Slemp," 94–99.
[68] *Times-Dispatch,* July 31, 1912.
[69] *Ibid.,* Aug. 2, 1912; George E. Mowry, "The South and the Progressive Lily White Party in 1912," *Journal of Southern History,* VI (July 1940), 237–47.

support and still woo the Southern white vote, Roosevelt issued an open letter on August 2 expressing his feelings on the situation. For the past forty-five years, wrote the Bull Moose candidate, the Republican party had attempted unsuccessfully to shape an organization in the Southern states based upon Negro leadership or upon that of whites who derived their power mainly through Negro suffrage. The Republican party had suffered badly as a result, and for the Progressives to repeat the past course of action would be senseless. Roosevelt appealed instead to

the men who have stood for securing the colored man his rights before the law, and they can do for him what neither the Northern white man nor the colored men themselves can do. Our only wise course from the standpoint of the colored man himself is to follow the course that we are following toward him in the North and to follow the course we are following toward him in the South.[70]

Publication of Roosevelt's letter all but ended hopes among Southern Negroes for representation at the Bull Moose Convention. Dismissed by the Republicans as well as by the Progressives, they had but one alternative left, to support the Democratic candidate. As yet the day had not arrived when the Negro vote would be courted openly by the Democratic party, but, according to Arthur S. Link, Wilson managers in Virginia made a bid for new support.[71] In September 1912 the Richmond Democratic Committee agreed to cooperate with the National Negro Wilson League. The purpose of the League was to provide Southern Negro orators for the Democratic National Committee in the North. The organization urged Southern Negroes to cooperate with their white brothers and to break the traditional allegiance to the Republican party. Giles Jackson, a Richmond attorney and formerly a Roosevelt Republican, called upon Negroes to back Wilson.[72] He predicted that in

[70] *Times-Dispatch,* Aug. 3, 1912; Arthur S. Link, ed., "Correspondence Relating to the Progressive Party's 'Lily White' Policy in 1912," *Journal of Southern History,* X (Nov. 1944), 480–88.

[71] "The Negro as a Factor in the Campaign of 1912," *Journal of Negro History,* XIII (Jan. 1947), 84–85.

[72] *Times-Dispatch,* July 10, Sept. 5, 29, 1912.

Richmond alone between 500 and 800 Negroes would vote Democratic. Jackson and others also busied themselves campaigning among colored "men of means" for funds to send speakers north.[73]

Dissatisfied with the three nominees who offered "colored voters of the country three dishes of crow," the Richmond *Planet* offered still another possibility to the discontented. "If the stomachs of the colored voters . . . are already upset and feverish then the Socialist dish of spring chicken [Eugene V. Debs] may prove to be an appetizing repast at the November elections." [74] It is doubtful that the attempts to form a Debs or even a Wilson following could have been extensive. The Negroes looked askance at Roosevelt because of his open letter prior to the Progressive convention. Thus, on election day most colored voters in Virginia remained begrudingly loyal to the Republican Taft.[75] Since mention of Negro voters appeared in but one of Virginia's leading newspapers, it is assumed that the Lynchburg *News* was accurate when it wrote that very few Negroes voted.[76]

Following Wilson's victory, the *Planet* commented blandly, "The election of Governor Wilson of New Jersey . . . should cause no uneasiness among the colored people of this country. He is not an extremist in either politics, religion, or the race question. He has given voice to no expression of antipathy to the colored people." [77] But Negroes in Virginia had little to cheer about during Wilson's first administration. Although born and raised a Southerner, the President failed to appreciate or understand the problems of the race and made little effort to win political rights for them. On two major occasions Negroes understandably condemned the administration for allowing race discrimination to spread.

[73] *Ibid.,* July 27, 1912; Norman P. Andrews, "The Negro in Politics," *Journal of Negro History,* V (Oct. 1920), 420–36.

[74] Oct. 26, 1912.

[75] Link, "The Negro as a Factor in the Campaign of 1912," 99; Tatum, *Changed Political Thought of the Negro,* 85; Meier, *Negro Thought in America,* 188. Meier contends that 60 per cent of the nation's Negroes voted for Roosevelt and the remainder divided their votes between Taft and Wilson.

[76] Nov. 6, 1912.

[77] Nov. 9, 1912.

This first occurred in 1913 when the President "submitted" to the policies of Postmaster General Albert S. Burleson and Secretary of the Treasury William Gibbs McAdoo of segregating workers, rest rooms, and lunch rooms of the Post Office and the Treasury Department.[78] Though many Negroes argued that Wilson was unaware of the situation, the general feeling was that the President "knows of the order and its execution, but refuses to interfere, thus approving it." [79] The National Association for the Advancement of Colored People filed a formal protest against "Jim Crowing" of federal employees and facilities, but only after many complaints was the segregation finally ended.[80]

In the second instance, Wilson became "an unwitting accomplice in the success of one of the most violent pieces of anti-Negro propaganda in modern American history," when he agreed to a private showing of the motion picture, *The Birth of a Nation.*[81] The movie, based on Thomas Dixon's novel, *The Clansman*, was a violent attack upon Negroes during the Reconstruction period and had become one of the most controversial topics of the day. Wilson's attendance at the showing, plus his involvement with segregation on the federal level, convinced such leaders of the Virginia Negro community as P. B. Young, editor and publisher of the Norfolk *Journal and Guide,* that a change was needed in 1916.[82] Young

[78] Arthur S. Link, *Wilson: The New Freedom* (Princeton, N.J., 1956), 243–52; John Hope Franklin, *From Slavery to Freedom: A History of American Negroes* (N.Y., 1947), 445–46; Carter G. Woodson, *The Negro in Our History* (Washington, D.C., 1922), 489–90.

[79] *Planet*, Aug. 23, 30, 1913.

[80] *Ibid.*, Aug. 13, 1913.

[81] Link, *Wilson: The New Freedom*, 252–54; John Hammond Moore, "South Carolina's Reaction to the Photoplay, *The Birth of a Nation*," *Proceedings of the South Carolina Historical Association* (1963), 36.

[82] P. B. Young remained active in Virginia politics until his death in 1944. He was one of the first to bolt the Republican party in 1928, and thereafter supported the national Democratic ticket. Under his guidance the *Journal and Guide* became the largest circulating Negro newspaper in Virginia, and was soon recognized for the excellence of its editorial page. Compared to the *Planet*, its writing was more temperate, better organized, and factually more reliable. Lewis, *Negro in Virginia*, 285; Boris, ed., *Who's Who in Colored America*, 232; Richard Bardolph, *The Negro Vanguard* (N.Y., 1959), 143–44, 216.

accused the administration of closing the civil service "door of hope" to the Negro and added that

during the last three and one-half years of the present Democratic Administration, there has been more segregation—or separation of colored from white employees—in the Executive Departments in Washington than in all of the 127 years of our Government's history, including the Cleveland Administration.[83]

The Norfolk editor complained that more than 100 federally employed Negroes, of a total of approximately 200 who received $1,800 or less annually, had been removed during the Wilson administration.[84]

Both Negro weeklies in Virginia predicted Wilson's defeat in 1916. The less condemnatory of the two, the *Planet,* in a general criticism did not denounce Wilson for his racial policies but claimed "his fault has been his attempt to be 'all things to all men.' " [85] The *Journal and Guide,* in giving its election results, had no tabulation of the number of Negroes who cast ballots but was certain that "almost to a man, [they] voted for Mr. Hughes." [86] If a mock election among women students at Hampton Institute, in which Charles Evans Hughes polled a total of 70 votes to 25 for Wilson and one for Theodore Roosevelt, can be accepted as verification of this, then the Republicans still held the Negro allegiance as of 1916.[87]

In political influence and power Virginia Negroes sank virtually to the bottom in the period from 1905 to 1916. Practically friendless in both parties in the state and nation, the best the Negroes could do was to criticize all parties. Most of this was done through the Norfolk and Richmond weeklies. Despite the low level to which their political fates had fallen, Negro participation in World War I and expected additional support resulting from women's suffrage gave hope that their fortunes might improve.

[83] *Journal and Guide,* Nov. 4, 1916.
[84] *Ibid.*
[85] *Planet,* Nov. 4, 1916.
[86] *Journal and Guide,* Nov. 11, 1916.
[87] *Southern Workman,* XLV (Dec. 1916), 702.

V

Temporary Political Awakening

1917-1921

AFTER the Negroes' longtime political exclusion by both parties in Virginia, an opportunity for their political awakening came with America's entry into World War I. Economic prosperity through job opportunity and a semblance of equality through participation in the war effort led Negroes to believe that political rights might follow. Coupled with these wartime gains was the adoption of the Nineteenth Amendment in 1920, giving women the right to vote. Hopes were high among Negroes that a boost in registration produced by women's enfranchisement might prod the men into action. The political revival, however, failed to materialize. The economic and social gains made during the war were soon lost in a wave of reaction against Negroes, a reaction which included a continuance of political exclusion. Disappointing, also, was the small number of Negro women who registered to vote. As of 1921 the total number of Negroes, male and female, registered to vote in the Old Dominion was estimated at less than 20,000.[1] Nevertheless, that year enough interest could be generated through a "lily-black" movement in protest of continued lily-white Republicanism. Virginia Negroes severed relations completely with the regular G.O.P. and ran a full slate of colored candidates for state offices. But election returns in November showed a pronounced defeat for the "lily blacks," and the movement ended

[1] *Times-Dispatch*, Nov. 1, 1921. Of the 690,017 Negroes in Virginia, approximately 260,000 were of voting age. The male-female ratio was about 130,000 each. *Fourteenth Census of the United States taken in the Year 1920* (Washington, D.C., 1922), II, 277.

as quickly as it had begun. Negroes again faded into the political background, not to reappear until the white primary cases in 1929.

American participation in World War I brought jobs and economic gains for many Negroes. Negro newspapers stressed the need of the race to improve itself economically by holding wartime jobs. Serialized accounts appeared regularly in the *Planet* depicting the northward migration of Southern Negroes because of the promise of steady employment in such cities as Pittsburgh and Detroit.[2] Countering such enticing opportunities, the *Journal and Guide* insisted that a more urgent need for manpower existed in the South, especially since 250,000 Negroes had been inducted into the armed services. The Norfolk weekly argued that employment in the North was temporary and migrating Negroes would find themselves jobless at war's end.[3] Whether in the North or South, however, the demand for Negro labor existed.

As Negro soldiers were shipped overseas to France, attention shifted from economic opportunity to the heroic feats of the boys over there. Army units remained segregated and Negroes actually saw limited battle action, but more important was the fact that they "moved about freely in France," with little regard for the color of their skin. This experience left a lasting impression on the minds of Negroes, evidenced by such comments in the *Planet* as, "Colored soldiers returning home are relating their experiences and they are telling some peculiar tales about conditions across the waters." [4] Hopes were raised that similar conditions would characterize postwar America. As returning Negro troops of the Veterinary Corps paraded down Broad Street in Richmond, the *Planet* was moved in a cartoon to have one of the veterans pleading with the woman warrior on the state seal, "YOUR HONOR, MISS—CUT DOWN THE

[2] April 7, 1917—Feb. 2, 1918, *passim*. For comprehensive coverage of the Negro in the war effort, see Emmett J. Scott, *Scott's Official History of The American Negro in the World War* (Washington, D.C., 1919); Franklin, *From Slavery to Freedom*, 444–68.

[3] April 7, 1917—Feb. 2, 1918, *passim*.

[4] March 29, 1919; Monroe N. Work, ed., "What Does the Negro Want or Expect after the War?" *Negro Year Book: An Encyclopedia of the Negro, 1918–1919* (Tuskegee, Ala., 1919), 120–22.

FLAGS AND THE HURRAHS, ABOLISH *Jim Crow* LAWS IN YOUR HOUSE. DO SOMETHING OF CONSEQUENCE FOR US." [5]

Oddly enough, during the war Negroes made little mention of their need for a political awakening. In one isolated instance in August 1917 an anonymous letter writer who signed as"Grumbler" urged prominent Negroes to run for office in Virginia. He emphasized that, with the wartime fervor, "the psychological moment" had arrived for the Negro to abandon his lethargy and get the habit of being a candidate.[6] Among those mentioned as possible candidates were John Mitchell, Jr., of Richmond for governor, J. Thomas Newsome of Newport News for attorney general, P. B. Young of Norfolk for councilman, and W. L. Lewis of Portsmouth for the House of Delegates. Response to the suggestion came from P. B. Young, editor of the *Journal and Guide,* who agreed that the idea had potential but would be feasible at a more opportune time. Perhaps in jest, Young concluded that he could not understand why he should merely be offered the candidacy for councilman while "our Journalistic contemporary, John Mitchell, Jr.," received the gubernatorial nod.[7] The matter was then laid to rest.

With the return of peace Negro opportunities diminished. Employment possibilities decreased and the competition for jobs became keener. Discriminatory practices, which had been forgotten temporarily, were revived. Negro soldiers returning from overseas duty where they had witnessed racial equality alarmed white citizens, who feared those veterans would attempt to gain similar privileges at home. In the summer of 1919 race riots erupted within a few weeks in Washington, Chicago, and Knoxville.[8] Lynchings increased sharply, with 36 Negro victims in 1917, 76 in 1919, and 59 in 1921. However, only three Negroes were lynched in Virginia during this period, evidence that violence was uncommon in the state.[9]

[5] June 21, 1919. [6] *Journal and Guide,* Aug. 11, 1917. [7] *Ibid.*
[8] *Planet,* July 26, Aug. 2, Sept. 6, 1919; Franklin, *From Slavery to Freedom,* 472–76; Newby, *Jim Crow's Defense,* 157–61.
[9] *The World Almanack and Book of Facts for 1927* (N.Y., 1928), 322; *ibid., 1923,* 300; *ibid., 1925,* 274.

There was an increase in the membership of the rejuvenated Ku Klux Klan, particularly in Richmond, Hopewell, Norfolk, Newport News, Danville, Lynchburg, and Roanoke, as well as in Princess Anne, Nansemond, and the southern tier of counties bordering North Carolina from Halifax to Patrick.[10] With the increasing industrialization in the cities, doubtless the influx of Negro farm hands created anxiety among white inhabitants. In Richmond, through the auspices of the Business Men's Club, the Klan attempted to recruit new members by sponsoring the following advertisement in the *News Leader*:

KNIGHTS OF THE KU KLUX KLAN.
If you are 100% American, believe in doing things, and want to get with a real bunch of Americans who love law and order, and will protect the pure womanhood, our Constitution, and enforce its principles,
Address State Secretary . . .[11]

On several occasions klansmen trooped down Richmond's Broad Street, throwing fear into the hearts of Negro onlookers.[12]

According to a Klan newsletter dated May 20, 1921, in Newport News the Invisible Empire controlled the chief of police, the police court judge, the postmaster, members of the city council, the managing editor of the leading newspaper, and many more prominent business and professional men. The Exalted Cyclops of Norfolk announced in a later newsletter that the Klan had also enlisted that city's chief of police within its ranks.[13]

Segregation laws were also strengthened. Between 1870 and 1900 there had been no consistent code of racial mores or "Jim

[10] Fredericksburg *Free Lance-Star*, Sept. 23, 1965; David M. Chalmers, *Hooded Americanism: The First Century of the Ku Klux Klan* (N.Y., 1965), 230–36; Arnold S. Rice, *The Ku Klux Klan in American Politics* (Washington, D.C., 1962), 39–41. For reaction against the Invisible Empire during the 1920's, see pages 101–3 of this volume.

[11] Nov. 12, 1920.

[12] *Planet*, Sept. 24, Oct. 30, Dec. 11, 1920, 1921.

[13] Henry P. Fry, *The Modern Ku Klux Klan* (Boston, 1922), 59–60; Rice, *Ku Klux Klan in American Politics*, 40. Charles B. Borland, chief of police of Norfolk, subsequently denied membership in the Klan.

Crow" legislation. In 1900 the Virginia legislature enacted a law requiring railroads to furnish separate coaches for Negroes and whites. Streetcars were included in a second act passed in 1906. The capstone came in 1925 when the General Assembly passed a bill introduced by Delegate G. Alvin Massenberg of Elizabeth City County separating the races in all theaters, opera houses, and other places of public assemblage. Consequently, "Negroes soon became accustomed to buying tickets and walking upstairs." [14]

Despite the postwar reaction, most of which was nonviolent in Virginia, this period was one of unaccustomed political activity among Negroes. Much of this resulted from the adoption of the Nineteenth Amendment. During the suffragist campaigns beginning as early as 1909, Negroes in the state remained in the background. The attempts to gain women's suffrage came almost wholly through the leadership of white women such as the socially prominent Richmond reformer, Mrs. Lila Meade Valentine, and writers Ellen Glasgow, Mary Johnston, and Kate Langley, who helped form the Equal Suffrage League.[15] In the struggle which lasted over a decade, the Negro gained the limelight only when opponents to women's suffrage charged that, as in 1902, white supremacy was endangered. To allow white women to vote was folly enough, but according to M. M. A. Williams, president of the Virginia Association Opposed to Woman Suffrage, to give Negro women the suffrage would inevitably compel whites to accept racial social equality and the intermarriage of blacks and whites.[16]

The Virginia Association Opposed to Woman Suffrage published a pamphlet entitled "The Virginia General Assembly and Women's Suffrage," which warned that Negroes, through better education, were becoming a threat to white supremacy. If the Negro illiteracy rate continued to decrease by 12 per cent a decade and older illit-

[14] Lewis, *Negro in Virginia,* 244; Wynes, *Race Relations in Virginia,* 68, 74–75; Woodward, *Strange Career of Jim Crow,* 97.

[15] Carrol H. Quenzel, "Is History Repeating Itself in Virginia?" (MS, Mary Washington College, Fredericksburg, Va., 1964), 2–3; Lloyd C. Taylor, "Lila Meade Valentine: The FFV Reformer," *Virginia Magazine of History and Biography,* LXX (Oct. 1962), 481.

[16] *Times-Dispatch,* Sept. 2, 1919.

erates died off, colored registrants would soon have few difficulties in passing "understanding tests." Then, "in the ensuing struggle to restore white supremacy, women would be involved in the old-time fraud in which . . . we are ashamed to have our men involved." [17] By the use of such arguments, antisuffragettes were able to defeat suffrage resolutions in the General Assembly during the 1912, 1914, and 1916 sessions.[18]

In the 1916 presidential campaign President Wilson adopted a federal suffrage amendment as a campaign plank. After an unsuccessful attempt in 1918 the proposal for submission of the amendment to the states was passed by Congress in the following year. The Nineteenth Amendment, with a recommendation for passage by Wilson, then went to the states for the necessary three-fourths approval. In Virginia opponents to the amendment continued to argue that white supremacy was endangered. In addition, they maintained that the federal amendment was a violation of states rights as expressed in the Tenth Amendment. In a question-and-answer type of editorial, the *Times-Dispatch* attacked the proposal:

Shall Virginia surrender the last vestige of its independence to the Federal Government? Shall it entrust to Congress the regulation of its suffrage, wherein, except for the few years of military occupation, it has been its own arbiter? Shall it stultify itself by subordinating Democratic principles to political expediency? Virginia stands ready to answer, and its answer is a thunderous chorus of "Noes" that reverberates from the mountains to the sea. . . . Virginia will not sell itself.[19]

Amid this criticism the amendment was presented by Governor Westmoreland Davis to the Virginia legislature on August 18, 1919. No recommendation by the Governor either for or against accompanied it. The fact that President Wilson had sent a telegram to the members of the Assembly on August 22 recommending ratification

[17] Jack T. Kirby, "Governor Westmoreland Davis and the Molding of the Twentieth Century," (Master's thesis, University of Virginia, 1964), 113.

[18] *Journal of the House of Delegates of Virginia, 1912,* 168, 364, hereafter cited as *Journal of the House; ibid., 1914,* 438, 872; *ibid., 1916,* 601; Quenzel, "Is History Repeating Itself in Virginia?" 7–8, 10.

[19] Jan. 22, 1920; Taylor, "Lila Meade Valentine: The FFV Reformer," 486.

only stiffened the opposition. Despite efforts by Senators E. Lee Trinkle and G. Walter Mapp to ratify the amendment in the senate, Senators Robert F. Leedy and William H. Jeffrey led a successful fight against it. Meanwhile, in the House of Delegates a resolution was passed denouncing the Nineteenth Amendment as "unwarranted, unnecessary, undemocratic, and dangerous interference with the rights reserved to the states." [20] Motions to modify the resolution were beaten by large majorities, and only parliamentary maneuvering by Senators Mapp and Trinkle averted a similar defeat in the senate. Rather than face a condemnatory resolution, Mapp successfully recommended postponement on the suffrage amendment until the regular legislative session in 1920.[21]

Between sessions Virginia political leaders faced the problem of how constitutionally to sidestep the Nineteenth Amendment, which seemed certain of adoption by autumn of 1920. If women's suffrage became the law of the land, what method would best restrict Negro women's suffrage? Congressman Henry Flood suggested implementing Section 19 of the 1902 state constitution.[22] "It did it in 1902 and '03 in the case of negro male voters, and it will do it again." Flood did not object to female suffrage being granted through state legislation, but he did consider it

of paramount importance to protect the electorate from the colored female voters. . . .

It looks as if the Federal amendment will be ratified before the State amendment would be adopted, and if so our General Assembly would have to use all of its wisdom to keep the 150,000 negro women in the State from getting on the registration books until the State Amendment with Section 19 in it is adopted.[23]

[20] *Times-Dispatch,* Aug. 29, 30, Sept. 1, 1919; Kirby, "Westmoreland Davis," 101–10; *Journal of the House, 1919 Special Session,* 146–47.

[21] *Journal of the Senate of Virginia, 1919,* 146–47, hereafter cited as *Journal of the Senate; Times-Dispatch,* Aug. 29, Sept. 1, 3, 4, 1919; Quenzel, "Is History Repeating Itself in Virginia?" 15–18.

[22] The section provided for age and residence requirements, armed services exemptions, property qualifications, and proof of literacy, i.e., that a person be able to read any section of the constitution submitted to him by the officers of registration and to give a reasonable explanation of the same. If unable to read the section, he should be able to understand and give a reasonable explanation thereof when it was read to him by the registrar.

[23] Flood to R. H. Willis, Feb. 25, 1920, Flood Papers.

Plans for an amendment to the state constitution loomed large when the regular session of the General Assembly convened in 1920. For a second time Governor Davis transmitted a copy of the proposed Nineteenth Amendment to the legislature on February 6, and again opposition to it quickly mounted. Senator Leedy and ten cosponsors in the senate and Delegate Thomas W. Ozlin with thirteen cosponsors in the house presented resolutions recommending defeat of the amendment. Senator Trinkle then challenged both resolutions and asked that they be bypassed in favor of a resolution approving the Nineteenth Amendment. His plan was promptly rejected on the same day, 24 to 10.[24]

As the legislative haggling continued, on March 12 Senator J. E. West offered a compromise to the Assembly. West proposed an amendment to the state constitution with basically the same requirements for voting placed upon females as already existed on males. His proposal had been submitted originally on the first day of the regular session but had not been pressed because West had preferred to allow the federal amendment to be disposed of first.[25] After hasty debate the West proposal passed both houses by sizable majorities, 67 to 17 in the house and 30 to 1 in the senate. A factor which doubtless limited debate and produced the wide margins was the knowledge that thirty-five states had ratified the Nineteenth Amendment, with but one more necessary for ratification. On the same day the West resolution passed the house, March 12, that body soundly rejected the federal amendment, 62 to 22. By state legislation, therefore, Virginia hoped constitutionally to sidestep national law as it had done in 1902. To prepare for such an eventuality, the West proposal stipulated that it would become operative only when the necessary thirty-six states passed the national amendment.[26]

In passing judgment on the constitutionality of the West resolu-

---

[24] *Journal of the Senate, 1920,* 41–42, 171–74; *Journal of the House, 1920,* 76; *Times-Dispatch,* Feb. 7, 1920. Also on February 6, a motion to submit the question of women's suffrage to popular referendum was voted down.

[25] *Times-Dispatch,* Feb. 8, March 13, Aug. 27, 1920.

[26] *Journal of the House, 1920,* 272–73, 806; *Journal of the Senate, 1920,* 55, 515, 802.

tion, John R. Saunders, Virginia's attorney general, declared it within the power of the General Assembly to enact such a measure making the qualifications of women the same as those already existing for men.[27] Thus, when the women's suffrage amendment became operative on August 26, 1920, the provisional West statute was automatically put into effect.[28]

Achievement of the suffrage by women meant that they could cast their first ballots in the presidential election of 1920. In preparation for the contest statewide registration dates were scheduled from September 1 through October 2. Whereas Negroes had not been vocal in the suffrage crusade prior to the adoption of the Nineteenth Amendment, during registration days they worked actively to register members of the race. Prominent Negro leaders such as attorney Joseph R. Pollard, candidate for the United States Senate, and Mrs. Maggie Walker of Richmond predicted a registration of at least 5,000 colored women in Richmond alone.[29]

As Negro activity stepped up, so too did that of the whites. Leaders such as Representative Henry Flood issued circulars urging white women not to be outdone in the registration drive. Flood warned that "Republicans will be active in their efforts to corral 'their own,' and the Democrats should be equally on the alert." Colored females, cautioned Flood, had more education than the males, and under Virginia's mild educational tests a much larger percentage of females than males might be registered. This increase "added to the solid Republican vote, . . . MIGHT materially affect the party status, and cast some uncertainty on the result of the coming election. This is not meant as a prophecy of evil. It is intended solely as an admonition to our party workers *to take no*

[27] *Times-Dispatch*, Feb. 28, 1920.
[28] *Ibid.*, Aug. 27, 1920.
[29] Roanoke *Times*, Sept. 29, 1920. Biographical material on Pollard is sparse. Mrs. Walker, better known in the Negro community, as executive secretary of an insurance company, the Independent Order of St. Luke, helped build its membership from 700 to 20,000. She established the St. Luke's Bank and Trust Company with assets of $300,000 and was also editor of the newspaper, *The St. Luke Herald*. Yenser, ed., *Who's Who in Colored America*, 210–11; Lewis, *Negro in Virginia*, 292–93; Horace Scott, secretary of the Independent Order of St. Luke to the author, Richmond, June 22, 1964.

risks." [30] In its concern the Norfolk *Virginian-Pilot* deemed it "the duty of every woman *in preserving the safety of Southern institutions* . . . to register and vote." [31] Disturbed by the turnout of Negro women at registration offices in Richmond, Rorer A. James, chairman of the Democratic Central Committee in Virginia, urged the Democratic white women of the state to register, "whether they favor equal suffrage or not, to maintain the prestige, the integrity, the traditions and honors of Virginia." [32]

There is little evidence to indicate that Negro women were rejected during registration in the wholesale manner that males had been in 1902 and 1904. On at least one occasion, however, "delaying tactics" were resorted to by election officials. In Richmond, where "an unprecedented rush of colored women" sought registration, two white clerks registered white women applicants on the main floor of the City Hall, while in the basement a deputy registrar did the same for Negro women. Daily reports in the Richmond *Times-Dispatch* depicted Mrs. Carter W. Wormley and Mrs. L. Jobson toiling away, almost as if competing against each other, "without pausing for rest or refreshment, . . . their task from 9 o'clock in the morning until 3:30 in the afternoon." They registered as many as 650 white women a day. Deputy Registrar Garland Taylor averaged below 100 Negro women daily. The Richmond daily attributed the small number to Taylor's being "less practiced." [33]

Mrs. Maggie Walker accused the registrars of partiality and, in an effort to speed up Negro registration, petitioned Judge D. C. Richardson of the Hustings Court. According to Mrs. Walker, when the City Hall doors closed at 4:00 P.M. daily, at least 100 colored women were turned away. She asked that Negro assistants be appointed as registrars, but despite her plea no formal action was taken by the court.[34]

[30] Carbon copy of two typewritten pages, Sept. 9, 1920, in Flood Papers. See also Charlottesville *Daily Progress,* Sept. 30, 1920, "BEWARE OF RADICAL AGITATORS," and Oct. 5, 1920, "HAVE A CARE, WOMEN OF VIRGINIA."
[31] Oct. 2, 1920.　　　[32] Roanoke *Times,* Sept. 29, 1920.
[33] *Times-Dispatch,* Sept. 25—Oct. 3, 1920. Also, "Negro Women, Women Suffrage," *Hampton Institute Political Scrapbook* (Hampton, Va., n.d.), IV.
[34] *Times-Dispatch,* Sept. 21, 1921.

Since news coverage of the voter registration in 1920 was far less complete than that in 1902, it is difficult to estimate how many Negro women were disqualified because of their inability either to fill out registration forms properly or to answer correctly questions pertaining to a voter's qualifications. In the few reports available it can be assumed rejection for these reasons was not unusual. In Lynchburg, with 320 Negro women listed as eligible to register, 91 failed to qualify. Norfolk had approximately 2,500 women who met poll tax requirements, but of that number 400 were rejected.[35] In Richmond the *Times-Dispatch* stressed the fact that Negro women could not fill out the simplest registration forms:

desire to regirst my nam is Mrs. Betsy Brown December 28, 1895 my age 24 Born in Darlington, S.C. 9 yrs, pritching 410 East 16St So Richmond va A Lady Bobber 6 in Precinct Madison Words.[36]

If this held true in the urban areas of Richmond, Norfolk, and Lynchburg, where registration requirements by 1920 were not overly restrictive, doubtless exclusion must have been greater in the rural, black-belt sections of the state.[37]

Whether or not restrictions were placed upon them, registration totals for Negro women were low. Richmond, with a female Negro population of 29,365, registered approximately 2,500; Lynchburg registered 421 of a 4,659 total; Petersburg estimated between 260 and 300 of 7,434; and Roanoke listed only 650 of a 20,098 total.[38] In smaller cities (total population of less than 25,000) such as Bristol, Charlottesville, Danville, and Fredericksburg registration stood at 34, 132, 614, and 33, respectively.[39] The *Times-Dispatch*

[35] *Virginia-Pilot*, Oct. 3, 5, 1920.   [36] Sept. 18, 1920.

[37] Interview with Roscoe C. Jackson, June 14, 1964, Richmond. The son of Giles Jackson, Roscoe Jackson entered Virginia politics in the early 1920's and was one of the first to break with the Republican party in 1928. Through his efforts the Richmond Democratic Voter's League was founded in 1929. He remained an active political leader in the Richmond area until the 1950's.

[38] *Fourteenth Census of the United States Taken in the Year 1920* (Washington, D.C., 1922), II, 47–49; *Times-Dispatch*, Nov. 2, 1920; Roanoke *Times*, Oct. 3, Nov. 2, 1920.

[39] Lynchburg *News*, Oct. 9, 1920; Charlottesville *Daily Progress*, Oct. 4, 1920; Danville *Register*, Oct. 3, 1920; Fredericksburg *Daily Star*, Oct. 4, 1920.

estimated that, in the state as a whole, 20,000 Negroes were registered to vote. The female vote, if it equaled the men's total, would be about 10,000.[40] The total Negro population was 690,017; approximately 260,000 were of voting age, half of whom were women. Therefore, only one out of every 130 Negro women over twenty-one years of age was eligible to vote in the Old Dominion.

The results of the election for United States Senator in 1920 illustrates the impact, or lack of it, the suffrage drive had on the Negro politically. Owing to the continued lily-whitism of the Republican party in Virginia, Negroes nominated attorney Joseph R. Pollard, state and Richmond chairman of the Negro faction of the G.O.P., for the Senate.[41] It was another attempt to show that Negroes could still muster votes which the lily whites badly needed. The regular Republicans did not offer a candidate, and the Democratic nominee, Carter Glass, easily won with 184,646 votes to 17,576 for Pollard. The Negro attorney fared well in his home city of Richmond, polling 2,791 ballots, but he could not approach Glass' total of 19,162. In Norfolk, Pollard polled 653 votes; in Portsmouth, 469; in Lynchburg, 446; and in Newport News, 406. He failed to gain 400 votes in any other city nor did he approach that figure in any county. In black-belt counties, where restrictions upon Negro suffrage were still most rigid, his total rarely exceeded 100 votes.[42]

Though efforts to register Negro women in 1920 had been unrewarding, and Pollard's showing left much to be desired, perhaps they acted as an incentive for further political action. Editor Mitchell of the *Planet*, undismayed at Pollard's defeat, placed more significance on the fact that the Negro candidate had polled over 17,000

[40] *U.S. Census, 1920*, 277; *Times-Dispatch*, Nov. 1, 1921. Approximations are used since the Census report categorizes the 20–24 age group as a whole. Age 20 must therefore be subtracted from the eligibles.

[41] *Times-Dispatch*, Oct. 20, 1920. At the Republican State Convention in Roanoke in March, Negroes were not consulted and not allowed seats in the convention hall for the selection of delegates to the national convention. As usual, protests at both the Roanoke meeting and the Chicago convention fell on deaf ears. *Ibid.*, March 17–18, June 1, 6, 1920; *Planet*, March 20, June 12, 1920.

[42] Alexander Heard and Donald S. Strong, *Southern Primaries and Elections, 1920–1949* (University, Ala., 1950), 198–99.

votes. Weighed alongside the 87,458 votes Republican presidential candidate Warren G. Harding received in Virginia, it represented approximately 20 per cent of the total G.O.P. tally, a high percentage in Mitchell's eyes.[43]

Pollard's candidacy failed to impress the lily-white faction of the Republican party. In fact, the gap between the two factions continued to widen in 1921. On July 14, at the Republican State Convention in Norfolk, it was openly declared that politically the Negro was of little or no value.[44] A week before the convention the Negroes had met at the True Reformers' Hall in Richmond and selected forty-five delegates and forty-five alternates, headed by J. Thomas Newsome and Joseph R. Pollard, to represent them at the Norfolk gathering.[45] But, with three exceptions, the Credentials Committee refused to seat the delegation. Little attention was paid to the threat made by Pollard afterward that the Negroes would hold a separate convention in Richmond. When Temporary Chairman Henry W. Anderson heard of the impending bolt, he was said to have remarked casually, "Fine." [46]

Chairman Anderson set the tone for the Norfolk meeting with his opening statement:

The white people of Virginia, constituting two-thirds of its population, holding nearly 95% of its property with centuries of discipline and training in the tasks of self-government, are charged with the solemn duty to all the people of this State to see that the State and local governments of the Commonwealth are conducted and administered in accordance with these self-evident principles.[47]

In an effort to assure whites of both political parties that Republicans were not attempting to reestablish the Negro as a political force in the state, he added:

Any suggestion that the colored people of Virginia, constituting

[43] *Planet,* Nov. 27, 1920. Ralph Bunche, while assisting Gunnar Myrdal in the research for *An American Dilemma,* contended that the Pollard candidacy was the last major effort by Negroes to work within the Republican party. Bunche, "The Political Status of the Negro" (MS, Library of Congress, 1940), V, 1181.
[44] *Times-Dispatch,* July 15, 1921.   [45] *Ibid.,* July 8, 12, 1921.
[46] *Virginian-Pilot,* July 15, 1921.
[47] *Times-Dispatch,* July 15, 1921; *Journal and Guide,* July 16, 1921.

less than one-third of its population can control our state and local government, or that they desire to do so is a patent absurdity, and a slander upon the intelligence of both races.[48]

At the convention Anderson, a successful corporation lawyer in Richmond recognized as the leader of eastern Virginia Republicans, received the nomination for governor. C. Bascom Slemp's biographer, Guy Hathorn, credits Anderson with attempting to keep his politics on a high level untainted by the race issue. The only issue before the people as he could see it was "the question of the management of state affairs."[49] Even the Democrats could find little fault with his candidacy, and the *Times-Dispatch* admitted that the choice was a wise one.[50] Nevertheless, the race issue was destined to play a major role in the campaign. It began with Democratic criticism of the Republican platform, which advocated reforms indirectly aiding the Negro. It remained in the forefront because the Negroes themselves opposed the regular Republicans and ran their own complete slate of candidates for state offices.

If one studies the Republican platform, he can understand why Democrats such as State Chairman Henry Flood cried out that Anderson proposed to "let down the bars of an unrestricted Negro vote, among men and women."[51] The platform advocated a revision and reform of the state's electoral laws, removal of the electoral machinery from the hands of the Democratic judges, and the abolition of the poll tax as a prerequisite to voting.[52] Active campaigning was hardly under way before Anderson was placed on the defensive concerning the reforms. In his keynote address at Clintwood on September 27, Democratic gubernatorial candidate E. Lee Trinkle denounced the Republicans for their Reconstruction policies in the past and for their political exploitation of the Negroes until the turn

[48] Bunche, "Political Status of the Negro," V, 1181.
[49] "C. Bascom Slemp," 161–62; Stanley Willis, "The Gubernatorial Campaign and Election: Virginia, 1921" (MS term paper, Edward Younger, History Course 115–16, University of Virginia, March 4, 1963).
[50] July 15, 1921.
[51] Lynchburg *News,* Sept. 23, 1921, cited in Horn, "Democratic Party in Virginia," 228.
[52] "The Republican Party in Virginia Platform, Adopted by the State Convention Held in Norfolk, Virginia, July 14, 1921," *Rare Virginia Pamphlets* (Richmond, 1921), 1–15.

of the century. Trinkle charged that Anderson's attempt to repeal the poll tax was but a sop to the Negroes, another Republican attempt to exploit their vote. The Democrat warned that poll tax repeal and restoration of the Negro franchise would set Virginia back a half century, "throwing wide open to the uneducated and ignorant Negro the broad door of our political life and seriously menacing the white man's supremacy in the 'black belt' of our State and probably in other positions as well." [53]

Anderson made a strong effort to defend both himself and his party, insisting that "the race issue is not involved in this campaign." [54] The Republican party in Virginia was "a party of white citizens," and if the 800,000 white voters in the state "cannot hold up the position they now occupy, then we have lost the capacity for self-government." To Anderson, suggesting that the race question was one "which the white people are not capable of dealing with is an insult to those to whom the statement is addressed." [55]

The G.O.P. candidate, forced to resort to racial politicking, attempted to shift the "party of the Negro" label to the Democrats, accusing the latter of furnishing Negroes with political appointments as election officials throughout the state. According to Anderson, at least twenty-five such appointments had been made, all by Democratic election boards. In Charlottesville two Negroes had been appointed who could neither read nor write. Anderson issued a challenge to Trinkle to join him in the removal of those officials, but according to the Republican candidate, "I have not heard from Mr. Trinkle, and I may say, in passing that I do not expect to hear from him." [56]

The Democrats paid little attention to such statements and con-

[53] *Times-Dispatch,* Sept. 28, 1921. A substantial collection of newspaper clippings on the 1921 gubernatorial campaign can be found in Slemp Scrapbook, Part II, 1921.
[54] *Times-Dispatch,* Oct. 11, 1921.
[55] *Ibid.,* Oct. 16, 1921.
[56] *Ibid.,* Oct. 11, 26, 1921. The Republicans took action against two Negro election judges in Charlottesville, charging they should be removed because they had voted Republican in the 1920 presidential election and therefore could not be appointed as Democrats to those positions. The Corporation Court decided in favor of the officials. Charlottesville *Daily Progress,* Oct. 29, Nov. 1, 7, 1921.

tinued to pressure Anderson with charges of aiding the Negro's return to Virginia politics. One of the sharpest criticisms came from the pen of Senator Carter Glass in the waning days of the campaign. His open letter, published on October 29 in many Virginia newspapers, credited the constitution of 1902 with having reduced Negro voter registration to less than 20,000, but cautioned that if Anderson was elected, he would undo that achievement. Virginia would then return

to the frightful period of reconstruction, when, to preserve our civilization, honest men were literally compelled to adopt methods of defense which were lawless and depraved. There is no record of Colonel Anderson ever having done anything to assist in the preservation of white supremacy in Virginia; now he proposes to tear down the barriers which the Constitutional Convention erected and thus clear the way to the ballot box for every shiftless and ignorant darky who may desire to exercise an unrestrained right to participation in the government of the State and the subdivision thereof.[57]

On the same day Senator Claude A. Swanson wrote a similar type of open letter.[58] As a result of this continuous barrage by the Democrats on the race issue, Anderson and the G.O.P. found little about which to be optimistic by election eve. The fact that the Negro vote, some 17,000 strong in the senatorial race of 1920, opposed the politics of the Virginia Republicans did not aid matters either.

As the battle lines were being drawn between the Democrats and the Republicans, for the first time in Virginia politics the Negroes made a complete break with the regular Republican party. In Richmond on September 6, as a protest against G.O.P. maltreatment, the Negroes nominated a lily-black ticket with John Mitchell, Jr., for governor; Theodore Nash of Newport News for lieutenant governor; J. Thomas Newsome for attorney general; Thomas E. Jackson of Staunton for treasurer; J. Z. Baccus of Lynchburg for secretary of the Commonwealth; Mrs. Maggie L. Walker for superintendent of public instruction; and J. L. Lee of Roanoke for commissioner of agriculture.[59] Defending the bolt in their party

[57] *Times-Dispatch*, Nov. 1, 1921.
[58] Petersburg *Index-Appeal*, Nov. 1, 1921; Roanoke *Times*, Nov. 4, 1921.
[59] *Times-Dispatch*, Sept. 7, 1921.

platform the lily-blacks insisted that for the past twenty years they had made no attempt either to lead the party or to gain social equality, as whites in both parties charged. They demanded, however, "to be treated as other citizens with all the rights, privileges, and immunities accorded them, including the rights to vote, and to be voted for." [60] The Richmond *Planet,* the spokesman for the lily blacks, boldly added that with a voting strength of approximately 20,000 Negroes behind them, those who were not permitted "to help nominate a Republican ticket will be permitted to help defeat a ticket in November that some of their white opponents inside the Democratic party nominate." [61]

Despite its full complement of candidates and the boasts of the *Planet,* the protest movement had major hurdles to overcome. As political leader Roscoe C. Jackson recalled, the lily blacks, first of all, lacked the voting strength to carry out their threats against the G.O.P. Secondly, the Negroes were not united behind the fight.[62] Leading the opposition was P. B. Young of the Norfolk *Journal and Guide,* who had declined the nomination for the position of lieutenant governor on the ticket. Originally, Young maintained that he had not had proper time to study the prospects of such a political movement.[63] As the campaign progressed, however, he openly opposed the move, calling it ill-timed and unwise. He complained that the lily-black candidates had drawn a color line by excluding whites from their party plans, thereby stirring racial antagonisms. The Norfolk newspaperman also attacked fellow-editor John Mitchell, Jr., as an inactive candidate, "rusticating in California while the other candidates for governor are stumping the State day and night in the interest of their respective tickets." [64]

To the charge that a color line had been drawn by Negroes,

[60] Work, ed., *Negro Yearbook, 1921–1922,* 39–40.
[61] Aug. 20, 1921.
[62] Personal interview, June 14, 1964, Richmond. That the Democrats were not concerned about the Negro contestants seems to be borne out by the paucity of material in such major collections as those of Henry D. Flood, then State Democratic Chairman, and of Senator Claude A. Swanson, whose records of 1920–22 are full ones.
[63] *Journal and Guide,* July 30, 1921.
[64] *Ibid.,* Oct. 8, 1921; *Virginian-Pilot,* Oct. 25, 1921; Lewinson, *Race, Class, and Party,* 177.

Mitchell replied that thousands of postcards had been mailed to whites as well as blacks inviting them to vote for the slate. The mailing list even included Anderson and State Chairman C. Bascom Slemp.[65] J. Thomas Newsome came to Mitchell's defense on the second accusation. Newsome declared, in Mitchell's absence, that Negroes should be proud of this civic leader who was not vacationing but attending the National Bankers' Association Convention in Los Angeles at the request of the whites as the only Negro delegate.[66]

Throughout the campaign P. B. Young appeared not so much to be opposing the lily-black movement, as he was the nomination of Mitchell. Perhaps it was little more than professional jealously between editors of the leading Negro weeklies in Virginia. At any rate, Mitchell was accused to employing "imperialistic and radical methods" in an attempt "to impose without reservation [his] judgment in matters political upon the intelligence of the colored electorate." [67]

Matters finally came to a head when the disputing factions met face to face at a political rally in Portsmouth on October 16. From the speaker's platform, J. Thomas Newsome let it be known that he was out "to get" two prominent Negroes opposing the lily blacks. One of the two was most certainly Young; the other is unknown to the writer. Newsome then boldly insisted that no self-respecting Negro could vote any ticket but the recognized one. A second speaker, Joseph Pollard, after paying his respects to the regular Republican candidate with the statement that "anyone who can swallow Anderson and Slemp must have a zinc-lined stomach," likewise tore into the Negro faction opposing the lily-black slate.[68]

At this point in the meeting, Young, seated in the audience, asked if he might be heard. Permission granted, he first declared that he had nothing further to say which would hinder the lily-black movement. He insisted, however, that, having enjoyed free speech all his life, to have a certain segment of the Negro press charge him with disloyalty warranted a defense on his part. Young then proceeded to recite a "history" of the colored race in Virginia

[65] *Planet*, Oct. 8, 1921.   [66] *Journal and Guide*, Oct. 15, 1921.
[67] *Ibid.*, Oct. 8, 1921.   [68] *Ibid.*, Oct. 22, 1921.

under the leadership of such men as Mitchell, Newsome, and Pollard. State Chairman Pollard abruptly issued orders to quiet the speaker, but this proved impossible as Young refused to submit. In a matter of minutes confusion reigned. Young was surrounded by those formerly on the speaker's stand, with everyone, Mitchell in particular, attempting to speak out at once. "In disgust," according to the *Journal and Guide*, "the audience left, followed by Mr. Young, who was unable to have one of Virginia's sacred traditions upheld." [69] Such is the evidence of the bedlam existing in the lily-black movement on the eve of the November elections.

Though the charge was never formalized against Mitchell and other lily blacks, there was the intimation that the Richmond editor ran as a candidate in the hire of the Democrats to steer votes away from the Republican candidate. Mitchell on one occasion praised Trinkle as "a fine Christian gentleman" and admitted in post-election statements that he had advised Negroes to vote for "our State ticket, and in all city and county contests to support the local Democratic nominees. It was understood that every vote for our State candidates was a half-vote for Senator Trinkle for Governor, and the other Democratic officials on the ticket with him." [70] Paul Lewinson, though unable to substantiate the accusation, called the lily-black movement not wholly an attempt to show up the Republican organization, but an effort to aid the Democrats planned at a conference with Democratic party officials. "The object was to provide an outlet for Negro indignations without compromising the Democratic ticket by a sudden adherence of Negro voters." [71] Since no proof has been discovered to support the allegation, it remains little more than "historical gossip." [72]

With the Negroes bolting the Republican party, as well as quarreling among themselves and the lily-white Republicans on the defensive over the race issue, the Democrats had little difficulty in sweeping the 1921 election by a substantial 70,000-vote majority. Trinkle polled 139,416 votes to 65,933 for Anderson and but

[69] *Ibid.*

[70] *Planet*, Dec. 3, 1921; Work, ed., *Negro Yearbook, 1921–1922*, 40.

[71] *Race, Class, and Party*, 158–59; Martin, *Negro Disfranchisement in Virginia*, 150–51; Hathorn, "C. Bascom Slemp," 161 n. 76.

[72] Tatum, *Changed Political Thought of the Negro*, 130–31.

5,046 for Mitchell. The latter's total fell well below the 17,000 polled by Pollard the previous year. Mitchell's major support came from Richmond, but even there the count was a mere 1,402 ballots of a possible 2,800 qualified voters. In Newport News, Danville, and Petersburg, his totals stood at 286, 124, and 124 respectively. Norfolk, with 1,600 registered Negro voters, gave a mere 90 votes to the Richmond editor.[73] Doubtless, P. B. Young's editorializing had its effect in the seaport city.

In dismay the *Planet* attributed the setback to the failure of "the 36,000 eligible Negroes" to satisfy poll tax and registration requirements.[74] Recollecting the campaign, Roscoe C. Jackson observed that though it was relatively easy to register in Richmond and other urban areas by 1921, many stayed away for fear they would be refused registration by white Democratic election officials. Others who had paid their capitation tax unfortunately had not done so six months before election day. And, inevitably, still others displayed no interest in playing a political game which they stood no chance of winning.[75]

Another source stressed illiteracy as a barrier to Negro political participation. According to the United States Census of 1920, 102,884 of the approximately 260,000 Negroes over twenty-one years of age in Virginia were illiterate. The simplest application blank, therefore, was sufficient to exclude almost one-half of the Negro voting potential.[76]

To the Norfolk *Journal and Guide* the defeat was inevitable simply because Negroes would not accept Mitchell's "radical leadership. There were certain objectives for which they were all striving, but they were not willing to jeopardize their prospects of reaching those objectives by adopting insane methods." [77] The ill feeling between the Norfolk and Richmond weeklies was to continue until 1938, when the *Planet* ceased publication and amalga-

[73] *Report of the Secretary of the Commonwealth for the Year ending September 30, 1921* (Richmond, 1921), 419–22; *Journal and Guide*, Nov. 12, 1921; Roanoke *Times*, Nov. 9, 10, 1921.
[74] Nov. 26, 1921.
[75] Personal interview, June 14, 1964, Richmond.
[76] McDanel, *Virginia Constitutional Convention*, 55.
[77] Nov. 12, 1921.

mated with the Baltimore *Afro-American* syndicate. Only then did the mutual antipathy simmer down.

As for the regular Republicans, they were so badly defeated that for the first time since 1898 the "Fighting Ninth" District went Democratic, favoring Trinkle over Anderson 20,329 to 18,659.[78] The headline, "Lily Black Outvote the Lily White Republicans," in the Danville *Register* added insult to injury by making special mention of the margin in that city of 20 votes, 161 to 141.[79] Finally, Carter Glass had the last word on the election of 1921 with the following comment: "Anderson has been buried in the same grave in which the people of Virginia in 1902 buried unrestricted Negro suffrage." [80]

The temporary flare-up by the Negroes in the early 1920's over women's suffrage and the lily-black movement had aroused mild interest among factions of the colored race, but hardly enough to sustain a permanent political drive. As 1921 gave way to 1922, there was a return to the status quo with little effort to maintain the Negro's interest. Though a minute nucleus of leaders including Mitchell, Newsome, and Pollard attempted to stir the political pot, results were unrewarding. One could not expect either Republicans or Democrats to be excited by the prospect of gaining 20,000 "probable" Negro votes. Consequently Negroes had little hope of being accepted by either party.

[78] *Report of the Secretary, September 30, 1921,* 419–22; Petersburg *Index-Appeal,* Nov. 10, 1921.
[79] Danville *Register,* Nov. 9, 1921.
[80] Roanoke *Times,* Nov. 10, 1921.

VI

Adrift toward the Democratic
Party, 1922-1928

THE 1920's marked the begin-
ning of a turning point for Negroes, when for the first time colored
voters became Democrats. Of course, in Virginia this did not apply
on the state and local level, since Negroes were not welcomed by
the Democracy. In presidential politics, however, a considerable
number of Negroes voted Democratic. The major cause of this
gradual change can be attributed to the G.O.P.'s continued lily-
white attitude, a policy adopted by William Howard Taft in 1908
to win white votes in the South and continued by President Warren G. Harding in 1920.

After the death of Harding in 1923, Negroes received a brief
respite under Calvin Coolidge. Though "Silent Cal" did not crusade for Negro rights, neither did he follow the course of Taft or
Harding. He merely remained quiet on the issue. In the presidential
election of 1928, because Al Smith was wet, urban, and Roman
Catholic, the Republican candidate, Herbert Hoover, broke the
Solid South for the first time since the Grant era. Attempting to gain
a foothold below the Mason-Dixon line, Hoover surpassed his
predecessors in promising to maintain a rigorous lily-white policy.
As a result, Negroes in sizable numbers abandoned the party of
emancipation and voted Democratic in that election.

To understand the beginning of this shift in party allegiance
during the late 1920's, it is necessary to examine the events of that
decade. Any hope that the lily-black protest of 1921 would convince the G.O.P. that Negro voters were needed within its ranks
was shattered in the following year at the Third Congressional

District Convention in Richmond and at the Republican State Convention in Roanoke. According to the *Planet,* Negroes were excluded from the Richmond meeting, which selected Channing M. Ward of Richmond as its congressional nominee. The Negro weekly also charged that "the gentleman nominating him [Ward] stated without equivocating that he believed in making the Republican party a white man's party." [1] At the Roanoke gathering on September 18 J. W. McGavock of Wythe County, a confirmed lily white, received the nomination for the United States Senate. [2]

In protest against the nomination of McGavock, Negroes met in Richmond on October 2 and nominated Matt Lewis, publisher of the Newport News *Star,* as the third candidate in the Senate race, the Democrats having already renominated Claude A. Swanson. [3] At the meeting State Chairman Joseph R. Pollard reaffirmed the Negroes' allegiance to the national Republican party but opposed the state G.O.P., which continued to thwart attempts by Negroes to affect a working agreement with the whites. [4]

Since no "antiwhite" candidate opposed Ward in the Third District campaign, the Negro press advised that colored voters support the Democratic candidate, "one of the brainiest Virginians in the State, Honorable Andrew Jackson Montague. . . . He comes from Virginia stock and is a statesman of transcendant ability. His friendship for colored people is proverbial and their support will be welcomed." [5]

The Democrats easily swept the state in the November elections, including the congressional seat in the Ninth District. Swanson had no difficulty defeating his opponents for the Senate, polling 116,393 votes to 42,903 for McGavock and 2,627 for Lewis.

[1] *Times-Dispatch,* Sept. 10, 1922; *Planet,* Sept. 16, 1922.

[2] Roanoke *Times,* Sept. 19, 1922.

[3] *Planet,* Oct. 7, 1922.

[4] *Ibid.* Coupled with this protest was an earlier rumor that the Negro leadership intended to nominate a candidate against Representative Slemp in the Ninth District. Hopes ran high that with aproximately 1,000 registered Negro voters and a strong Democratic candidate, the Republican State Chairman could be defeated. *Journal and Guide,* April 22, 1922. Slemp, however, did not run in that year's contest and subsequently became private secretary to President Coolidge.

[5] *Planet,* Oct. 28, 1922.

Analysis of the vote reveals that Negroes displayed little interest in the election. Lewis received his highest totals (167 and 125) in Richmond and Norfolk respectively.[6] As a postscript, the *Journal and Guide* suggested that those results ought to be a final lesson for those who still believed there was major sympathy for a Negro party.[7]

In the Third District race Montague won handily over Republican Ward by 7,746 to 847. In this contest, Negroes, according to one source, "either voted for Congressman Montague, the Democrat, or scratched the Congressional part of the ticket." [8] But that they figured appreciably in the Montague victory is unlikely.

Then, oddly enough, in the two years prior to the 1924 presidential race the G.O.P. in Virginia appeared to have a change of heart toward the Negroes, and once again they were accepted within the Republican ranks. In 1921 and 1922 the party had been firmly lily white. Negroes bolted the party as a result, and in both years Republican candidates had been badly beaten at the polls. Perhaps the possibility of Negro voting strength caused Republicans to reevaluate their potential.

More amicable political relations between the races as the 1924 election approached did not necessarily mean that the Negroes had forgiven the lily whites. When President Calvin Coolidge appointed C. Bascom Slemp as his secretary on August 14, 1923, a Norfolk newspaper saw the appointment as an attempt by Coolidge to win Southern delegates in the 1924 Republican convention. The newspaper summarily denounced Slemp as "a millionaire and a notorious referee of Republican patronage in Virginia." Slemp was further characterized as the " 'whip horse' of the Republican lily whites in the South, and sponsor of the things considered by the race as unAmerican and undemocratic in American politics." [9]

[6] Heard and Strong, *Southern Primaries and Elections,* 198–99.
[7] Nov. 11, 1922.
[8] *The World Almanac and Book of Facts for 1922* (N.Y., 1923), 881; *Times-Dispatch,* Nov. 8, 1922.
[9] *Journal and Guide,* Aug. 18, 1923; Slemp Scrapbook, 1923.

However, criticism slackened considerably as G.O.P. political doors began opening to Negroes. On January 29, 1924, at the Norfolk convention for the selection of delegates to state and district conventions, Negroes were invited to attend. The schedule of activities was published well in advance so that no one would be neglected, and no attempt was made to exclude Negroes from the meeting.[10] A week later, on February 5, Negroes attended the Republican State Convention in Roanoke without difficulty. Negro delegates from Petersburg were even seated in preference to an all-white delegation which had held its district convention in a hotel which excluded Negroes. When a white delegate received the congressional nomination for the Sixth Congressional District, Negro B. F. Crowell seconded the party's choice.[11]

At the Roanoke meeting Negro State Chairman Joseph R. Pollard urged Negroes to vote Republican in the 1924 election.[12] C. Tiffany Tolliver, a relative newcomer on the political scene, also worked for reconciliation. He was described as "a young man of the progressive type" and as especially concerned with developing the interest of younger Negroes in state politics. Allegedly, after a meeting with C. Bascom Slemp, Tolliver revealed that Negroes would have no further difficulty in attending Republican meetings throughout the state and urged them to attend all such political conventions.[13]

Though they found little reason to praise the deceased Harding, Negroes remained loyal to the Republican party in 1924. As chief executive in 1921 Harding had urged Congress to pass a federal antilynch law, but he did not follow up this request when a Southern bloc in the Senate threatened to stifle the proposed legislation

---

[10] *Journal and Guide*, Feb. 2, 1924. According to the Norfolk newspaper, by 1924 apathy was so great that even opening conventions to Negroes did not interest them. Only one Negro, C. L. Williams, city editor of the paper, is reported to have attended the convention.

[11] *Planet*, Feb. 16, 1924.

[12] *Journal and Guide*, Feb. 16, 1924.

[13] *Ibid.*, Jan. 12, 26, Feb. 16, 1924. Tolliver's role was brief and little information pertaining to his career and influence after the 1928 campaign can be found.

by a filibuster. The bill was killed without ever coming to a vote.[14] On another occasion, while speaking in Birmingham on October 26, 1921, Harding appeared to endorse Southern lily-whitism when he declared that "a fundamental, eternal, and inescapable difference [exists] between the Negro and the white man." He urged the Republican party "to lay aside any program that looks like lining up with the black man as a mere political adjunct." [15]

Harding also came under heavy fire for failing to appoint Negroes to federal positions of responsibility. On July 18, 1921, at a meeting with dignitaries of the N.A.A.C.P. attempting to sound out his patronage plans for Negroes within the administration, the President closed the door on appointments of Southern Negroes. He commented explicitly,

I am not going to appoint any colored men to public office in the southern states, but there will be some appointments in the northern states. This thing called "race prejudice," you cannot down by battling it, and the only salvation as I see it, for the colored man in the South is to fall into the ranks behind white leadership until he can, acting through Southern legislatures work out his own destiny. This is my policy and I am going to follow it live or die, sink or swim.[16]

Such policies aroused criticism from the Negro press, particularly from the Baltimore *Afro-American,* the New York *New Crusade,* New York *News,* the N.A.A.C.P. publication *Crisis,* and the National Urban League organ *Opportunity,* as well as from the *Planet* and *Journal and Guide.* Harding had not been in office six months when the *Planet* accused him of surrendering to the "anti-Negro oligarchy. . . . So far as colored folks are concerned, Honorable Warren G. Harding, Goodnight and goodbye!" [17] *Opportunity* agreed that his actions "left no good blood in the veins

[14] Richard B. Sherman, "The Harding Administration and the Negro: An Opportunity Lost," *Journal of Negro History,* XLIX (July 1964), 151–68 *passim; Journal and Guide,* Dec. 9, 1922.

[15] Tatum, *Changed Political Thought of the Negro,* 95; *Journal and Guide,* Nov. 5, 1921; "Politics-Presidents, Harding and the Negro," Dec. 1921–23, 2 vol. Scrapbook, Hampton Institute.

[16] *Journal and Guide,* July 31, 1921; Sherman, "Harding Administration and the Negro," 164–65.   [17] *Planet,* July 31, 1931.

of the Negroes for him," and the New York *News* concluded that had Harding lived Negroes undoubtedly would not have supported him in 1924.[18]

Coolidge, however, was received more favorably by the Negroes, perhaps simply because he did not commit himself for or against the race. Moreover, Negroes again found acceptance in the ranks of the Virginia Republican organization. A Norfolk weekly attributed this acceptance to Republican fears that Northern Negroes protesting against Southern lily whites might vote in 1924 either for the Democratic candidate, John W. Davis, or the Progressive, Robert La Follette. The increase in Negro votes since World War I in such states as New York, New Jersey, Illinois, and Indiana could mean the difference between victory and defeat. For example, New York City prior to the war had 125,000 registered Negroes, but in 1924 the count had risen to 200,000 and Tammany Democrats hoped to make inroads into that vote. Democrats also eyed the 250,000 to 300,000 Negro ballots in Illinois and Indiana.[19]

"Concern" over Negroes' political welfare appeared evident at the Republican National Convention in Cleveland on June 10, 1924, when Negro delegates from Georgia and Mississippi were seated. A Negro newspaperman noted that not even Virginia State Chairman Slemp betrayed any evidence "whatever of his 'lily white' proclivities" and fraternized with the Negro group "upon a basis of equality that reminds one of the former days of Republican ascendancy." This same reporter considered the G.O.P. platform acceptable to most Negroes. It advocated an antilynch law and recommended a commission for the investigation of social and economic conditions and the promotion of mutual understanding and confidence.[20]

Both Negro weeklies in Virginia endorsed Coolidge. The Norfolk newspaper steered a more "independently Republican" course

[18] Tatum, *Changed Political Thought of the Negro,* 98; New York *News,* Jan. 9, 1923, cited in Sherman, "Harding Administration and the Negro," 166–67.

[19] *Journal and Guide,* Aug. 18, 1923, June 21, 1924; *Planet,* Jan. 5, 1924.

[20] *Planet,* June 14, 1924.

and backed "Silent Cal" mainly because the colored vote was unwanted by the Democrats.[21] Though allowed to vote in general elections, Negroes were still excluded from participation in Virginia primary voting. Since primaries nominated the Democratic candidate to run against his Republican opponent and the latter stood little chance of winning in predominantly Democratic Virginia, the general election was usually of little significance. Though Negro political organizations supporting Davis sprang up in Norfolk, Portsmouth, Richmond, and Roanoke, there is no evidence proving they were influential. In the Old Dominion, it can be safely assumed that Negro voters followed the slogan, "Keep Cool with Coolidge." [22]

As President in his own right, Coolidge won the approval of most Virginia Negroes. He received credit for inducing Slemp, the "High Priest of Lily Whitism," to adopt a conciliatory attitude toward the Negro. Colored citizens also expressed relief that Slemp was not appointed to a cabinet position, a political prize which he sought.[23] Coolidge certainly did not crusade for the rights of Negroes, but neither did he encourage the lily whites. Thus, though the President may have been "a disappointment in the main, . . . he was far from wholly unsatisfactory." [24] One Negro newspaper even characterized Coolidge as "one of the greatest statesmen who ever occupied a seat in the White House of the Nation." [25]

In 1928, directed by State Chairman Slemp, Herbert Hoover received the hearty endorsement of Virginia Republicans at their state convention in Roanoke on March 17. Few colored delegates were present and little attention was paid to them.[26] Negroes aired their grievances, however, at the national convention in Kansas City. In most of the Southern delegations where there were contests between lily whites and Negroes, the credentials committee awarded seats to the former. Negro leaders, among them Walter

[21] *Journal and Guide,* Sept. 13, 1924.
[22] *Ibid.,* Sept. 13, Nov. 8, 1924; Lewinson, *Race, Class and Party,* 158.
[23] *Journal and Guide,* Jan. 31, Nov. 28, 1925.
[24] *Ibid.,* March 2, 1929; Tatum, *Changed Political Thought of the Negro,* 99.
[25] *Planet,* Aug. 6, 1927.
[26] *Times-Dispatch,* March 18, 1928; *Planet,* March 24, 1928.

L. Cohen of Louisiana and "Gooseneck Bill" McDonald of Texas, though personally seated, were unable to gain official acceptance for fellow Negro delegates. As a result McDonald, the owner of a Fort Worth newspaper, became one of the first to break with the "new" Republicanism and declare himself for the Democrat Al Smith.[27]

Herbert Hoover was criticized for his silence during the controversy and also because, as the party nominee, he appeared to condone investigations into the political honesty of Southern Negro leaders. During the 1928 campaign a special Senate subcommittee charged Benjamin J. Davis with selling postmasterships in Georgia. A second party regular, Perry Howard, who held a federal patronage refereeship, was indicted by a special grand jury in Biloxi, Mississippi, for the alleged sale of public offices.[28] Both men were cleared after an extensive investigation, but the suspicion aroused against them was hard to overcome. Since Hoover offered them no aid, his inactivity indicated to Negroes that he intended to court Southern white votes and shake "colored rule in the South from his coat-tails." [29]

In Northern states with large Negro voting populations, major defections from the Republican party seemed certain in the 1928 election. Negro newspapers in various sections of the nation, among them the Baltimore *Afro-American,* Atlanta *Independent,* Chicago *Defender,* and Boston *Guardian,* bolted the party and backed Smith.[30] Governor Al Smith of New York, as a Roman Catholic and thus himself a member of a minority group, came to be looked upon by Negroes as a fellow sufferer in the prejudiced South.[31] He had done a commendable job as a progressive leader in New York, had openly opposed the Ku Klux Klan, and had taken a definite stand against prohibition. Most of all, Negroes believed he was sincere in his fight for the underprivileged.[32]

[27] *Journal and Guide,* June 9, 17, 23, 1928; Lewinson, *Race, Class, and Party,* 172–73.
[28] *Journal and Guide,* July 21, 1928.
[29] *Planet,* July 28, 1928, cited in Washington *Post,* July 18, 1928.
[30] Moon, *Balance of Power,* 198.
[31] *Journal and Guide,* July 7, 21, 1928.
[32] Tatum, *Changed Political Thought of the Negro,* 99, 103.

The threatened bolt also took hold in Virginia. On July 3 Negro Thomas L. Dabney organized a "Smith for President" club in Richmond.[33] A month later for the first time "in many years" Negroes at their annual statewide political meeting at Buckroe Beach did not unanimously back the Republican candidate. Thomas H. Reid of Portsmouth waged a hard fight for Hoover and only reluctantly accepted a compromise proposal by J. Thomas Newsome, which recommended neutrality and selection according to individual preference.[34] Late in the campaign, the Newport News *Star* and, more importantly, the Norfolk *Journal and Guide* made definite commitments for Smith.[35]

The defection to Smith, however, was by no means complete. Party regular C. Tiffany Tolliver acted as Negro campaign manager for Hoover in Virginia.[36] The Richmond *Planet* initially adopted a policy of "we shall see what we shall see," but during the waning weeks of the campaign it became more vocal in its attacks against the Democrats, especially for their policy of segregating Negro delegates at the national convention in Houston. The Richmond Negro newspaper complained of segregated sections for Negroes, fenced off with chicken wire, causing "many heartburnings among the colored people who had been trapped into believing Smith and his supporters would treat them fairly." [37] In an attempt to depict Smith as bowing to the South's demands, the *Planet* published a political cartoon showing Smith addressing a Negro audience. As the Democratic candidate shouted fourth, "I'M FOR YOU, HARLEM AND GIN," his colored audience queried, "BUT WHAT ABOUT THE REST OF THE COUNTRY? AND WHAT ABOUT THAT GANG BEHIND THE CURTAIN?" Behind the curtain peering through rather sheepishly were Carter Glass, Cole Blease, Claude Swanson, and Hoke Smith counseling Smith, "Stay off the South, Al." [38]

While Negroes went their separate ways on the Smith-Hoover

[33] *Journal and Guide,* July 7, 1928.
[34] *Ibid.,* Aug. 28, Sept. 8, 1928.
[35] *Ibid.,* Oct. 27, 1928; Van Deusen, "Negro in Politics," 256–74.
[36] *Journal and Guide,* Aug. 28, 1928.
[37] *Planet,* Sept. 15, Oct. 13, 1928.
[38] *Ibid.,* Oct. 20, 1928.

candidacies, one source contends that their vote was sought by both parties, though generally undercover "to avoid the damning 'nigger-lover' charges." [39] Such accusations were held in readiness, especially by the "Hoovercrats," a group of bolting Democrats opposed to the wet, Roman Catholic, New York City candidate. They accused Smith of being aligned with the Pope, as well as of being a tool of the Tammany bosses and a friend to the Negro. In the South the race issue was pressed as hard as the religious issue.[40]

Smith had the reluctant backing of party regulars, Governor Harry Flood Byrd and Senator Carter Glass, but the pressure brought to bear by the Republicans, the Hoovercrats, and the Protestant clergy led by Bishop James Cannon, Jr., was difficult to combat. The Democracy was placed on the defensive concerning the race issue and was forced to justify Smith's stand on the Negro. After approximately fifty years of being dubbed "the party of the Negro," the Republicans had the opportunity to use the phrase as political ammunition against the opposition. Particularly effective were the serialized accounts by Jennings C. Wise in the Richmond *Times-Dispatch.* In one such article entitled "The Truth about the Smithite Negro Policy," Wise insisted that

as soon as Smith was nominated, Negro agents of Tammany Hall appeared in Virginia and caused the Negro politicians to meet in convention at Bay Shore to declare their independence of the Republican party, which seven years before had declared itself independent of them! This was, of course, but a patent scheme to enable Negro Smith clubs to deliver the Negro vote to Smith. Prompted by Tammany, everywhere the Negroes now began speaking of wielding in Virginia the balance of power just as they wield it in New York and elsewhere.[41]

When Senator Glass attempted to defend Smith's candidacy, Wise challenged Glass with a series of embarrassing questions. Typical of those asked was "Did he [Glass] approve the organization of Negro Smith Clubs in Virginia?" [42] Needless to say, replies were not forthcoming.

[39] Lewinson, *Race, Class, and Party,* 158.
[40] Bunche, "Political Status of the Negro," V, 1153; Moon, *Balance of Power,* 106.
[41] *Times-Dispatch,* Oct. 11, 1928.   [42] *Ibid.,* Oct. 25, 1928.

The attacks of Methodist Bishop James Cannon, Jr., the cleric termed by many "the most powerful ecclesiastic ever heard of in America," [43] were equally damaging to the Democrats. For over forty years "the Dry Messiah" had opposed demon rum, and the thought of an urban, wet, Roman Catholic in the White House appalled him. Further, it was alleged that Cannon had been at odds with Governor Byrd since 1925. The feud began when Byrd, the nephew of machine politico Henry D. Flood, after having served ten years in the state senate, announced himself as a gubernatorial candidate. His decision was opposed by Cannon, who preferred state Senator G. Walter Mapp, an ardent spokesman of the Anti-Saloon League in Virginia. Byrd badly defeated Mapp in the Democratic primary, 107,317 to 67,579, and went on to become governor, quickly establishing himself as the head of the party organization. During Byrd's term as chief executive, Cannon severed his relationships with the Democratic leadership.[44]

During September and October 1928 Cannon canvassed the state, campaigning feverishly against Smith, attacking the bigotry of the Catholic church and the anti-prohibition movement in America.[45] The race issue was not excluded, though Cannon insisted he opposed injecting it into the campaign. At Lynchburg on October 20 the Bishop charged that Tammany had deliberately campaigned for Negro votes by publicizing the story that a Negro civil service commissioner in New York City was supervisor to a white stenographer and that Negro teachers were teaching white students there.[46]

Again Senator Glass took up the defense, this time in a two-

[43] Virginius Dabney, *Dry Messiah: The Life of Bishop Cannon* (N.Y., 1949), vii. For complete coverage of the 1928 campaign, see Chapter XIV, "The Bishop and the Brown Derby." Julia E. Caldwell, "The Presidential Election of 1928 in Virginia" (Master's thesis, Howard University, 1953), 39–120.

[44] Edward T. Folliard, "The Man at the Throttle," Washington *Post,* June 16, 1957. This article is the eighth in a series of eleven entitled "The Byrd Machine." Election figures are from Heard and Strong, *Southern Primaries and Elections,* 193. For Byrd's achievements as governor and "organization" leader, see Leslie Lipson, *The American Governor from Figurehead to Leader* (Chicago, 1939), *passim;* Key, *Southern Politics,* 19–35; Eckenrode, "Virginia since 1865," chap. xvi, "The Byrd Administration."

[45] Dabney, *Dry Messiah,* 177.

[46] Lynchburg *News,* Oct. 21, 1928; Newby, *Jim Crow's Defense,* 162–63.

and-a-half-hour radio address on October 23. Glass attacked Bishop Cannon for his obvious bias and his prejudiced statements, such as the one that conditions in Harlem dance halls were deplorable. The Senator from Lynchburg insisted this bias intimated that

Smith and Tammany are responsible for these deplorable conditions. If the Bishop's taste persists, and he wants to be further amused, he can go to the Republican cities of Chicago, Philadelphia, Pittsburgh, and Cincinnati, and Hoover's own city of San Francisco, and find things much worse.[47]

The Democrats also had to defend Smith against attacks from the Ku Klux Klan. Despite criticism against the organization, such as that presented to the governor in 1921 by the Richmond chapter of the United Daughters of the Confederacy protesting the Klan's establishment, or that by the state Democratic party's insertion of a strong plank for religious liberty in its 1924 platform, the Invisible Empire gained a foothold in the Commonwealth. Further, by 1924 it was making inroads along the Eastern Shore in Cape Charles, as well as in Winchester, Staunton, and Shenandoah Caverns.[48] However, general resentment against the Klan was aroused after citizens witnessed a rash of intimidation and violence in 1926 and 1927.

On August 15, 1926, Raymond Bird, a Negro accused of raping a white girl, was taken forcibly from his jail cell in Wytheville by 50 masked men and lynched.[49] On September 1 another group seized and interrogated a Roman Catholic priest, Father Vincent D. Griffin, while he was conducting an outing for Negro boys near Princess Anne Court House. In the same month, it was charged that Klansmen near Bristol flogged three white women.[50] On November 30, 1927, Leonard Woods, a Negro accused of murder, was shot and publicly burned by a mob along the Virginia-Kentucky border.[51]

[47] *Virginian-Pilot*, Oct. 24, 1928.
[48] Rice, *Ku Klux Klan in American Politics*, 41; Chalmers, *Hooded Americanism*, 232–33.
[49] *Journal and Guide*, Aug. 21, 1926; Chalmers, *Hooded Americanism*, 234.
[50] *Journal and Guide*, Sept. 11, 1926.
[51] *Ibid.*, Dec. 10, 24, 1927; John Hohenberg, ed., *The Pulitzer Prize Story* (N.Y., 1959), 77.

Though these acts could not be traced back directly to the Klan, the onus of guilt generally appeared to rest with the hooded organization. In the aftermath of the kidnapping of Father Griffin, the Norfolk city council enacted legislation making it a crime to wear masks in public places.[52] The leading newspapers of the state denounced the lynchings and prominent citizens urged the governor to sponsor an antilynch law. Among the most vocal was Louis I. Jaffe, editor of the Norfolk *Virginian-Pilot,* who subsequently received a Pulitzer Prize in 1929 for his editorials against mob violence. According to one source, his writings were instrumental in convincing Byrd of the need for such legislation.[53] The governor, who was sympathetic to Jaffe's cause, initially moved cautiously because he feared that an antilynch law violated the state constitution. For example, he had been unable to employ state investigatory forces in the Wytheville killing unless so requested by county officials.[54] Coupled with Jaffe's entreaties and the second lynching in 1927, a final incentive for a state law came on December 7 when President Coolidge recommended a national antilynch law, whose passage might have meant intervention in Virginia's affairs. In addition, though Byrd was opposed to any Negro political resurgence, he was equally against violence toward either race.[55] In an almost paternal manner, the Democratic leader frowned upon rabble-rousing and Negro-baiting of any kind. Key described such sentiments as those of a Virginia gentleman maintaining political decorum at all times.[56] Finally, since it was likely that Smith would be nominated by the Democrats in 1928, the antilynch legislation seemed well timed. It afforded the Democrats with an opportunity to discredit the clandestine group which opposed its Presidential candidate. On March 10, 1928, the Byrd proposal became law, making lynching a crime punishable by death with the Commonwealth's attorney general acting as prosecutor against offenders.[57]

[52] *Journal and Guide,* Sept. 11, 1926.
[53] Jaffe, "Virginia Again Disgraced," *Virginian-Pilot,* Dec. 2, 1927; Hohenberg, *Pulitzer Prize Story,* 77.
[54] *Times-Dispatch,* Aug. 17, 1926; Hohenberg, *Pulitzer Prize Story,* 77.
[55] Lipson, *American Governor,* 131.   [56] Key, *Southern Politics,* 26.
[57] *House* and *Senate Journals, 1928,* see Senate Bill 191; *Times-Dispatch,* March 13, 1928.

The Hooded Empire denounced Byrd as much as it did Smith. Aside from the antilynch law, among the many other reforms Byrd advocated the short ballot particularly irritated Klansmen. It made several hitherto elective offices appointive, thereby reducing the number of positions available through ballot to Klan-favored candidates. In 1925 the Klan had opposed unsuccessfully Roman Catholic John M. Purcell, the Democratic candidate for state treasurer. Byrd's ballot reform in 1928 threatened to end their chances to unseat Purcell and others like him in the future. The Klan was so bitterly against Byrd that in 1928 it burned a cross in protest at Covington near where he was speaking. It even threatened the governor with a flogging.[58]

The Democratic party was clearly on the defensive throughout the campaign. Though they accused the Republicans of conducting a "whisper campaign" against Smith, denounced Republican State Chairman Robert H. Angell for using the pro-Klan newspaper, *Fellowship Forum,* as campaign literature, and condemned the G.O.P. for secretly sending out circulars to Negro women explaining why they should vote for Hoover, the Democrats faced defeat in Virginia for the first time since Readjuster days.[59]

Unfortunately for the Negroes, no matter which candidate won on November 6, possibility for advancement was slight. Neither party openly sought their votes. Perhaps Colonel Henry W. Anderson, speaking as "a private citizen" in a plea for a two-party system in the Old Dominion, best summed up the situation:

We know and every intelligent person knows, that whatever party may be in power in this nation or in this state, there will be no change in the relations between the races in Virginia. The white people control the government agencies in Virginia, and will continue to do so, regardless of what party is in power.[60]

On election day Hoover not only won the electoral votes of forty states, but he also split the Solid South by carrying Florida, North Carolina, Tennessee, Texas, and Virginia, and the border states of

---

[58] Fredericksburg *Free Lance-Star,* Sept. 23, 1965; Chalmers, *Hooded Americanism,* 233.
[59] *Times-Dispatch,* Oct. 9, 10, 1928; Lynchburg *News,* Oct. 21, 1928; Danville *Register,* Oct. 24, 28, 1928; Chalmers, *Hooded Americanism,* 234.
[60] *Times-Dispatch,* Nov. 4, 1928.

Kentucky and West Virginia. The Republican candidate defeated Smith by a vote of 164,609 to 140,146 in the Old Dominion. It was estimated that no more than 5,000 Negroes voted.[61] That none of the leading daily newspapers in Richmond, Norfolk, Roanoke, Lynchburg, or Danville offered approximations of Negro voting strength indicates that their role was minor. Roscoe C. Jackson, a founder of the Richmond Democratic Voters' League, estimated that between 200 and 300 Negroes in his city registered as Democrats for the election, but resentment against the Democratic party died hard. Even when confronted by lily-white Hoover, most Negro voters were unwilling to defect to Smith.[62]

The low Negro total in the presidential election of 1928 was typical of overall voter participation in the Commonwealth. The 304,755 votes cast were the most since 1900, but still below the high of 308,415 ballots cast in the 1888 presidential election. The 1928 figure was approximately 50,000 more than the 264,095 total of 1900,[63] but Virginia's population had increased considerably, from 1,854,184 in 1900 to 2,309,187 in 1920.[64] Women had also been granted the right to vote in 1920. Not until 1936, with a state population of 2,421,851, when 334,790 voted in the presidential election, was the 1888 total exceeded.[65] Thus, though the Negro remained disfranchised, political interest among both races was minimal. In 1924 the *Times-Dispatch* summed up Richmond's political situation, commenting that since the adoption of the 1902 constitution no more than 20 per cent of the whites of voting age ruled the city; "20 per cent at the maximum. . . . And it is called democracy!" [66]

Moreover, contrary to the belief that a genuine two-party sys-

[61] *Statement of the Vote for President, 1924* and *1928; Journal and Guide*, Nov. 10, 1928.
[62] Personal interview, June 14, 1964, Richmond.
[63] *Warrock-Richardson Almanack for the Year 1893*, 73; ibid., *1902*, 65.
[64] *Twelfth Census of the United States, 1900: Population, Part II*, (Washington, D.C., 1902), 171; *Fifteenth Census, 1930* (Washington, D.C., 1931), 10.
[65] *Ibid.*, 10; *Statement of the Vote for President, November 3, 1936;* McDanel, *Virginia Constitutional Convention*, 50–56.
[66] *Times-Dispatch*, Nov. 8, 1924, cited in Woodward, *Origins of the New South*, 345.

tem would return to Virginia once the Negro had been eliminated from politics, the opposite had occurred. Only once since 1902 had a Republican presidential candidate carried the Old Dominion —Hoover in 1928. In congressional contests, only in the Ninth District could the G.O.P. consistently gain a lone seat in the House of Representatives.

The 1920's were not politically rewarding for the Negro in Virginia. After a temporary renewal of amicable relations with the state G.O.P. from 1922 through 1924, with the election of Herbert Hoover to the presidency in 1928 Negroes witnessed the renewal of Republican lily-whitism. The *Planet* glumly predicted "more of the same" during the next four years.[67]

[67] Nov. 10, 1928.

VII

The Virginia Negro Becomes a Democrat, 1928–1936

In an effort to strengthen the G.O.P. in the South, Hoover continued the lily-white policy during his administration. In Virginia this strategy failed, for not only did the Republicans lose in the 1929 gubernatorial election but many Negroes abandoned the party in the 1932 presidential election. Hoover's racial stand partially alienated Negro voters and the Great Depression completed the rupture. That the administrations of Harding and Coolidge were as much to blame for the nation's economic plight as Hoover's meant little to needy Negroes. To them the Hoover administration, which bore the brunt of the responsibility, failed to provide desperately needed relief. Therefore, they took what appeared to them to be the only alternative and voted for a Democrat in anticipation that he would end the depression. The record of Franklin D. Roosevelt's first administration encouraged more and more Negroes to change their party affiliations in 1936.

Another factor which accelerated this shift was the elimination of the Democratic party's closed, or white, primary. Exclusion of Negroes from party primaries had been established as Democratic policy in 1905 and made law by the General Assembly in 1912. This legislation fulfilled its purpose until 1928, when the first successful court case for admittance into the closed voting circle was won by Negroes. After a series of court battles, colored voters by 1936 had no further difficulty voting in the primaries. As a result, despite the hostility of many white Democrats, Negroes made their way into the Virginia Democracy.

It was not long after Hoover became President that his policy toward the Negro turned the race against him. On March 27, 1929, he issued a statement commending the Republican organizations of the lily-white states of Alabama, Arkansas, Louisiana, Texas, Florida, North Carolina, and Virginia for their work in the past campaign. In South Carolina, Georgia, and Mississippi, however, where racially mixed or "black-and-tan" organizations were guilty of patronage abuses, he recommended reorganization. If such political housecleaning failed through the present leadership, he then cautioned that the federal departments would be compelled to seek advice about the selection of federal employees from other sources.[1] Hoover's statement was tantamount to endorsement of white Republicanism, the same policy long since practiced by the Democrats. Consequently, Negroes considered themselves deserted, "cast adrift" without a party even on the national level.[2]

Negro Republicans received a second setback with the breakdown on the state level of Republican reconciliation which had begun during the 1923–24 period. The party once again emphasized its lily-white policy. Henry W. Anderson, keynote speaker at the Republican State Convention in Roanoke on June 26, 1929, excluded Negroes from party plans and declared that "the political and social relations between the races were not to be disturbed, no matter what party succeeded." On the following day President Hoover endorsed Virginia's state organization as a model for other Southern states to follow.[3]

If the President expected a permanent G.O.P. revival in the Old Dominion under the lily-white banner, the gubernatorial race of 1929 ended such expectations. On the surface, there appeared little difference between the candidates of both parties. The nominee of the regular Democrats, John Garland Pollard, was a former state attorney general and currently chairman of the Department of Government and Citizenship at the College of William and Mary. He promised to reduce taxes, continue the "pay-as-you-go" road program, protect the seafood industry, improve education

[1] Lewinson, *Race, Class, and Party,* 174–75; *Journal and Guide,* March 30, 1929.   [2] *Journal and Guide,* July 6, 1929.
[3] *Times-Dispatch,* June 26, 27, 1929.

for Virginia's children, help the farmers, and support welfare agencies more adequately. His opponent, William Moseley Brown (himself a lifetime Democrat), a professor of psychology and education at Washington and Lee University, issued a similar platform. In addition Brown charged that if Pollard was elected, he would return Virginia to the policies of the repudiated Al Smith. Brown initially received his nomination from an "anti-Smith" convention, consisting mainly of Hoovercrats led by Bishop James Cannon. The Republicans then jumped on the bandwagon, and the contest became one of anti-Smith Democrats allied with Republicans against the regular Democrat Pollard.[4]

The gubernatorial race offered little comfort for Negroes, as neither candidate solicited their votes. The leading Negro weeklies conceded they were "wholly unable to discover any difference in attitude towards the Negro on the part of the two platforms or the two candidates." [5] Even the Socialist party's choice, John J. Kafka, "has not made any special bid for the votes of this class of people." [6] One observer, nevertheless, expressed the opinion that the Democrats secretly sought the Negro vote. In Richmond unnamed sources from both parties allegedly admitted that Democrats wooed that city's 18,000 potential Negro voters.[7]

The role of the Negro, however, was not to be a voter but an issue. As of old, he was depicted as a threat to white supremacy. Late in October, when the Republicans had little opportunity to counter the charge, a Richmond daily carried a story accusing Brown of catering to the Negro vote. The article claimed that the Republican candidate sought revision of state election laws, particularly the repeal of the poll tax. Allegedly Brown also had distributed among colored voters a political pamphlet which included a photograph of Chicago's Negro congressman, Oscar DePriest, campaigning in Virginia for the Republican candidate.[8]

[4] Alvin L. Hall, "Virginia Back in the Fold: The Gubernatorial Campaign and Election of 1929" (MS term paper for Edward Younger, University of Virginia, March 4, 1963), 6–30 passim.
[5] Journal and Guide, Sept. 21, Nov. 2, 1929.
[6] Planet, Oct. 19, 1929.
[7] Lewinson, Race, Class, and Party, 159–60.
[8] "Can White Supremacy Be Preserved in Virginia If Our Election Laws

Campaign manager Henry W. Anderson charged that the Democratic state organization had sponsored the newspaper article expressly to intimidate white voters. Democratic headquarters director T. McCall Frazier flatly denied this accusation. But, by this time, the campaign was in its last days, and undoubtedly the original charge against Brown had its effect. The vote, though not heavy, was a decisive victory for Pollard, 169,329 to 99,650.[9] As a result, Republican long-range victory plans in Virginia failed to materialize in 1929, blocked partly by the ever-present label of "friend of the Negro."

Coupled with the Republican failure in Virginia, nationally many Negroes who opposed Hoover as a lily white now also blamed him for the Great Depression. The normally pro-Republican *Planet* noted critically that owing to economic distress resulting from the depression, lynching had increased.[10] Because of Hoover's pussyfooting, no federal legislation was enacted to end this nefarious crime, despite 12 recorded lynchings in 1929 and 25 in 1930. That no one was lynched in Virginia was attributed primarily to the Byrd administration's antilynch law of 1928.[11] Nevertheless, Negro weeklies in the Old Dominion asked for protection by the federal government.

In 1930 Hoover was further castigated for nominating Circuit Court Judge John Parker of North Carolina to the United States Supreme Court. Ten years earlier, as the gubernatorial nominee in that state, Parker had openly condemned the Negro in politics as "a source of evil and danger to both races . . . and not desired by the wise men of either race or by the Republican party of North Carolina." [12] Later as circuit judge he upheld the yellow-

---

are Liberalized to Meet the Views of Dr. Brown, the Republican Candidate for Governor, and Colonel Anderson, His Chief Supporter?" Richmond *News Leader*, Oct. 28, 1929.

[9] *Statement of the Vote for Governor, November 5, 1929.*

[10] Tatum, *Changed Political Thought of the Negro*, 114; *Planet*, Oct. 4, 1930.

[11] *Journal and Guide*, Jan. 18, 1930; Tatum, *Changed Political Thought of the Negro*, 291.

[12] Tatum, *Changed Political Thought of the Negro*, 118–28; Moon, *Balance of Power*, 109.

dog contract. Because of his stand against the Negro and organized labor, the American Federation of Labor and the N.A.A.C.P. protested Parker's nomination. After intensive lobbying by both organizations, the Senate refused to confirm him 41 to 30. Among Negroes, much of the credit for Hoover's defeat was given to the executive secretary of the N.A.A.C.P., Walter White.[13] Later he was to spearhead the Negro shift to the Democratic party.

In still another complaint Negroes excoriated the President for not taking suitable action against Secretary of War Patrick J. Hurley's bungling of a proposed trip to France by American Gold Star Mothers. Negro mothers, hopeful of visiting the graves of their sons, had protested to the Secretary against the segregated accommodations arranged for them in New York City. While white mothers were lodged in the finest hotels, colored women were offered poor boarding houses. Similar quarters were also scheduled on board ship. In an attempt to smooth over the difficulty, Hurley declared that the group could be mixed if women of both races were agreeable. Confident that the white mothers would refuse this offer, colored women decided to avoid the humiliation, and of the 450 Negroes scheduled to make the trip, only 58 sailed.[14]

Because of these developments, even die-hard Negro Republicans were sorely tempted to bolt the party in 1932. A shift toward the Democratic party had begun, especially in the North, as early as 1930.[15] Commenting on the presidential election of 1932, the Negro press in Norfolk explained that Negroes who voted for Governor Franklin D. Roosevelt of New York would not do so out of admiration for him but out of disapproval of Hoover. Little favor-

[13] *Journal and Guide,* April 5, 19, May 10, 1930; Richard L. Watson, "The Defeat of Judge Parker: A Study in Pressure Groups and Politics," *Mississippi Valley Historical Review,* L (Sept. 1963), 213–34.

[14] *Journal and Guide,* June 7, 1930; Van Deusen, "Negro in Politics," 272; Franklin, *From Slavery to Freedom,* 515–16.

[15] In 1930 two Negroes were elected to judgeships in Harlem. Negroes contributed to the defeat in close elections of two pro-Parker Senators, McCulloch of Ohio and Allen of Kansas. Negroes were also reportedly shifting to the Democratic party in Rhode Island, Delaware, and New Jersey. *Journal and Guide,* Nov. 8, 15, 1930.

able could be discovered in Roosevelt's attitude toward the Negro. It was charged that to win the Democratic nomination in 1932 he had made a concession to the "Bourbon South" by accepting Texan John Nance Garner as his running mate. The Negro press accused F.D.R., as Assistant Secretary of the Navy during the Wilson administration, of aiding in the unjustifiable seizure of the black republic of Haiti by American marines. As governor of New York, commented the *Journal and Guide,* he paid little attention to Negro problems and had not appointed Negroes to prominent state positions. Furthermore, the Democratic platform of 1932 adopted at the Chicago national convention made no specific reference to Negro needs. Though thousands of people attended the Chicago convention, allegedly less than ten Negroes did so officially.[16] Lastly, Negroes were reluctant to desert the party of Lincoln because they retained the feeling "that the 'best people' voted Republican; and it meant a great deal to many Negroes to be identified with that group." [17]

Unimpressed with Roosevelt, desirous of remaining loyal to the G.O.P., but unwilling to vote for Hoover, once source counseled Negroes to steer a course of militant independence, advising solidarity behind "any party or candidate as long as—only as long as —a solid vote [pays] back individual dividends in justice, fair play, and full equality of all citizenship rights." [18]

Roosevelt scored a stunning victory in Virginia, amassing 203,-980 votes to 89,637 for Hoover and 2,382 for Socialist Norman Thomas.[19] How Negroes cast their ballots is uncertain, though Roscoe C. Jackson thinks they still voted Republican.[20] Regardless

[16] *Ibid.,* May 26, July 9, Oct. 22, 1932; Moon, *Balance of Power,* 17; Van Deusen, "Negro in Politics," 256–76; William E. Leuchtenburg, *Franklin D. Roosevelt and the New Deal* (*The New American Nation Series,* ed. by Henry Steele Commager and Richard B. Morris; N.Y., 1963), 185–86.

[17] Franklin, *From Slavery to Freedom,* 516; personal interview with David E. Longley, Sept. 13, 1965, Richmond. Dubbed by fellow Negroes as "Mr. Republican," Richmond insurance executive Longley remained in the G.O.P. from 1930 through 1958.

[18] *Journal and Guide,* Oct. 8, 1932.

[19] *Statement of the Vote for President, Nov. 8, 1932.*

[20] Personal interview, June 14, 1964, Richmond.

of whom they voted for, the following fragmentary figures of potential Negro voters in 1932 illustrate that their influence was minor:

Alexandria	279
Danville	345
Fredericksburg	144
Lynchburg	300
Norfolk	1,000 approximately
Petersburg	150–200 approximately
Richmond	1,500–2,300 approximately [21]

In all, Negroes probably cast less than 20,000 votes in the presidential election. The *Journal and Guide* calculated in a "liberal estimate" that approximately 13,168 of the 329,000 Negroes over twenty-one voted in 1932.[22]

Evidence of Negro loyalty to the G.O.P. is found in the returns from major Northern cities where they voted in large numbers. Detroit, Cleveland, and Philadelphia returned majorities for Hoover; and, while Roosevelt gained 59 per cent of the the the white vote in Chicago, only 23 per cent of the Negroes voted for him. In Cincinnati's heavily Negro-populated Sixteenth Ward, the Democratic candidate received only 29 per cent of the vote.[23]

Virginia Negroes had little to cheer about in the 1932 election, but during the next four years they deserted the "party of emancipation," proclaimed their "declaration of independence," and moved into the ranks of the Democracy. Franklin D. Roosevelt's New Deal, though it made no special efforts to aid them as a race for fear of alarming Southern Democrats such as Senator Carter Glass of Virginia, seemed to indicate through its legislation and

[21] *Journal and Guide,* Feb. 10, Oct. 20, 1934, May 23, 1936; *Planet,* Sept. 1, 1934. These figures are estimates. To illustrate, while the Lynchburg figure is 300, C. M. Bowman of the Lynchburg Board of Registrars recorded only 137 Negro ballots cast in the 1936 election. Registration Records, June, 1932, to Aug. 3, 1937.

[22] Josephus Simpson, "Are Colored People in Virginia a Helpless Minority?" *Opportunity,* XII (Dec. 1934), 373–75; *Journal and Guide,* May 23, 1936.

[23] Leuchtenburg, *F.D.R. and the New Deal,* 185; Franklin, *From Slavery to Freedom,* 516; Tatum, *Changed Political Thought of the Negro,* 135–41; *Planet,* Nov. 17, Dec. 1, 1934.

patronage that the Negroes had found a friend in the White House. To most Negroes, during Roosevelt's first term there was "No Forgotten Man." [24]

Nationally, the Negro press praised the chief executive for appointments made to prominent Negroes, something Hoover had not done. Among those selected for F.D.R.'s "Black Cabinet" were Robert L. Vann, editor of the Pittsburgh *Courier,* as special assistant to the Attorney General; Robert Weaver as special adviser on the economic status of Negroes; and John A. Langford as architectural engineer in the Public Works Administration's Housing Division.[25] The Richmond *Planet* commended the Democratic administration for including Negroes in such relief programs as Federal Emergency Relief Administration scholarships to Negro schools and colleges ($281,000) and Atlanta and Chicago slum clearance programs ($2,000,000 and $7,000,000). Front-page coverage was allotted the dedication of the new $626,000 chemistry building constructed by the Public Works Administration at Howard University. A series of articles in a leading Negro weekly on the Tennessee Valley Authority carried the headline, "Predict That Lives of Four Million Negroes Will Be Affected by the Great TVA Experiment." [26]

The New Deal program in Virginia likewise was greeted favorably by Negroes. By mid-March 1934 over 2,000 Negroes had been accepted in the Civilian Conservation Corps; and, although they were segregated from white workers, the fault was not Roosevelt's but that of the state's political machinery.[27] The Homestead Project, through the Resettlement Administration, received $280,-000 for housing redevelopment in Newport News. The project,

---

[24] For extensive coverage of the New Deal period, see Franklin, *From Slavery to Freedom,* 512–32; Moon, *Balance of Power,* 17–219 *passim;* Gunnar Myrdal, *An American Dilemma: The Negro Problem and Modern Democracy* (N.Y., 1944), *passim;* Arthur M. Schlesinger, Jr., *The Age of Roosevelt: The Politics of Upheaval* (Boston, 1960), 425–38; Frank Freidel, *F.D.R. and the South* (Baton Rouge, La., 1965), 71–102.

[25] *Planet,* Sept. 29, Nov. 17, Dec. 1, 1934; *Journal and Guide,* Sept. 29, 1934.

[26] *Journal and Guide,* March 21—April 11, Oct. 24—Nov. 3, 1934, *passim;* Franklin, *From Slavery to Freedom,* 522–28.

[27] *Journal and Guide,* March 17, 1934; Lewis, *Negro in Virginia,* 343.

staffed with Negro personnel from the civil engineers down to the common laborers, was a first for the nation. Virginia Negroes were included in the National Youth Administration, "granting aid to needy students [which] also has rendered valuable aid in redeeming Negro youth in city and country." [28] The W.P.A. gave $60,000 of $141,000 spent for improvements on the Booker T. Washington High School in Norfolk. Furthermore, construction by the P.W.A. of the Norfolk Community Hospital for Negroes [29] caused colored citizens seriously to reconsider their loyalty to the G.O.P.

Perhaps as influential as programs and benefits in winning Negroes to the Democratic party was the friendship for them exhibited by the first lady, Mrs. Eleanor Roosevelt. It had been rumored that as President, Hoover refused to have himself photographed with Negroes. When the President's wife was photographed being escorted by two R.O.T.C. cadets at Howard University, Negroes publicized the event as an example "of the broad equalitarianism" of the occupants of the White House.[30] Her invitation to the Hampton Institute Singers to perform at a White House function and her visit to the Negro patients at the United States Veterans Hospital in Hampton, followed by an informal visit to Hampton Institute,[31] won many Negro votes for the Democrats. Much more than political gain was involved, for the First Lady had a genuinely sympathetic interest in the Negroes' welfare which was reflected in their great admiration for her.[32]

During Roosevelt's first term, Negro voter sentiment took a decided turn toward the Democratic party. The *Planet* reported that the 1934 off-year congressional elections had been won by that party because of 200,000 Negro votes. In Harlem two Negro Democrats won seats in the state legislature, while in Pittsburgh and "old staid Philadelphia" Negroes were elected to the state assembly.

[28] Lewis, *Negro in Virginia*, 343–44; *Journal and Guide*, March 9, 1935, Feb. 29, 1936.

[29] Thomas Jefferson Wertenbaker, *Norfolk: Historic Southern Port* (Durham, N.C., 1931, 1962), 341–43.

[30] Franklin, *From Slavery to Freedom*, 517.

[31] *Journal and Guide*, Feb. 23, 1935, April 1, 1936.

[32] Personal interview with Roscoe C. Jackson, Aug. 14, 1964, Richmond; Franklin, *From Slavery to Freedom*, 517–20; Lewis, *Negro in Virginia*, 346–47; Freidel, *F.D.R. and the South*, 73, 86–88.

The extent of the shift was further demonstrated in Chicago by the victory of Negro Congressman Arthur W. Mitchell, the first colored Democrat ever to sit in the United States Congress. Mitchell defeated Negro Republican incumbent, Oscar DePriest.[33] It was not surprising, therefore, when the *Journal and Guide* in 1934 endorsed the Virginia Democratic ticket headed by Senator Harry F. Byrd and Colgate W. Darden, Jr., incumbent congressman for the Norfolk area. This backing was not meant to aid the Virginia candidates especially, but "a vote for these men is a vote for the New Deal. . . . What voter wants to dismantle the New Deal and return to the Old Order? Or, what has any political party or candidate offered as a substitute for the New Deal?" [34]

As the Negro made his decisive shift from the G.O.P., his vote was sought by both parties. Even in Virginia, where only an estimated 29,250 Negroes were registered to vote,[35] in 1936 Democrats and Republicans alike appeared to make all-out efforts for the first time since 1900 to win that handful of votes. Although previously Negro weeklies had received little political advertising, impressive full-page advertisements for the reelection of Roosevelt and for Republican candidate Alfred Landon appeared in them as early as August. The Democrats characterized the G.O.P. as the party which, during the twelve years of Harding-Coolidge-Hoover, appointed only seven Negroes to federal positions. F.D.R., however, had already made fifty such appointments. Under Coolidge and Hoover, over 7,000 banks had failed. The toll was only 61 during the New Deal. Because of the Democratic administration, C.C.C. boys were sending home $1,000,000 monthly to dependents. Twenty-six thousand Negroes benefited from the N.Y.A.[36] Not to be outdone, the Republicans charged that of the 340,000 patronage jobs in the New Deal, Negroes had received fewer than 100. If colored citizens benefited from the New Deal, they did so at a lower scale than the whites. For example, while white laborers

[33] *Planet,* Nov. 17, 1934; Myrdal, *An American Dilemma,* 494–95; John G. Van Deusen, *The Black Man in White America* (N.Y., 1944), 134–36.
[34] *Journal and Guide,* March 14, 1934.
[35] *Estimated Number of Voters, April, 1938, State Board of Elections,* hereafter cited as *Estimated Number of Voters.*
[36] *Journal and Guide,* Oct. 17, 1936.

received $86.50 monthly working for the W.P.A., Negroes earned but $29.50.[37]

The *Journal and Guide,* Democratic since 1928, pledged itself again to Roosevelt. The *Planet,* however, opposed to "the boondogglers, office holders, Santa Claus enthusiasts, college professors, dreamy-eyed social workers, and all of the mongrel host who are advocating Roosevelt and Ruin," remained faithful to the "party of Emancipation." [38] The Richmond weekly also held the Roosevelt administration responsible for Jim Crowism on various federally sponsored projects. The New Deal, it insisted, had accomplished little; and, while there had been 4,000,000 families on relief in 1933, a year later the figure rose to 5,000,000.[39]

Roosevelt swept the nation in the 1936 presidential election, and for the first time the Negro majority in America favored a Democratic candidate. Samplings of the Negro vote showed F.D.R. carrying Pittsburgh's Third Ward by nearly ten to one and Cincinnati's Sixteenth Ward with over 65 per cent of the vote.[40] Of the 16 Negroes elected to state legislatures in 1936, 11 were Democrats. An authority on the Negro commented that of the 15 colored wards in nine Northern cities, Roosevelt won 9 in 1936, whereas he had carried only 4 in 1932.[41]

In Virginia, F.D.R. won by a sizable margin, 234,980 to Landon's 98,336. The heavily Negro-populated 21st Precinct of Norfolk, which had never in its political history voted for a Democratic presidential candidate, cast 202 votes for Roosevelt to 131 for Landon. To an influential Negro paper the results signified Negro faith in the Democratic party. Only once before had any Democrat won in that precinct—when Harry F. Byrd defeated his Republican opponent in the 1934 Senate race, 66 to 64.[42] Two politically

[37] *Planet,* Oct. 24, 1936.
[38] *Journal and Guide* and *Planet,* Oct. 31, 1936.
[39] *Ibid.,* Nov. 10, 1934, March 14, 1936.
[40] Leuchtenburg, *F.D.R. and the New Deal,* 187; Moon, *Balance of Power,* 18–19; Schlesinger, *Politics of Upheaval,* 598–600.
[41] Myrdal, *An American Dilemma,* 238; V. O. Key, Jr., "The Future of our Political Parties: The Democratic Party," *Virginia Quarterly Review,* XXVIII (Spring 1952), 163–65.
[42] *Statement of the Vote for President, Nov. 3, 1936; Journal and Guide,* Nov. 7, 1936.

prominent Negroes, Roscoe C. Jackson of the Richmond Democratic Voters' League and Dr. J. M. Tinsley, former state secretary of the Virginia branch of the N.A.A.C.P., also agreed that the 1936 election was the first in which the Negro majority voted for a Democrat for President.[43] Thus, as a result of continued lily-whitism, the G.O.P. "responsibility" for the Great Depression, and the gains made during the New Deal, the Virginia Negro deserted the party of Lincoln for the Democracy.

There appeared concurrently another avenue by which Negroes entered the Democratic party—the destruction of the white primary in Virginia. Judging from the paucity of material in the leading Negro weeklies of the state, after their initial exclusion from the primary little action was taken by Negroes from 1912 through 1925 to contest the law. Though a handful of "worthy Negroes" continued to vote in Richmond, Norfolk, Portsmouth, and Newport News, their influence was minimal.[44] Periodically other Negroes in the early 1920's unsuccessfully attempted to vote in the primaries. For example, in Richmond in June 1925, when a delegation of colored citizens inquired of the Richmond Democratic Committee why they were not allowed to vote, they were told simply that it was against party rules. According to the *Journal and Guide,* the best remedy for such exclusion was for Negroes to register in as large numbers as possible for general elections in order to illustrate to the Democratic party their potential value.[45]

In 1925, while Negroes were kept from voting in the primaries, the total turnout in the general election was so small that only 8.6 per cent of the entire adult population was needed to elect the governor. The average participation in Virginia from 1925 through 1945 in gubernatorial primaries ranged between 5 and 7 per cent of the adult population. This evoked V. O. Key's witty remark that by contrast Mississippi, whose Democratic gubernatorial nominees won the votes of from 12.4 to 16.4 per cent of its adults, was

[43] Personal interviews with Jackson and Tinsley, Aug. 14, 1964, Richmond.

[44] Bunche, "Political Status of the Negro," I, 66; personal interview with Roscoe C. Jackson, June 14, 1964, Richmond; *Journal and Guide,* April 8, 1916.

[45] *Ibid.,* July 27, 1925.

"a hotbed of democracy." [46] In Virginia, a Negro weekly observed, the Democratic party needed no platform. Its candidate for governor, nominated in a closed primary, was the platform. The task of the candidate and the party was to keep the Negroes in Virginia poor and ignorant so that they could not meet either economic or educational qualifications for voting. More than one critic believed the Byrd organization purposely discouraged a high vote count, black or white, to promote manageability of the electorate. [47]

Not until 1927 was the white primary successfully challenged in a United States Supreme Court decision, *Nixon* v. *Herndon*. In this case against the Democratic party in Texas the Court upheld the contention of Dr. L. A. Nixon of El Paso that his exclusion from the primary election constituted a denial of equal protection of the law under the Fourteenth Amendment. [48] Though no mention of violation of the amendment which prohibits the denial of the right to vote on account of race or color was made, Negroes in the Old Dominion hailed the decision as the beginning of the end of the white primary. However, when Richmond Negroes attempted to vote in the mayoralty primary on April 3, 1928, Democratic party officials asserted that the Texas decision did not apply in Virginia. [49] The primary law in Texas specifically barred Negroes but the Virginia statute was less specific and gave parties the right to make their own regulations. Since there had been no discrimination by the state, any discrimination must therefore be charged against the Democratic party—a private organization which had the right to control its own affairs. [50] Negroes then took advantage of Section 21 of the 1912 Primary Law and argued that since the

[46] Key, *Southern Politics*, 20; Heard and Strong, *Southern Primaries and Elections*, 193. For an account of machine-controlled primaries, see Horn, "Democratic Party in Virginia," 245–58.

[47] *Journal and Guide*, Oct. 31, 1925; Benjamin Muse, "The Durability of Harry Flood Byrd," *The Reporter*, XVII (Oct. 3, 1957), 27; Key, *Southern Politics*, 20; Folliard, "Shadowy Oligarchy Rules over Virginia," Washington *Post*, June 9, 1957.

[48] *Nixon* v. *Herndon*, 273 U.S. 536 (1927), cited in Key, *Southern Politics*, 621–22; Charles Staples Mangum, *The Legal Status of the Negro* (Chapel Hill, N.C., 1940), 405–14.

[49] *Planet*, March 19, 1927.

[50] *Times-Dispatch*, March 23, 1928.

state defrayed the cost of the primary, it must be considered part of the state election machinery and subject to the rules governing elections.[51]

In spite of these persuasive arguments, Negroes did not easily gain the right to vote in primaries. A group of Richmond Negroes, led by Joseph Pollard and Theodore W. Jones, president of the Non-Partisan League for Colored Voters, were denied the vote in a Democratic primary in April 1928. Upon appeal to the hustings court, Jones was informed by Judge Beverly T. Crump that if party officials cared to do so, they might allow Negroes to cast their ballots.[52] There is no record to show that this was done. In another suit resulting from the same primary, James O. West charged that his rights, as guaranteed by the Fourteenth and Fifteenth Amendments, had been abridged by the election judge of the First Precinct, Madison Ward.[53] Tried before the United States Federal District Court for Eastern Virginia, Judge Lawrence D. Groner presiding, the case was decided in favor of West. According to the decision, since state funds financed party primaries, those elections must be considered a valid state function. Therefore, the legislative statute which authorized discrimination by party officials was invalid as a violation of Fourteenth and Fifteenth Amendments to the federal Constitution.[54] When challenged, this decision was subsequently upheld by the United States Circuit Court of Appeals, with basically the same dictum that if all political parties incorporated the same qualifications in their rules as did the Democratic party, nobody would participate in the primary except white persons, and other persons would be deprived of the right guaranteed them under the United States Constitution.[55]

No further appeal was made by the state to the United States Supreme Court within the required forty-day time limit; therefore, the Circuit Court decision became binding. In correspondence on

---

[51] *Planet*, March 31, 1928.
[52] *Ibid.*, April 8, 1928.   [53] *Ibid.*, April 31, 1928.
[54] *West* v. *Bliley*, 33 F.2d 177 (E.D. Va. 1929); Duncan Lawrence Groner Papers, University of Virginia; Mangum, *Legal Status of the Negro*, 414–15.
[55] *West* v. *Bliley*, 33 F.2d 177, 42 F.2d 101 (1930); Mangum, *Legal Status of the Negro*, 414–15.

the matter, Attorney General John R. Saunders conceded that the decision was final. The Democratic party acquiesced to the state's financing the primary because the expense was far too costly for any private organization. Thus the Democratic primary was now open to all citizens.[56]

Although there were approximately 385,000 Virginia Negroes of voting age, only about 10,000 voted in 1930,[57] so that the percentage who registered for Democratic primaries must have been exceedingly low. Moreover, available reports indicate that most Negro voters remained Republicans, despite the circuit court decision, Negro opposition to the Hoover administration, and the organization of such clubs as the Richmond Democratic Voters' League. According to the Richmond *Times-Dispatch,* a year after the Negro won the right to participate in the Democratic primary only a few bothered to do so. Only with reluctance did any Negro admit he had joined the enemy camp.[58] Another Richmond daily commented, "At present, the Negro would be far more enthusiastic if he had won the right to participate in the Republican mass meetings and conventions." [59] Some Negroes, notably in Suffolk and Hampton, still hesitated to register for fear that local officials might turn them away. In the Suffolk primary of August 1933, Edward Lowe, principal of a Negro high school,[60] and L. E. Wilson, secretary of the People's Building and Loan Association,

[56] Key, *Southern Politics,* 624; correspondence from Attorney General Saunders to O. M. Price, June 30, 1931, in *Report of the Attorney General to the Governor of Virginia from July 1, 1930 to June 30, 1931,* 80. Though the closed primary became a dead letter thereafter, even as late as 1947 the Democratic party included in its rules the voting right to only white Democrats. According to Key, revision of the outdated rule was considered "at a recent convention," but party leaders deemed it unwise to revive the issue as it would "have created an opportunity for intolerant elements to sound off, unnecessarily and undesirably opening the whole race issue, which is little discussed in Virginia politics."

[57] *Journal and Guide,* July 13, 1930.

[58] Virginius Dabney, "The Negro and the Franchise: Their Participation in the Primary," Richmond *Times-Dispatch,* Aug. 30, 1931, cited in *Journal and Guide,* Sept. 12, 1931; Lewinson, *Race, Class, and Party,* 271 n. 55.

[59] *News Leader,* Sept. 12, 1939, cited in *Planet,* Sept. 20, 1930.

[60] *Journal and Guide,* May 20, Aug. 12, 1933.

charged they had been deprived of their votes. Dr. and Mrs. Thomas T. Turner, members of the Hampton Institute faculty, were also barred.[61] Aside from this rash of incidents, other exclusions by officials were mainly in general elections and not in primaries.

An examination of random figures indicates that the Negroes' lethargic attitude toward voting continued. In 1931, in Richmond only about 2,000 to 3,000 qualified to vote by paying their poll taxes. Only "several hundred" Negro tax payers voted in the primary of August 1932.[62] In 1933 Portsmouth listed 239 Negro men and 95 women registered for the primary, and in the following year the figures were 177 and 112 respectively.[63] The estimate of Negro voters in the August 1936 Democratic primary in Norfolk and Portsmouth combined was "not less than 700." [64] Though a Richmond weekly boasted that at least four councilmen were elected in that city's primary by the Negro balance of power on April 3, 1934, research has not substantiated the claim.[65]

The results of the 1936 mayoralty primary in Richmond further contradict this boast. In the contest, incumbent J. Fulmer Bright opposed Roy Dudley. Negroes resented the fact that Bright's administration had refused to employ them, even in the City Social Service Bureau which received $5,085 monthly from the federal government for salaries. They further objected to Mayor Bright's failure to investigate police brutality against Negroes.[66]

The race issue was injected into the campaign when the Dudley

[61] *Ibid.,* Aug. 5, 24, Oct. 14, Nov. 18, 1933; Lewis, *Negro in Virginia,* 245. Considered to be the last major white primary case in Virginia, the contest was decided by the Elizabeth County Circuit Court in favor of Wilson.

[62] *Journal and Guide,* Sept. 12, 1931; *News Leader,* April 6, 1932; Bunche, "Political Status of the Negro," IV, 948.

[63] *Journal and Guide,* Feb. 17, 1934.

[64] *Ibid.,* Aug. 29, 1936.

[65] *Planet,* April 7, 1934; Moon, *Balance of Power,* 177, asserts that the Negro vote in the Second Congressional District was credited with the victory of "a New Deal candidate" over an organization man in the 1936 primary.

[66] *Times-Dispatch,* April 4, 5, 1936; *Planet,* April 7, June 30, 1934; Bunche, "Political Status of the Negro," VI, 1492.

forces accused the opposition of circulating a mimeographed sheet which asserted that Dudley, if elected, would put Negroes on the city payroll and discharge white employees. Dudley branded it a lie and described it as a deliberate attempt to incite racial antagonism.[67] The *Times-Dispatch,* though agreeing that Dudley had acted wisely in bringing the issue into the open and forcing acknowledgment of the circular's origins from the Bright forces, nevertheless requested that Dudley clarify his position on Negro employment. The question seemed pertinent since the Bright administration had not employed even one of the city's 53,000 Negroes.[68] The newspaper's challenge, however, was issued too late. Dudley was apparently able to sidestep the issue and failed to make his position known.

On April 7, even with the majority of Negro voters supporting Dudley, he lost by 9,277 votes to 7,910. To the Negro press it was the same old story—only 2,000 Negro voters went to the polls.[69] This defeat undoubtedly could be attributed in part to the anti-Negro attitude of white Richmonders, but Negro apathy certainly influenced the results.[70] Thus, even when Negroes had the opportunity to rid themselves of an unsympathetic administration, they failed.

Four years later, however, Richmond Negroes claimed that through the efforts of approximately 2,400 Negro voters Mayor Bright had been finally defeated by Gordon B. Ambler, 13,089 to 7,727. In that campaign a concerted voter registration drive was

[67] *Times-Dispatch,* April 4, 1936; Bunche, "Political Status of the Negro," IV, 948. Roscoe C. Jackson claimed this charge was totally unfounded, and despite the fact that the Negroes of the city intended to vote for Dudley, he did not solicit their votes. Personal interview, Aug. 14, 1964, Richmond.

[68] April 4, 1936. On the following day, the paper corrected its original statement and wrote that there were 61 Negroes on the payroll as attendants or orderlies or cooks at the City Home, City Library, Pine Camp Hospital, and other locations. Of a total of 2,000 city employees, only one of every 32 was a Negro.

[69] *Planet,* April 18, 1936. City registration figures set the Negro total at 1,800 registered Negro voters. Martin, *Negro Disfranchisement in Virginia,* 158–59.

[70] Personal interview with Roscoe C. Jackson, Aug. 14, 1964, Richmond.

led by Dr. J. M. Tinsley of the N.A.A.C.P. and Roscoe C. Jackson of the Richmond Democratic Voters' League.[71] Such victories were seldom repeated. Though the Negro had gained admittance to the Democratic primary, he was neither active as a participant nor welcomed as a voter by white Democrats.

[71] *Times-Dispatch,* April 3, 1940; Richmond *Afro-American,* April 6, 1940, hereafter cited as *Afro-American;* personal interviews with Jackson and Tinsley, Aug. 14, 1964, Richmond.

VIII

Combating Voting Restrictions

1930–1950

DESPITE the fact that Negroes had gained the right to participate in the Democratic primary and a majority of those registered had voted for the Democratic presidential candidate in the 1936 election, some Negroes in Virginia still were excluded from the polls. The major hurdles remaining were the blank white paper registration form, obstacles to registration set by local registrars, and the yearly poll tax payment for three consecutive years as a voting prerequisite. Of the three barriers, the latter proved to be the most permanent, persisting into the 1960's.

During the early 1930's, the questions local officials posed pertaining to their qualifications as electors proved to be a major obstacle for Negro registrants. Negroes insisted that even the registrars could not answer the questions they asked. Despite coaching by Negro citizens' leagues, would-be registrants could not name the counties which constituted the 27th Judicial District of Virginia nor recite Article X, Section 3, of the state constitution.[1] When Charles Butts from Portsmouth attempted to register to vote in 1931, he succeeded only after the following ordeal:

Three times I went to register and three times I was refused. The first time, my form was all right, but he asked me how many signed the Declaration of Independence and who was President of the Senate (at the time of my registration) . . . . I didn't know and I wasn't registered. The second time I went to the polls,

[1] Lewis, *Negro in Virginia*, 245; Bunche, "Political Status of the Negro," IV, 956.

the registrar told me that the "sun was down" and so I wasn't registered. The third time, I hadn't signed my name enough times on the blank form he gave me and I wasn't registered. I knew the machine was run at the time by Dr. Brooks, who was anti-Negro and so I figured it would be best for me to take a politician along with me the last time I went. I took over our ward leader, a man who was "in the know." I registered this time. I almost got out of the notion of voting, though.[2]

When Mrs. Samuel Jones filed for voting rights, she was informed that her name had not been signed in the required place on the blank application form. Because, furthermore, she did not know how many men had signed the Declaration of Independence, she was denied registration. As a result, Mrs. Jones resorted to the courts. During her appeal, her lawyer asked the judge if

he could ask Mr. Parker [the registrar] a question. The judge told him yes and whereupon Mr. Melvin [her attorney] asked the registrar how many signed the Declaration of Independence. Parker couldn't answer. The judge gave me the privilege of going to register without further difficulty.[3]

Because of such obvious attempts to keep them from registering, Negroes were forced to resort to the courts as they had done in the white primary cases. In Hampton, where it was charged that even professors at Hampton Institute were turned away for failure to pass registration requirements, the Negroes scored their first significant victory. The case of *Davis v. Allen,* decided in September 1931, resulted from the refusal of white registrar Thomas C. Allen of Hampton to register W. E. Davis two years earlier,[4] because the Negro allegedly lacked a basic knowledge of the state constitution. According to Registrar Allen, Davis had been unable to answer the following questions properly: (1) What is meant by legal residence in Virginia? (2) When is payment of the poll tax not required? (3) What are the prerequisites to enable one to register in Virginia? Davis appealed to the Circuit Court through his at-

---

[2] Bunche, "Political Status of the Negro," IV, 958.

[3] *Ibid.,* 959.

[4] *Cases Decided in the Supreme Court of Appeals of Virginia: September and November Terms, 1932,* 84–93; Key, *Southern Politics,* 11, 67, 564; *Journal and Guide,* Aug. 8, Oct. 10, 1931.

torney A. W. E. Bassette, Jr. (who had been involved previously in forty similar cases), on the basis that the questions asked pertained to the obsolete "temporary understanding" clause in Section 19 of the state constitution.[5]

The Circuit Court sustained the action of Allen,[6] but on September 17, 1931, the State Supreme Court of Appeals reversed the decision. The court ruled that questions two and three had been asked in the form of the "understanding and educational" requirement which had expired on January 1, 1904. Question number one was allowed as a fair inquiry relating to Davis' "qualifications as an elector," and his answer, "All persons who have lived in the State for one year and a legal Residenter," while showing his lack of education, was basically a correct one.[7]

According to Executive Secretary of the Virginia N.A.A.C.P. W. Lester Banks, the decision marked a turning point in the Negro's attempts to register in both primary and general elections. The case had a "far-reaching" effect on local registrars, who thereafter became more selective in their questions, making certain they related only to the Negro's "qualifications as an elector." [8]

Employment of unfair questions by local registrars persisted until the early 1940's, after which Negroes encountered few "understanding and educational" requirements except in Isle of Wight, Princess Anne, Nottoway, Dinwiddie, Prince Edward, and Surry counties.[9] When such instances occurred, the Virginia branch of

[5] *Journal and Guide*, March 29, 1930.
[6] *Ibid.*
[7] *David* v. *Allen* (16 S.E. 85), cited in Martin, *Negro Disfranchisement in Virginia*, 156; *Journal and Guide*, Oct. 10, 1931.
[8] Personal interview with Banks, Aug. 27, 1964, Richmond. See also Lewis, *Negro in Virginia*, 245.
[9] *Third Annual Report, The Voting Status of the Negro, 1942* (Petersburg, Va., 1943), 8, hereafter cited as *Annual Report, Voting Status;* Allen W. Moger, Department of History, Washington and Lee University, Lexington, Va., to the author, Aug. 17, 1964. Professor Moger indicated that "about fifteen years ago" Professor Luther P. Jackson of Virginia State College and president of the Virginia Voters' League informed him that "registrars generally in the state were no longer discriminating against Negroes, as they once did, and that low Negro registration was due primarily to Negro apathy." Dr. J. M. Tinsley and Roscoe C. Jackson substantiated this in interviews on Aug. 14, 27, 1964.

the N.A.A.C.P. and the Virginia Voters' League acted to correct the situation, either through persuasion or through the courts. Of the two organizations mentioned above, the N.A.A.C.P. possessed more statewide influence. It began inauspiciously, with chapters established in Richmond and Falls Church in 1915. Two years later there were but 1,097 members in the state, and additions during the 1920–35 period only raised the number of branches to twenty.[10] In an effort to increase enrollment and stimulate interest in the organization, as well as to coordinate the activities of the existing branches, the State Conference of Branches was formed in 1935. The results during the next fifteen years showed a steady growth to over sixty branches.[11] Leadership in the Virginia N.A.A.C.P. for the next two decades rested mainly with Dr. J. M. Tinsley of Richmond. Working in conjunction with civic organizations throughout the state, the organization sought as a major goal the elimination of the "understanding and educational" questions asked by local registrars. It also campaigned throughout the years from 1936 to 1940 to register 10,000 N.A.A.C.P. members as voters—a mark the organization was not to achieve until the post-World War period.[12]

Working many times in coordination with the N.A.A.C.P. to end voter discrimination was the nonpartisan Virginia Voters' League. Organized in May 1941, primarily through the efforts of Luther Porter Jackson, professor of history and political science at Virginia State College,[13] the purpose of the Voters' League was

[10] *Annual Report of the N.A.A.C.P. for the Years 1917 and 1918* (N.Y., 1919), 85.

[11] Personal interview with W. Lester Banks, Aug. 27, 1964. Richmond; *N.A.A.C.P.: Virginia State Conference of Branches, Twenty-Fifth Anniversary Issue, 1935–1960* (Richmond, 1960), 14–15.

[12] Personal interview with Dr. J. M. Tinsley, Aug. 27, 1964, Richmond.

[13] Born in 1892, Jackson acquired an M.A. degree from Columbia and Ph.D. from the University of Chicago, joined the faculty at Virginia State College in 1922, and remained there until his death in 1950. Jackson had his hand in almost every area concerning the betterment of the Negro. Among his many publications are *Virginia Negro Soldiers and Sailors in the American Revolution, Negro Officeholders in Virginia, 1865–1895,* and *Free Negro Labor and Property Holding in Virginia, 1830–1860,* the latter published as the annual selection by the American Historical Association in 1942. In constant correspondence with historian Carter Woodson, editor of

to persuade Negroes to pay their poll taxes and then follow through by registering to vote. Jackson maintained that though many counties and cities had organized voters' leagues and civic associations, they had not banded together under a central head from whom they could receive directions, information, and encouragement.[14] That central head became the Virginia Voters' League. Originally begun in 80 counties and 24 cities, the League rapidly covered the remaining 20 counties in the state. This did not mean that the local and state civic leagues already formed were subordinate to the League. They worked in coordination with the League. W. Lester Banks commented that on more than one occasion both groups worked side by side in voter registration and in opposition to voter discrimination.[15]

Professor Jackson stressed the point that by 1940, with but scattered exceptions, Negroes were encountering few restrictions in registering. Most of the remaining disfranchisement was self-imposed owing to Negro apathy and nonpayment of the poll tax. When "exceptions" did arise, Jackson would usually correspond with the individual or group involved. Often he made trips with lawyer Robert Cooley, Jr., to the office of the particular registrar involved in an attempt to rectify the situation. On one occasion a woman in Princess Anne County wrote that registrar Andrew Shipp informed Negroes who came to his home to register that he

---

The Journal of Negro History, he worked to advance Negro scholarship. He was a member of the Negro Business League and Secretary of the Virginia Teachers' Association, a position he used to advantage in attempting to induce Negro teachers to vote and also to teach citizenship in the classroom. Jackson wrote a weekly column during most of the 1942–50 period for the *Journal and Guide* entitled "Rights and Duties in a Democracy," as well as carrying on the mountainous correspondence of the Virginia Voters' League. The Jackson manuscript collection, a valuable source for the 1940–50 period in Virginia history and as yet untapped by scholars, is available at Virginia State College. J. H. Johnston, Jr., "Luther Porter Jackson, 1892–1950," *Negro History Bulletin,* XIII (June 1950), 195–97; G. James Fleming and Christian E. Burckell, ed., *Who's Who in Colored America* (7th ed., N.Y., 1950), 291–92.

[14] Jackson to President Weldon Henderson of Alpha Phi Alpha Fraternity, May 8, 1941, Jackson Papers.

[15] Personal interview, Aug. 27, 1964, Richmond.

did not have a registration book and that they would have to wait until the Electoral Board forwarded him one. Registrar Shipp told others that the only time he was supposed to register people was before the August primary election at the courthouse.[16] Before directly intervening in the case, Jackson wrote Shipp. He noted that Negroes had been denied the registration right and was certain this had been an oversight which would not reoccur. If, however, it persisted, court action would have to be resorted to.[17] After such indirect pressure had been employed against another registrar in Martinsville, Professor Jackson received the following letter from a Negro who previously had been denied registration: "The attitude of the registrar in the city has completely changed. Everyone who attempted to register on the 7th of October was successful. He even helped those who has some difficulty in making application. I think the "Little Hitler" has been conquered." [18] As late as 1948 Jackson, in his capacity as president of the Virginia Voters' League, received complaints of discrimination by local registrars.[19] By then, though, such grievances were infrequent.

[16] Laura M. Cooper to Jackson, May 19, 1942, Jackson Papers.

[17] Jackson to Andrew W. Shipp, May 16, 1942, Jackson Papers. For a case in which Jackson worked in coordination with the Nottoway Branch of the N.A.A.C.P., see W. Winston to Jackson, April 24, 1943, and Jackson to W. Winston, May 4, 1943.

[18] C. P. Jeter to Jackson, Nov. 2, 1944.

[19] Jackson to Oscar W. Epps, June 17, 1946; Willis Allgood to Jackson, Sept. 15, 1948. See also an undated case study in the Jackson collection, *Confidential Report on Interview with Registrars in Isle of Wight County* (presumably 1946), by a white field worker of three registrars in Isle of Wight County. The worker, Joanne Farrell, wrote that in those cases "the situation is not at all conducive to easy registration of the Negro voters in the area, either because of the location of the registration place, the economic status of the Registrar, or in at least one case, open anti-Negro feeling on the part of the Registrar." In one case, Mr. Zollie Johnson, registrar for Windsor District in the town of Windsor, insisted that "them Communists" attempted to "register the niggers working in the lumber mill there, but I told them where to get off at." When asked how he knew one of the men was a Communist, Mr. Johnson replied, "Why, I could tell by talking to him! He was from the union over there one of them CIO'ers . . . he came over to the store (Mr. Johnson's drugstore in town where he registers people) and got to actin' smart . . . he almost got himself in trouble too, talking so uppity, they liked to jumped him in the store before he got away from there."

Not only had certain Negroes through persistence done much to eliminate this barrier, but the Democratic organization headed by United States Senator Harry F. Byrd, frowned upon this type of intimidation. According to V. O. Key, in the virtual monopoly which the Democratic organization in Virginia enjoyed, if one wished to succeed in high-level state politics,

a person must enjoy a relatively high social status commanding at least a measure of respect. In a word, politics in Virginia is reserved for those who can qualify as gentlemen. Rabble-rousing and Negro-baiting capacities, which in Georgia or Mississippi would be a great political asset, simply mark a person as one not to the manner born. A public attitude favorable to this type of leadership combined with organization discipline represses most of the crudities commonly thought to be characteristic of southern politics.[20]

Key also asserted that in cities where Negroes voted in large numbers and tended to be allied with the local arms of the Byrd machine, the latter protected their right to the suffrage. "Virginia's white citizens in and out of the machine have demonstrated a relatively acute sense of responsibility toward the Negro—an attitude that may account in part for the fact that its race relations are perhaps the most harmonious in the South." [21]

A second registration roadblock, erected by the blank paper application form, continued to be common in rural areas, but by the end of the decade the standardized printed application form had been adopted in most cities, mainly for convenience of processing.[22] For example, in Richmond, "blacks and whites alike are given printed application forms; if they can read and write well enough to fill out the form, they are registered." During this period the Byrd "machine" appeared to frown upon the use of the blank form. Three times it was declared to be in violation of the state constitution. On the third occasion Attorney General J. Lindsay Almond added that it was the duty of the registrar to explain to the potential voter what questions he should answer.[23]

After the elimination of the white primary in the mid-1930's

[20] Key, *Southern Politics*, 26.   [21] *Ibid.*, 32.
[22] Personal interviews with Roscoe C. Jackson, Aug. 14, 1964, and W. Lester Banks, Aug. 27, 1964, Richmond.
[23] Key, *Southern Politics*, 564.

and with the relative ease with which a Negro could register in a primary or general election by the early 1940's, the remaining obstacle to the Negro's voting, other than his own apathy, was the $1.50 yearly poll tax payable for three consecutive years preceding any election. Investigations of Negro payment by Professor Jackson from 1939 through 1950 showed that it was irregular. Many citizens paid the tax for one or two of the years, but comparatively few had met the full requirement. In Brunswick County, for example, approximately 1,260 Negroes paid the capitation tax for either 1939, 1940, or 1941, but only 492 had done so for all three years. Throughout the state approximately 75,000 Negroes paid the tax for 1942, but only 28,845 paid for each of the three years to meet the registration requirement. Two years later, again in Brunswick, 1,489 Negroes made payment for either 1941, 1942, or 1943, but only 541 or 36 per cent paid for three years. In the state as a whole, only 41,385 of the 100,000 colored citizens who paid the tax for 1944 did so for three required years.[24] The city of Newport News in 1946 had 4,548 Negroes as poll tax payers for one or more years, but only 1,458 for the period necessary for registration. In the same year approximately 124,000 Negroes paid their taxes in the Old Dominion, but only 48,448 for all of the years required.[25]

Coupled with the monetary obligation was the requirement that capitation taxes be paid three months prior to any primary election and six months before any general election. It has been contended that those who might be interested in voting did not do so because the tax fell due six months prior to the campaign, before the candidates had announced and before political interest could be aroused.[26] According to one observer, at one time during the 1930's notices were mailed out to prospective Richmond voters informing them when taxes were due in order to qualify for the vote, but the practice was discontinued.[27] The *Journal and Guide*

[24] *Third Annual Report, Voting Status, 1942,* 3; *ibid., 1944,* 5.
[25] *Seventh Annual Report, Voting Status, 1946,* 5.
[26] Key, *Southern Politics,* 505, 587; Bunche, "Political Status of the Negro," III, 636.
[27] Interview by James Jackson with Roscoe C. Jackson, Oct. 12, 1939, Richmond, cited in Bunche, "Political Status of the Negro," III, 636.

in 1933 charged that poll tax bills had been mailed to white citizens of Richmond, but Negroes were required to pick theirs up at the collector's office.[28]

Another complaint against the capitation tax was that since payment was optional, little effort was made by officials to collect it. Negroes, therefore, might unknowingly have missed payment before the required time deadline. Luther P. Jackson commented that among Virginia tax collectors this was known as giving the Negroes the "pay-if-you-wish" message.[29]

It was further contended that on many occasions propertyholders were not informed that they had met their voting requirement by payment of the poll tax as part of their real and property tax assessment. Assuming the bill to be property taxes, the payee did not realize that he had also met the chief requirement for voting. "Fully one-half the poll tax paying by Negroes in rural Virginia [in 1941] is done under these circumstances." [30] In 1942 Professor Jackson estimated that at least 40 per cent of the 32,-504 poll-tax-paying Negroes did not register to vote. Knowingly and unknowingly, therefore, that year at least 13,000 Negroes who paid the poll tax had disfranchised themselves.[31]

Defenders of the capitation tax insisted, as they had since 1904, that if a citizen was not conscious of the time factor in payment or was unwilling to pay $1.50 yearly for the privilege of citizenship, then he did not deserve to vote. Proponents also decried the allegation that the poll tax discriminated against lower-income Negroes. The tax was levied against whites as well as Negroes, so that it could hardly be construed as a tactic for exclusion of anyone on account of race.[32] Negro leaders had to agree that members of the race were apathetic. On one occasion in 1937 it was reported that only 826 of the total Negro population of Norfolk

[28] Dec. 9, 1939.

[29] *Seventh Annual Report, Voting Status, 1946,* 6; Frederick D. Ogden, *The Poll Tax in the South* (University, Alabama, 1958), 65, 76.

[30] *Third Annual Report, Voting Status, 1941,* 3.

[31] *Fourth Annual Report, Voting Status, 1942,* 6.

[32] Key, *Southern Politics,* 585. Ralph Bunche, however, charged that the poll tax was an attempt by whites to dominate the "black belt" area of Dinwiddie, Amelia, Nottoway, Brunswick, and Prince George counties; "Political Status of the Negro in the South," III, 700. See also Virginius Dabney, *Below the Potomac* (N.Y., 1942), 113–14.

bothered to pay the tax. To this sad showing a Negro teacher of history in one of the city's high schools could only reply, "They just don't bother about it." [33] Urgings and proddings by civic organizations and the Negro press met with little success, and even chiding the indifferent delinquents was of no avail. A typical editorial in this vein, under the heading "YOU AND YOUR DOG," read as follows:

Your dog license will cost you $3 per year, if you have a female dog, and $1 if your pet is a male.
Your poll tax, which qualifies you to vote, is only $1.50 per year. . . . The right to vote is surely as important to you, your family and your community, as your dog. The right to have a voice in the government of the city in which you live is certainly just as important as your dog.[34]

Another claim advanced by tax proponents was that the funds collected as revenue were used for whites and Negroes alike in the Virginia public school system. But on this point they stood on untenable ground. Opponents of the tax, whose forces had been building steadily since the mid-1930's, charged that the revenue gained was minimal. For example, in 1937 the state received approximately $700,000 from poll tax collection while $1,315,528 remained delinquent.[35] In 1940, when $821,609 was collected, editor Virginius Dabney commented that if the poll tax was elimi-

[33] Interview by Wilhelmina Jackson with Mr. [or Mrs.] Fulford, Norfolk, Oct. 21, 1939, cited in Bunche, "Political Status of the Negro," II, 584.

[34] *Journal and Guide,* Nov. 24, 1945. Numerous accounts of Negro apathy to paying the poll tax are found in the Jackson Papers, accounts which complain of the unwillingness to pay the tax because "it is not warthwhile. So thire you are, and yet sumphting must bedon about it." H. J. Williams to Jackson, Aug. 26, 1941. A Negro leader in Roanoke commented, "Why the Negroes don't take advantage of some of the opportunities that are given them in Virginia I can't see. I suppose they will arouse themselves from this slumber one bright day, but I hope it won't be too late." H. T. Penn to Jackson, April 6, 1944. Another wrote in dismay, "I am ashamed to write you the facts. The truth is our people are very slothful and, we are not making any progress as far as I can see. . . . Our Professional men are not interested or, won't take the time to direct the people. I hope that you won't think me too harsh but, I feel that I can only tell you the truth." Lilliam Simms to Jackson, May 8, 1947.

[35] "The Poll Tax, A Burden upon Education," *Southern Planter,* XCIX (Jan. 1938), 5; Jesse P. Guzman, ed., *Negro Year Book . . . 1941–1946* (Tuskegee, Ala., 1946), 262.

nated in favor of a required annual head tax, Virginia could raise between two and three million dollars a year, as in Massachusetts and Connecticut.[36] For the fiscal year ending in June 1954 poll tax revenue was equivalent to only 1.44 per cent of the state expenditures for public schools. Poll tax revenue accounted for only 0.86 per cent of the total tax receipts. Virginia spent $67,653,976 for public free schools, while the amount received from the yearly capitation tax was but $1,458,976.[37]

Tax proponents also warned that floods of Negroes in the black-belt areas of Virginia would overwhelm the white voter if the suffrage was more easily attainable. The *Southern Planter* refuted this line of reasoning by comparing voter registration in nonpaying North Carolina to that of the Old Dominion. The former had repealed its poll tax in 1920, and since then the Democratic majority had risen from 100,000 to 300,000, and the so-called black counties had increased their white majorities. This agricultural journal insisted that those who oppose repeal

in North Carolina, Virginia, or anywhere else, are not afraid of the Negro, they are afraid of democracy. They are unwilling that government shall be of the people, by the people and for the people. . . . There are more Negroes in North Carolina than there are in Virginia (918,647 to 650,165), but poll tax repeal has not even rippled the race question in this State, but it has set white men free from a poll tax which denied citizenship to poverty.[38]

Whether poll tax proponents were actually "afraid of democracy," rather than the Negro vote, V. O. Key hypothesized that the Byrd

[36] Dabney, *Below the Potomac*, 117, and *Liberalism in the South* (Chapel Hill, N.C., 1932), 408–9. The *Times-Dispatch*, which during the 1901–2 constitutional convention favored a poll tax, under the guidance of Dabney in the 1930–40 period moved strongly against it. Similar campaigns were made by the *News Leader*, edited by Dr. Douglas S. Freeman, and the *Virginian-Pilot*, headed by Pulitzer Prize-winning editor Louis I. Jaffe.

[37] *Report of the Comptroller to the Governor of Virginia, Fiscal Year ending June 30, 1954,* cited in Ogden, *Poll Tax in the South,* 57.

[38] "Highlights of Virginia Suffrage History," *Southern Planter,* C (Feb. 1938), 7. The *Planter* was the oldest agricultural journal in America, and under the direction of Westmoreland Davis, former governor of Virginia, had become an active political organ.

machine during the 1925–45 period owed its existence to a competent management and a restricted electorate. Small voting totals alone did not necessarily ease the task of controlling election results, but in Virginia the low number of voters contributed to the manageability of elections.

Abolition of the poll tax as a voter prerequisite became a major issue during the 1940's. Earlier unsuccessful attempts dated back to those made by Virginia Republicans in 1906. Henry Anderson, the Republican candidate for governor in 1921, had campaigned against the capitation tax, and the Democrats immediately brought out "the old 'scarecrow' of Negro domination." After the resounding defeat of Anderson, little action against the poll tax had been taken during the remainder of the 1920's with the exception of that by crusading daily newspapers. In the following decade, however, the movement for repeal gained momentum.

Opponents to the tax in Virginia appeared to be steering along the course similar to that of Congress, which from 1939 onward yearly proposed at least one bill to abolish the capitation requirement in federal elections. In January 1938 Governor-elect James H. Price came out in favor of poll tax repeal. It was reported that Price, while lieutenant governor in 1937, had announced his gubernatorial candidacy without previous organization sanction. Because he was considered more sympathetic toward national administration policies than was Senator Byrd, perhaps the Virginia leadership had not intended him for the governorship. Price, however, had "an impressive network of personal friendships" and when it appeared that his victory in a primary would be assured, he received the reluctant endorsement of the state's Democratic leaders. His action for repeal hardly constituted a major revolt against the organization, but Price later became one of the few governors who attempted to initiate legislation contrary to machine wishes.[39] With his backing the Virginia Federation of Labor introduced a resolution in the House of Delegates to abolish the poll tax. The measure was killed in

[39] Key, *Southern Politics,* 23; Muse, "The Durability of Harry Flood Byrd," 26; Folliard, "Shadowy Oligarchy Rules over Virginia," Washington *Post,* June 9, 1957.

the pro-organization House Privileges and Elections Committee,[40] but the fight for repeal continued. Both Negro weeklies crusaded actively against the tax during the next two years as did the N.A.A.C.P., the Richmond Democratic Voters' League, and the Independent Voters' League.[41]

Further action came from a group of liberal anti-Byrd Democrats headed by Francis Pickens Miller of Fairfax, Moss Plunkett of Roanoke, and Martin A. Hutchinson of Richmond. Led primarily by Plunkett, the newly formed Virginia Electoral Reform League charged that the Byrdites were not responsive to the popular needs of the state. Opposed to what it termed the organization's support for restricted suffrage, the League began a program of education with the purpose of applying pressure on the General Assembly for a constitutional amendment abolishing the poll tax as a voting prerequisite. Members of the League also ran for political office against machine candidates, with capitation tax abolition as a platform plank. Though Plunkett was badly beaten in the 1941 primary for lieutenant governor by organization-backed William Tuck, 98,744 to 23,732, the defeated candidate stressed the significance of the contest as being that Tuck was opposed and that citizens had begun to voice their dissent against machine politics. Plunkett later ran unsuccessfully against Tuck for governor in 1945 as did Martin Hutchinson against Byrd for the Senate in 1946.[42]

In March 1941, at the request of Governor Price, the Virginia Advisory Legislative Council appointed a subcommittee to study the poll tax situation. Its members, Professor Robert K. Gooch of the University of Virginia Political Science Department, Roanoke attorney Colonel James P. Woods, and Theodore R. Dalton, a Radford attorney, were not regarded as organization men. They reported that, because of the capitation tax, a restricted suffrage had become part of the people's habits and therefore "a consequent inertia exists which takes the form of unquestioning accept-

[40] *Journal of the House*, 1938, 33; *Journal and Guide*, Jan. 22, 1938.
[41] *Journal and Guide*, March 5, 1938; personal interviews with Dr. J. M. Tinsley, Aug. 14, 1964, and W. Lester Banks, Aug. 27, 1964, Richmond.
[42] Key, *Southern Politics*, 28–29, 659; Fredericksburg *Free Lance-Star*, Aug. 6, 1941.

ance and of unreasoning hostility to change." The report did not hold any group or political party within the state directly responsible for such a condition, but it did conclude that "certain elements . . . regard the *status quo* as being to their continued advantage." [43] In all likelihood those "elements" referred to the Byrd organization.

Replying to the timeworn bromide that the poll tax was needed to keep the Negro disfranchised and to prevent the election of "Black Republicans," the committee report asserted that "the simplest conclusion concerning the Negroes in relation to suffrage is that the whole situation is permeated with pretended or unfounded fears." Setting aside the fear of Negro officeholders and "Black Republicans," the committee attempted to point out by a comparison of voting in North Carolina and Virginia that there was little danger of an upsurge in Negro voting.[44]

As a result of their findings, Gooch and Dalton proposed that the poll tax be abolished by a constitutional amendment. Colonel Woods filed a minority report recommending lowering the tax but not abolishing it. Despite the majority's recommendation, the General Assembly did not initiate legislation to repeal the tax during the 1942 session. In fact, the subcommittee's findings were not even published, though those of two other such investigatory groups had been before the legislature convened in January. Because of the "thunderous silence" on the part of the General Assembly, the *Times-Dispatch* concluded that the Gooch report contained "a minimum of whitewash and a maximum of forthright criticism of the *status quo,*" and its contents did not find favor with the powers that be. Though Moss Plunkett of the Virginia Electoral Reform League had caused a minor sensation by unexpectedly reading the report before the House of Delegates

---

[43] *Report of the Subcommittee for a Study of Constitutional Provisions Concerning Voting in Virginia,* 6–7; Ogden, *Poll Tax in the South,* 203.

[44] *Report Concerning Voting in Virginia,* 14–15; Key, *Southern Politics,* 659. Comparison was made between two adjoining counties, Mecklenburg County, Va., and Warren County, N.C. In 1936, in Mecklenburg, more than 1 per cent of the Negroes voted but less than 17 per cent of the whites did, whereas in Warren, 1/3 of 1 per cent of the Negroes voted while 40 per cent of the whites did so.

and senate committees on privileges and elections on February 12, no further action was taken on the matter.[45]

The matter lay dormant until March 1945, when Governor Colgate W. Darden, Jr., suggested the creation of a commission to study state suffrage laws. A nine-man committee was formed with Representative Stuart B. Campbell of Wythe County as chairman.[46] After months of probing and investigation the committee reported its findings to Governor Darden on December 15, 1945. By a vote of 7 to 2 this body also recommended a constitutional amendment to abolish the capitation tax as a prerequisite to voting. To compensate for the loss of revenue the committee recommended a school tax of no more than $3.00 on all residents over twenty-one years of age, with payment made a prerequisite for obtaining any license or permit. To replace the poll tax as a voting requirement, the committee suggested that annual registration be adopted for all voters registered since January 1, 1904. This registration was to be conducted four months prior to any election in the Commonwealth. Voters would also be required to meet literacy tests and other such requirements as the General Assembly might prescribe.[47]

The recommendations, passed by 34 to 3 in the senate and 57 to 37 in the House of Delegates during the 1946 session, became known as the Campbell Amendments.[48] According to law, amendments had to be approved by two successive legislative sessions before being submitted to the people, therefore they were brought to a vote again in the 1948 session and passed. On the final day of the session the General Assembly ruled that the Campbell Amendments should be submitted to the people in the November 1949 elections.[49] The year and a half delay was necessary, according

[45] *Times-Dispatch,* Feb. 12, 14, 1942; Ogden, *Poll Tax in the South,* 203–4.

[46] *Journal and Guide,* March 24, 1945; Ogden, *Poll Tax in the South,* 204; Horn, "Democratic Party in Virginia," 239.

[47] *Report of the Commission to the Governor and the General Assembly of Virginia, Senate Document No. 8* (Richmond, 1946), 11, 14–15.

[48] *Journal of the Senate, Regular Session, 1944–1945, Extra Session, 1945, Regular Session, 1946,* 529–41.

[49] *Journal of the Senate, 1948,* 1034–35; *Journal of the House, 1948,* 1274; *Times-Dispatch,* March 18, 1948.

to the legislative body, so as not to interfere with the presidential and congressional elections of 1948. It was speculated, however, that the Byrd organization did not wish passage of suffrage amendments in 1948 for fear they might hamper the machine in the following year's gubernatorial race.[50] Apparently there was some truth in such speculation, as Francis Pickens Miller, basing the brunt of his campaign in the Democratic primary on an anti-Byrd appeal, came within 24,000 votes of defeating organization candidate John S. Battle. Allegedly Miller would have won the nomination had election officials not closed their eyes to primary rules and allowed some 25,000 Republicans to vote for Battle. The closeness of the race was accentuated by the fact that Battle received less than a majority of the votes (about 43%), while Miller garnered about 35% and the rest were split between two lesser candidates.[51]

One would expect that the Negroes who had campaigned against the poll tax would have welcomed this development. Instead, Negroes and whites alike joined ranks against the proposed amendments. Negro leaders insisted that the new requirement of registering four months prior to any election, along with the insertion of a literacy test, would be as effective a disfranchiser as had been the capitation tax.[52] Leading Negro organizations, headed by the N.A.A.C.P., the Virginia Voters' League, and the Virginia Civil Rights Organization, all opposed the amendments. Local groups, such as the Norfolk Democratic Club and the Non-Partisan League, also spoke out against the change. The Virginia Teachers' Association joined in the opposition and the Negro Baptist Ministers Conference voted that clergymen should speak for three minutes on Sunday against the Byrd manipulations.[53] Both Negro weeklies denounced the amendments, and the *Afro-American*

[50] Key, *Southern Politics,* 660; Ogden, *Poll Tax in the South,* 208; personal interviews with Roscoe C. Jackson and W. Lester Banks, Aug. 14, 27, 1964, Richmond.

[51] *Times-Dispatch,* Aug. 4, 5, 1949; William Peters, *The Southern Temper* (N.Y., 1959), 154–5.

[52] Personal interviews with Roscoe C. Jackson and W. Lester Banks, Aug. 14, 27, 1964, Richmond.

[53] Ogden, *Poll Tax in the South,* 209; *Journal and Guide,* Nov. 5, 1949.

boldly warned Negroes, "DON'T BE A SUCKER! There's a String TIED TO IT!" [54]

Senator Harry F. Byrd and John S. Battle, the Democratic candidate for governor, stood behind the proposed amendments, but they faced a formidable coalition. With the Negroes were the AFL-CIO, the Virginia Right to Vote League, the Republican gubernatorial candidate, Walter Johnson, the College of William and Mary Voters' League, and the Richmond Citizens' Association.[55]

On election day the Campbell Amendments were soundly defeated by a vote of 56,687 to 206,542. They failed to win approval in even one county or city, the county with the closest vote being Rappahannock with a 314 to 307 count. Even ordinarily pro-organization counties such as Lunenburg, Mecklenburg, Nansemond, Powhatan, and Prince Edward opposed the amendments 1,418 to 177, 1,315 to 243, 823 to 310, 534 to 45, and 1,156 to 323 respectively.[56] Aside from the opposition previously mentioned, a Richmond daily attributed the decisive setback in part to the Byrdites' halfhearted campaigning for the amendments. Perhaps the backing had been meant as a token indication that the organization favored electoral reform. Equally responsible was the fact that hitherto loyal organization Democrats, particularly in the rural areas, preferred to retain the poll tax rather than contend with more stringent voting qualifications. The Campbell proposals might have maintained a curb on Negro voting, but they could very well disfranchise many of the white voters upon whom local organization candidates depended for election.[57]

There were no further serious attempts to repeal the poll tax until the late 1950's. It therefore remained a hindrance to the Negro. True, the number who met the three-year requirement increased by approximately 50,000 from 1941 through 1950; but expressed in terms of the 442,663 Negroes of voting age, the 1950 figure represented only 18.6 per cent who had met the first requirement

[54] Afro-American, Oct. 8, 1949; Journal and Guide, Nov. 5, 1949.
[55] Ogden, Poll Tax in the South, 210–11; Times-Dispatch, Oct. 9, 1949.
[56] Statement of the Whole Number of Votes Cast for and against Certain Proposed Amendments to the Constitution of Virginia, November 8, 1949; Heard and Strong, Southern Primaries and Elections, 206.
[57] Times-Dispatch, Nov. 9, 1949.

for voting.[58] Payment of the poll tax was not necessarily followed by registration. Of the 76,448 Negroes who satisfied the three-year requirement in 1950, the State Board of Elections estimated that 40,376 had registered to vote.[59]

That the poll tax was one of the factors influencing the lack of voter participation is certain. Weighing its effect, though, was "somewhat like trying to decide what proportion of the score of a football game can be attributed to the effects of any one player." [60] According to the Virginia Voters' League, the poll tax could be paid by any conscientious citizen. Also, the small number of registered Negroes could not be attributed to the local registrars' opposition, since "less than 70 [of over 1,770 in 1950] seek to prevent a Negro from registering because of his race." The League maintained that "custom and dull indifference," rather than the poll tax, remained the outstanding obstacles.[61] Whatever the reasons, politically the Negro was still not "vote conscious" by 1950.

[58] *Third Annual Report, Voting Status, 1942,* 3; *ibid., 1946,* 5; *ibid., 1950–1951,* 4, 13, 15.

[59] *Report of Estimated Number of Voters, April, 1950.*

[60] Key, *Southern Politics,* 599.

[61] *Eleventh Annual Report, Voting Status,* 1950–1951, 14–15. The recent study, *Negroes and the New Southern Politics* (N.Y., 1966), 38–39, by Donald R. Matthews and James W. Prothro, attributes this lack of interest or vote consciousness in part to the Negroes' attitude that politics is white man's business.

IX

The Negro as Office Seeker in the 1940's

No WHITE MAN IS GOING TO JEOPARDIZE HIMSELF POLITICALLY FOR THE RIGHTS OF NEGROES UNLESS NEGROES HAVE SUFFICIENT VOTING STRENGTH TO PROTECT HIM. . . . Vote-language is the only language spoken in the realm of politics." [1] This statement by Gordon B. Hancock, professor of theology at Virginia Union University, in August 1935 forcefully points out the cause of Negro political disabilities then and throughout most of the 1940's. Negro voting strength remained negligible until after World War II, and, though it was estimated that 30,967 Negroes had met all voting requirements in 1940, at best only 15,000 actually voted. Few white office seekers were bold enough to engage openly in the precarious activity of soliciting Alexandria's 338 Negro votes, Charlottesville's 255, Danville's 632, or even Richmond's 5,200 and Norfolk's 2,891.[2] That the anticipated votes might not materialize and the probability of being labeled a "nigger lover" by the opposition were sufficient reasons to disregard Negroes as potential voters.

Telling examples of Negro-baiting had occurred in the previously mentioned 1936 Richmond mayoralty contest and the 1938 Second District congressional campaign. In the latter Colgate W. Darden, Jr., was opposed by incumbent Norman R. Hamilton, editor of the Portsmouth *Star,* who had defeated Darden in 1936.

[1] *Journal and Guide,* Aug. 10, 1935.
[2] *Estimated Number of Voters, April, 1940;* Luther P. Jackson, "Race and Suffrage in the South since 1940," *The New South,* III (June–July, 1948), 3, 25; Margaret Price, *The Negro and the Ballot* (Atlanta, 1950), 9.

Hamilton, allegedly in gratitude for Negro support in the past election, set up an imposing campaign headquarters, complete with a Negro secretarial staff, on Effingham and High Streets, the heart of the Portsmouth Negro district. The Darden forces in turn used this tactic to their advantage by printing a circular charging Hamilton with favoring Negro employees over whites. Approximately 10,000 copies are said to have been distributed to white neighborhoods in Portsmouth and outlying regions. One page in the circular had a photograph of a Negro stenographer working at the Hamilton headquarters, with the caption beneath the photo reading: "Look, Hamilton's a nigger lover . . . ! See, the niggers are set up better than your own people by him. . . . If you vote for Hamilton, niggers will be teaching your children soon." According to Hamilton, after his defeat by less than 2,000 votes, that circular was "one of the things that cost me the election." [3] This incident taught the lesson that white candidates seeking Negro votes would do so most safely at group rallies where all or most of the candidates appeared before the Negro audiences, made short prepared speeches, and perhaps concluded with how they had been nursed as a child by a beloved colored "mammy." [4]

Neither party courted the Negro vote. The Republicans had not altered their lily-white policy appreciably since the 1920's and continued the charge that the Virginia Democracy, by allowing Negroes in its primaries, was now the party of the Negro. As late as the 1937 gubernatorial campaign, not a single Negro delegate was present at the Republican State Convention in Richmond, and no mention was made of the Negro in the party platform.[5] Negroes also failed to make headway in the Democratic party. Small wonder that the Richmond *Planet* editorialized in 1938 that Negroes did not stand a chance of exerting any semblance of power in any state or local election. The best they could do was resort to denunciation of white candidates in the Negro weeklies. For example, when Senator Carter Glass opposed the Wagner–Van Nuys anti-

---

[3] Bunche, "Political Status of the Negro," V, 1172.

[4] *Journal and Guide,* Aug. 3, 1935.

[5] Palmer Weber, "The Negro Vote in the South," *The Virginia Spectator,* C (Nov. 1939), 22; *Times-Dispatch,* Aug. 28, 29, 1937.

lynch bill, the *Planet* had to content itself with admitting that Glass would meet no resistance in Virginia "except by death. . . . The aged United States Senator of Virginia has a rendezvous with his conscience as the inevitable hour rapidly approaches. We are positive that his meeting place will be harassed by ghosts of remorses and regrets for his inhumanity to his fellowmen who by chance were born colored." [6]

On the national level, the presidential election of 1940 followed a pattern similar to the contest four years earlier. The *Journal and Guide* advocated a third term for Roosevelt, while the Richmond *Afro-American,* after having backed La Follette in 1924, Smith in 1928, and Roosevelt in 1932 and 1936, shifted to the Republican candidate, Wendell Willkie.[7] In the heaviest criticism of F.D.R. to date, the *Afro* accused his administration of not solving the unemployment problem and of allowing Jim Crowism on federal projects, such as in the Civilian Conservation Corps and the armed forces. Negroes in the military were passed over and not made officers but were relegated instead to positions of top sergeant or officer's steward. In one instance the President promoted a number of colonels to the rank of general, but passed over Negro Colonel Benjamin O. Davis, who had seniority over many of the white officers.[8] In contrast Willkie was portrayed as an opponent of discrimination in the military and other governmental agencies. Furthermore, even if Willkie "were not the giant of energy, tolerance, enthusiasm, patriotism that he is, we should still advocate his election, because long perpetuation is the stuff out of which royalty, dictators and tyrants grow." [9]

Despite the opposition the majority of Negroes remained loyal to the party of the New Deal. Perhaps Bishop R. R. Wright of

[6] Feb. 12, 1938.

[7] Oct. 19, 1940.

[8] Roosevelt promoted Davis to the rank of general just prior to the November election. The *Afro-American* denounced the move as a political maneuver for the Negro vote, while the *Journal and Guide* editorialized it as "Our Improved Status in Our Armed Forces." *Journal and Guide,* Nov. 2, 1940; *Afro-American,* Oct. 19, Nov. 2, 1940.

[9] *Afro-American,* Oct. 19, 1940.

Richmond best characterized Negro sentiment for Roosevelt as follows:

We KNOW him and we do not know Willkie. Roosevelt has started on a work which he has not completed. We want him to complete it. . . .
Willkie has done nothing for the government. Most of his reputation has come from fighting the government's New Deal plans. He has never held public office. He would not know what to do with it if he had. He would be just another Hoover—smart in business, but dumb in politics, and a tool of those who keep back the social advance.
But there is another, a more personal reason. The Roosevelts have always been kind to the Negroes. They are not personally afraid of the Negroes. They have hired Negroes all of their married life. Mrs. Roosevelt's maid and Mr. Roosevelt's valet are colored. It means much to the race to have a man and his wife of this type in the White House who know us first hand.[10]

According to poll results released by the American Institute of Public Opinion prior to the 1940 campaign, Negroes in the states where they were politically influential favored the Democrats over the G.O.P. by 66 per cent to 34 per cent, but approved of Roosevelt personally over a Republican possibility by 82 per cent to 18 per cent.[11] Though there are no specific data to indicate that Negroes in the Old Dominion voted in this manner, Negro leaders agree that F.D.R. was their people's choice in 1940.[12] Even so their possible 30,967 votes, out of a total of 364,224 Negroes over twenty-one, were insignificant in Roosevelt's Virginia victory over Willkie, 235,961 to 109,363.[13]

The political situation did not improve appreciably during World War II years. Though voter registration totals increased,

[10] "No Hope for the Race in a Willkie Candidacy," *Journal and Guide,* Oct. 26, 1940.

[11] *Ibid.,* Feb. 17, 1940.

[12] Personal interviews with Roscoe C. Jackson, Dr. J. M. Tinsley, W. Lester Banks, Aug. 14, 27, 1964, Richmond.

[13] *Estimated Number of Voters, April, 1940;* Moon, *Balance of Power,* Appendix II, 238. For Negro participation nationally, stressing the Northern states, see James E. Allen, "The Negro in the 1940 Presidential Election" (Master's thesis, Howard University, 1955), 97–122 *passim.*

they did so slowly. Only in 1945, as indicated by the figures below, did the number jump markedly, undoubtedly because of discharged servicemen returning to civilian life.

1941	30,748
1942	31,490
1943	33,406
1944	32,889
1945	38,020

The increase over the five years appears less significant when it is compared with the 365,717 Negroes of voting age in the Commonwealth.[14]

Continued Negro apathy and the subordination of political activity to the war effort were the major reasons for the snail-like pace of voter registration. This conclusion appears to be borne out by the sharp decrease of political news in the Negro weeklies. Interest shifted instead to the weekly press coverage of the war by on-the-spot Negro correspondents such as Thomas W. Young of the *Journal and Guide.* Feature stories receiving priority included the launching of the Liberty Ship, *Booker T. Washington,* the first to be commanded by a Negro, Captain Hugh Mulzac. Equally inspiring were the exploits of the all-Negro 99th Fighter Squadron in the Italian campaign and the bravery of the 24th Infantry Regiment battling in the jungles of New Georgia. Attention also turned to the breaking down of Jim Crow barriers in the armed services and in defense employment. Amid the patriotic efforts of blood donors and civil defense workers, the motto of Negroes became "give us the chance." [15]

Few gains were made by Negroes on the political homefront. Luther P. Jackson, in his weekly newspaper column, "Rights and Duties in a Democracy," constantly reminded his race that "a

[14] *Estimated Number of Voters, 1941–1945; Sixth Annual Report, Voting Status, 1946,* 5.

[15] *Journal and Guide,* Sept. 19, 1942, Nov. 11, 1944, *passim.* For a full account of the Negroes' role in World War II, see Franklin, *From Slavery to Freedom,* 560–90; Ulysses Lee, *The Employment of Negro Troops: United States Army in World War II* (Washington, D.C., 1966).

voteless people is a voiceless people," but his efforts met with little success. He complained of Negro apathy not only among the laboring class but also among the educated. He could hardly be optimistic with figures revealing that only 4.6 per cent of the adult Negroes in Virginia registered to vote, that 95 per cent of the ministers failed to register, or that fewer than 2,000 of the state's 4,000 Negro school teachers were registered by 1943. How could Negroes be expected to perform their civic duty, queried Jackson, if educated leadership was lacking? Furthermore, though it was estimated that 33,406 Negroes met all voting requirements in 1943, Professor Jackson contended that less than 4,000 actually voted.[16]

Local civic clubs, among them the Richmond Democratic Voters' League, Young Men's Civic Organization of Portsmouth, and the Civic League of Hampton, continued their efforts to stimulate the political interest of the race, but here too the wartime pressures were felt. President Roscoe C. Jackson of the Richmond organization recalled that during this period political activity took second place to his work on the city draft board. Dr. J. M. Tinsley of the Virginia N.A.A.C.P. also attested to the difficulty of motivating Negroes politically during the war years.[17]

Some enthusiasm was mustered for the presidential election of 1944. The *Afro-American* renewed its attack on the Roosevelt administration where it had left off in 1940, chastising F.D.R. for not having done enough to end discrimination against the 800,000 Negroes in the armed forces. According to that weekly, one-half of the Negro work force still was excluded from social security benefits. Its editors also complained that the President had made concessions to the South by permitting the nomination of Harry S. Truman of Missouri for the vice presidency over their choice, Henry Wallace. The *Afro* chose as its standard-bearer the Republican candidate, Governor Thomas E. Dewey, who pledged "full citizenship for colored citizens," including correction of Army-Navy segregation, a federal antilynch law, and the establishment

[16] *Fourth Annual Report, Voting Status, 1943*, 8; *ibid., 1944*, 8; *ibid., 1945*, 7.

[17] *Journal and Guide*, Sept. 19, 1942, Nov. 13, 1943; personal interviews, Aug. 14, 27, 1964, Richmond.

of a permanent Fair Employment Practices Commission.[18] These promises did not shake the loyalty of either the Norfolk *Journal and Guide* or the majority of the Negroes in Virginia. Once again they voted to return F.D.R. to the White House, regarding him as "the best President since Lincoln." [19]

With the end of the war, Negro political participation increased markedly. Among the factors spurring Negroes to action were the economic gains during the past four years, the migration of Negroes northward, and the feeling that, since Negroes had served the nation in its time of need, they should be allowed to do so in time of peace. The founding of the United Nations in which countries of all races were represented doubtless gave Negroes a feeling of participation in world politics. The defeat of Nazi Germany, with its philosophy based on the supremacy of the Aryan race, implied that as a nation Americans did not consider one race superior to another. Political opportunity in the future should be equal to all.[20] C. Vann Woodward has remarked that the revitalization of the Negro in the postwar years initiated a "Second Reconstruction" in the United States. Unlike the first, which ended in failure shortly after the Civil War, the second appears to hold the promise of success. The increasing power of the Negro vote in both political parties, especially in the North, has been a major factor in this new development.[21]

Virginia was affected by the "Second Reconstruction." This is evidenced most clearly in the increase of registered voters and the growing number of Negro candidates for office. Professor Luther P. Jackson believed that increased Negro voting and candidacies were interrelated. Negroes ran for office primarily because of the

[18] *Afro-American,* Oct. 14, 28, 1944; Moon, *Balance of Power,* 33.

[19] *Journal and Guide,* Oct. 28, Nov. 4, 11, 1944; Franklin, *From Slavery to Freedom,* 584; personal interviews with Roscoe C. Jackson and Dr. J. M. Tinsley, Aug. 14, 27, 1964, Richmond.

[20] Franklin, *From Slavery to Freedom,* 560–92; Woodward, *Strange Career of Jim Crow,* 129–34; Benjamin Quarles, *The Negro in the Making of America* (N.Y., 1964), 215–30 *passim.*

[21] Woodward, *Strange Career of Jim Crow,* 128–29, and "From the First Reconstruction to the Second," *Harper's Magazine,* CCXXX (April 1965), 127–34.

increase of Negro registrants, mainly in urban areas.[22] The number of Negro voters statewide increased from 38,020 in 1945, to 43,945 in 1946, 45,737 in 1947, 53,035 in 1948, and 65,286 in 1949. Richmond and Norfolk, where Negro candidates ran regularly during these years, showed typical increases. In the capital city registration doubled from 6,374 in 1945 to 12,518 in 1949, while in Norfolk it climbed from 3,964 to 6,390 during the same years.[23]

The increase in voter participation plus interest in the Negro as an aspirant for office marked the postwar years as the first real awakening of the race to Virginia politics in the twentieth century. Prior to 1945 Negroes rarely sought political office. When they did run, as in the lily-black campaign of 1921, their purpose was not victory but stimulation of political awareness among Negroes. Other examples of such attempts can be seen in the June 1936 Portsmouth councilmanic election. Two Negroes, the Reverend C. C. Somerville of Jefferson Ward and Dr. A. C. Johnson of Harrison Ward, entered the race in districts where "most" of the 463 qualified Negroes were located. Their platforms were similar to those advocated by previous and subsequent Negro candidates: equal schooling, free textbooks for all students, better streets and lighting, and equal jobs for Negroes. When cautioned by friends that they would become political goats because their candidacies were premature, Dr. Johnson replied, as many had before and would after him,

that the Negro, even if he polled only one vote, had to take the step forward in those sections, where conditions were favorable and the Harrison Ward, due to the predominance of Negroes, was certainly such a section. I ran to prove a point that Negroes weren't politically asleep. I lost, but hope the point was proved.[24]

Concurring with Johnson, the Reverend Mr. Somerville declared he was dismayed and angry because for the past forty years no

---

[22] *Seventh Annual Report, Voting Status, 1945,* 8; personal interview with Roscoe C. Jackson, June 14, 1964, Richmond.

[23] *Estimated Number of Voters, 1945–1949.*

[24] Interview by Wilhelmina Jackson with Johnson, Portsmouth, Va., Sept. 6, 1939, cited in Bunche, "Political Status of Negroes," IV, 960–61.

Negroes had held political positions in Portsmouth. Yet even as a candidate, Somerville did not appear to take the role seriously, as evidenced by the following statement:

I did not attempt to campaign. I simply contacted my friends and relatives. None of the Negro organizations in town supported me. When the votes were counted, Dr. Johnson and I both had the same number—eight apiece. This appeared to me as a very strange thing so I'm going to make a bid for the support of Negro organizations in Portsmouth.[25]

The handful of votes received by the Negro candidates left them at least 100 votes behind their nearest opponent. If there was any satisfaction in the election, it was that the Negro vote in the Twenty-first Precinct had helped elect to city council D. J. W. Reed, a white sympathetic to Negro needs, over his opponent George R. Abbott.[26]

Attempts such as these prior to 1941 usually were disappointing. Not until 1942 did Negroes in Roanoke make a creditable showing. Sponsored by the Roanoke Civic League, Dr. Harry T. Penn became the first Negro candidate for councilman in the history of the city. Advocating improvement of the school system, the police department, and the recreational system and speaking out for adequate city planning and straightening of the city's thoroughfares, Penn polled 424 votes in the primary.[27] Unsuccessful in this first attempt, he ran for a second time in 1944; and, though again defeated, his total reached 537 votes.[28] While praising Penn's efforts, Luther P. Jackson could not help being dismayed at the low turnout in a city as large as Roanoke. He estimated that only 12 per cent of the Negroes eligible to pay the poll tax had done so and that 7,000 others had not paid their capitation tax for three years.[29]

Even when an issue arose which directly concerned the Negroes, they did not organize as a body and protest by means of the ballot.

[25] Interview by Wilhelmina Jackson with Somerville, Sept. 15, 1939, in *ibid.*, 962.
[26] *Ibid.; Journal and Guide,* June 13, 1936.
[27] *Journal and Guide,* Feb. 7, March 14, 1942, April 18, 1942.
[28] *Ibid.,* April 8, 1944.
[29] *Ibid.,* March 25, 1944.

A case in point was the Newport News race for councilman in 1944. Negro attorney Wendell R. Walker, the first of his race to run for office in that city in twenty years, did so in protest of the school board's lack of any stated reason for dismissing six Negro teachers. Backed by the Grace Independent Voters' League, the Eastern Voters' League, and the Ministers' Alliance, Walker campaigned on the school dismissal issue. Contesting for one of three vacancies on the city council, he polled sixth in a field of nine. His vote total was 1,039 of the 3,802 cast for all candidates.[30]

In the following year Negroes ran for state offices for the first time since the early 1920's. The Reverend W. B. Ball, pastor of Goodwin Baptist Church in Richmond, threw his hat into the ring as a candidate for the House of Delegates in the August 1945 Democratic primary. His platform advocated a permanent F.E.P.C., abolition of the poll tax, repeal of segregation laws on public carriers, increased educational facilities for all, strengthening of the juvenile court system, and a health program to eradicate venereal disease. In the same primary, attorney Thomas H. Reid of Portsmouth also campaigned for a house seat. However, both candidates were defeated. Hall placed fourteenth in a 17-man race for seven seats in the Richmond area, and Reid ran last in a 5-man race for one seat.[31]

After World War II the combination of young Negro leaders, renewed efforts by civic organizations to interest the race politically, and the steady rise in poll tax payment led Negroes to believe they could win elections. Instead of running for office to stir up the apathetic and the indifferent, Negro candidates campaigned to win. Four candidates came forward in 1946 for the city council— Victor Ashe of Norfolk, Dr. Bernard A. Coles of Charlottesville, C. K. Coleman of Danville, and C. V. Wilson of Lynchburg.[32]

Though not one of the candidates was successful, their total vote increased over that of previous years. The *Afro-American* commented that candidates Coleman in Danville and Wilson in

[30] *Ibid.,* Feb. 12, April 1, 8, 1944; Newport News *Daily Press,* April 5, 1944, in Jackson Papers.

[31] *Afro-American,* June 30, 1945; *Journal and Guide,* Nov. 10, 1945.

[32] *Journal and Guide,* Feb. 16, 23, July 13, 1946; *Afro-American,* July 6, 1946.

Lynchburg polled 956 votes between them, almost one-fourth of the 4,187 votes cast in the two cities.[33] In Charlottesville, Dr. Coles ran third to white candidates Mayor Roscoe S. Adams and Gus K. Tebell, polling 448 votes to their 1,838 and 1,751 respectively.[34] Coles, the first Negro candidate "in recent times" to run in a primary or general election in Charlottesville, declared he was not dismayed with the results. In 1946 the city had 317 registered Negroes, and the fact that he received over 100 white votes and that he "had some very prominent whites sponsor him" was encouraging.[35] Professor Luther P. Jackson commented that the favorable showing by Coles was owing to the Negro turnout for their candidate. Whereas in 1941 only 126 Negroes had paid their poll tax, in 1946 the number rose to 570. Two hundred of the latter paid almost at the deadline, after hearing that a colored candidate was running for office. Two days before the election "the leaders of this town swamped the churches on a Sunday in a plea for a big increase in the number of qualified voters—an increase sufficient to land Dr. Coles in office." When churches opened their doors and ministers advocated participation in political affairs, citizens would soon become interested. And even in defeat, when Negroes sought office, some Negroes would "become concerned, and a number will qualify and [hope to] put a member of their race in office." [36]

In the same election Norfolk attorney Victor Ashe made the strongest race by a Negro for city council. Well-known in the community, a World War II veteran, chairman of the Colored Democrats in the Second Congressional District, and legal adviser to the Norfolk N.A.A.C.P.,[37] Ashe offered a platform similar to those previously mentioned. Unlike most Negro candidates before him, the Norfolk attorney campaigned actively through press, radio,

[33] *Afro-American,* July 6, 1946. The figures do not appear as impressive when compared with the total number of eligible Negroes in Danville and Lynchburg, 1076 and 1080 respectively.

[34] Charlottesville *Daily Progress,* March 26, April 3, 1946; *Journal and Guide,* April 20, 1946.

[35] Personal interview with Dr. B. A. Coles, Aug. 25, 1964.

[36] *Journal and Guide,* Feb. 2, 1946.

[37] Fleming and Burckel, eds., *Who's Who in Colored America,* 15.

and personal appearances. Full-page political advertisements appeared in the *Journal and Guide;* a typical one depicted Ashe inspecting city slum areas and included his pledge to work for reform and slum clearance.[38]

The 3,101 votes polled by Ashe appeared slight when compared with the totals of those elected: Richard D. Cooke, 7,334; Pretlow Darden, 7,971; and John Twohy II, 7,383. Considering, however, that his total was about two-thirds of the 4,235 Negroes registered to vote in Norfolk, the figure appears impressive.[39] Negroes had taken an active part in a Virginia election. There was also an indication, as in the candidacy of Dr. Coles, that a number of whites voted for Ashe. The following anonymously written letter to the candidate bears this out:

First off I am a white man and you must secure some of the white vote if you hope to be elected to the City Council. . . . There are not enough qualified colored voters to elect you or nay [*sic*] other colored person to any public office in Norfolk.

Now I know that considerable number of white people are going to vote for you, but not enough to elect you, unless you can win more of their votes. You can do this if you will go on the air and make radio addresses, and vigorously attack the present City Council. You are an intelligent man and a fine public speaker. If you will go on the air twice a week from now until June 11th you can win 2,000 or more white votes. You can win if you get 1,500 votes, but not with less. . . .

Best of luck
A White Friend [40]

Despite backing by some whites, rarely did Negroes get open campaign support. The fear of being labeled "friend of the Negro" still lingered in Virginia.[41]

The race by the four candidates in 1946 was followed by a closer contest in 1947 in which attorney Oliver W. Hill of Richmond came within 191 votes of being nominated in the Demo-

[38] *Journal and Guide,* June 8, 1946.
[39] *Ibid.,* June 15, 1946; *Estimated Number of Voters, April, 1946.*
[40] Undated letter, 1946 Councilmanic campaign, in Victor Ashe Scrapbook, Norfolk, Va.
[41] Personal interviews with Dr. B. A. Coles, Aug. 25, 1964, Charlottesville, Va., and Victor Ashe, Sept. 2, 1964, Norfolk, Va.

cratic primary to the General Assembly. The candidacy of Hill had aroused interest in the Negro community, and a concerted effort was made by various civic and political organizations in his behalf. Late in 1946 the Richmond Civic Council, which consisted of over eighty Negro church, civic, fraternal, labor, business, and educational groups, fostered a drive to get out the vote.[42]

Hill, a veteran of World War II, known and respected by members of both races, hoped to win support by campaigning on a biracial platform. He appealed for hour and wage legislation, tenure and minimum annual salaries of $2,400 for teachers, a revision of the child labor act, increased appropriations for hospitals, and a public health program, as well as the establishment of a state department for race relations and the abolition of the poll tax as a voting prerequisite. The candidate received the support of the United Labor Political Action Committee, the political arm of the C.I.O., the A.F.L., and the railroad brotherhoods. The organization reportedly had 2,500 votes, most of them white, at its disposal. In return for its support, it was assumed that Negroes would back W. H. C. Murray, the labor candidate.[43]

The registration drive was an intensive one. On May 1, the final day for poll tax payment, tax officials in Richmond and in Henrico and Chesterfield counties granted Dr. Tinsley a two-day extension so that as many Negroes as possible might be added to the rolls. Despite the concerted drive the N.A.A.C.P. goal of 10,000 voters fell short by about 4,000.[44] Nevertheless, the result was a marked improvement over previous years.

On election day 150 Negro volunteers on foot and in a score of automobiles canvassed the city for Hill votes, and at day's end the tally showed the Negro candidate had polled 6,313 votes, to place eighth in a field of seventeen for seven Assembly seats.

[42] *Afro-American,* Dec. 28, 1946. In Richmond, though 40,000 Negroes were of voting age, the State Board of Elections claimed only 8,122 were registered. *Estimated Number of Voters, April, 1947.*

[43] *Journal and Guide,* March 15, July 25, 1947; Moon, *Balance of Power,* 159.

[44] *Times-Dispatch,* May 1, 2, 1947; *Journal and Guide,* June 21, 1947. The Norfolk weekly estimated that 5,000 Negroes registered, while Moon's figure was 6,230. Moon, *Balance of Power,* 159.

Seventh position was won by W. H. C. Murray with a 6,500 total.[45] According to discontented Negroes, Murray had been elected because the colored vote had backed him; but white labor union members had not reciprocated and backed candidate Hill.[46] This group of malcontents was in the minority, though, and estimates soon appeared indicating that between 700 and 1,500 whites had cast ballots for Hill. Both Hill and Dr. Tinsley denied as false the charge that the Murray forces had abandoned the Negro candidate. The N.A.A.C.P. advocated a continuation of the alliance with labor, calling it unwise and foolish "to discontinue our friendly relations with labor at this time because we need the support of white as well as colored people if we hope to win in the next election." [47]

One of the seven successful candidates, Charles H. Phillips, in protest of what he termed "single shot" electioneering by the Negroes, charged that the latter had resorted to bloc voting, casting their ballots for Hill and leaving the remainder of the ballot unmarked. Rumor had it that he threatened to introduce a bill in the legislature prohibiting such a practice.[48] The Richmond *Times-Dispatch,* less alarmed about single shotting and the possibility of victory by future Negro candidates, commented:

We do have a democratic tradition which holds that American citizens are entitled to vote and to hold office. It is natural, thus, that our Negro citizens should exercise that right. Furthermore, it seems inevitable that as they rise higher in the educational and cultural scale, they will succeed in doing so. . . . So we may as well accustom ourselves to the thought that the Negro citizens of the Old Dominion may send one of their number to the General Assembly before many years are past.[49]

Another Negro candidate who had run for city council in 1946,

45 Moon, *Balance of Power,* 159; *Times-Dispatch,* Aug. 7, 1947.
46 *Afro-American,* Aug. 9, 1947.
47 *Crisis,* LIV (Sept. 1947), 265; *Afro-American,* Aug. 9, 16, 1947; personal interviews with Dr. J. M. Tinsley, Aug. 27, 1964, Richmond, and Oliver W. Hill, Sept. 23, 1965, Washington, D.C.
48 *Times-Dispatch,* Aug. 17, 1947. Apparently, nothing came of the threat since no follow-up was uncovered.
49 *Ibid.,* Aug. 7, 1947; *Crisis,* LIV (Sept. 1947), 265.

Victor Ashe of Norfolk, tried again in 1947, this time for a seat in the House of Delegates. In the primary election on August 5 he placed far behind the winners, polling only 2,733 votes as compared to the 4,858 of the lowest successful candidate. Ashe's total, 300 less than he had polled in 1946, was only about half the 5,412 registered Negro voters in the city.[50]

Thus far when Negroes ran for office regardless of their chances for election there had been little intimidation. Much of the credit for the minimal amount of rabble-rousing and Negro-baiting, according to Key, belonged to the state "organization" headed by Senator Byrd, which frowned upon such tactics. Only rarely was a Negro candidate or voter intimidated as in the Nansemond County Board of Supervisors election of November 1947. One of the candidates, Negro school teacher William A. Lawrence, reportedly had the backing of G. C. Mann, the white principal of the local high school in Cypress Chapel. Local citizens, however, allegedly opposed backing a Negro. On the night of September 15, a Ku Klux Klan type of cross was burned on the lawn of Mann's residence. Across the street was the home of the registrar for the Cypress District, Emmett Rogers, and Negroes attempting to register, therefore, had to pass the spot where the cross was burned. The night of the burning the Independent Voters' League had assisted in registering thirty-seven Negroes. Despite this singular incident, Lawrence defeated his white opponent, F. E. Harrell, by the close vote of 292 to 290.[51]

With virtually no intimidation of the Negro and with hostility by white registrars all but eliminated, by 1948 the only obstacles to the growth of a Negro electorate sufficiently large to put a Negro in public office were the payment of the yearly poll tax and the filing of a voter application form. According to statistics of the Virginia Voters' League, 62,457 Negroes met the three-year poll tax requirement in 1948, an increase of 17,396 since 1945. The State Board of Elections estimated that the number of Negro

[50] *Journal and Guide*, June 21, Aug. 9, 1947; *Estimated Number of Voters, April, 1947.*

[51] *Journal and Guide*, Sept. 27, Nov. 29, 1947. Because of disputed ballots on the first tally, the victory came on a recount.

registrants over the three-year period had climbed from 38,020
to 53,035.[52] Increases in the number of Negro voters in the major
cities were especially noteworthy,[53] as the following table shows:

City	1945	1948
Charlottesville	385	645
Clifton Forge	120	205
Danville	764	1,469
Fredericksburg	170	225
Newport News	1,468	2,062
Norfolk	3,964	6,118
Petersburg	497	978
Richmond	6,374	11,127
Roanoke	1,146	1,768
Suffolk	117	428

As indicated, registration was particularly high in Richmond,
almost doubling to reach 11,127. A major reason for the gain was
the candidacy of Oliver W. Hill for city council. Hill ran as an
independent because the interracial Richmond Citizens' Association, feeling the time "was not ripe" for a Negro candidate,
declined to back him.[54] A second Negro, Samuel Kelley, general
chairman of the Committee for Justice in Virginia, was also listed
as one of the twenty-nine contestants for nine councilmanic seats.
According to the *Afro-American,* unsuccessful attempts had been
made to convince one or the other of the candidates to withdraw,
since two Negroes in the race reduced the possibilities of victory.
Hill, who conducted a singlehanded campaign in white as well as
Negro areas, polled 9,097 ballots of the 28,143 total on election
day, enough to win ninth place and a seat in the city council. He
was the first Negro to be elected to this body since Henry J. Moore
won in 1898.[55] The *Afro-American* attested to the willingness of
some whites to vote for a Negro candidate, estimating that approximately 3,000 had cast their ballots for Hill.[56]

[52] *Ninth Annual Report, Voting Status, 1948–1949,* 4; *ibid.,* 1946, 4;
Estimated Number of Voters, 1945, 1948.
[53] *Estimated Number of Voters, 1948.*
[54] Personal interview with Oliver W. Hill, Sept. 23, 1965, Washington,
D.C.
[55] *Afro-American,* April 24, June 12, 1948. Kelley received only 618
votes.   [56] *Ibid.,* June 12, 19, 1948.

Hill's victory, however, proved to be the only one for Negroes that year. Defeated candidates included Raymond L. Valentine, who aspired to the city council of Petersburg,[57] and Mrs. Nancy Thomas Wheeler and William W. Miles of Portsmouth, also contestants for city council.[58] In Danville, Charles K. Coleman, who had run unsuccessfully for city council in 1946, fared no better two years later; Isaac Johnson and Dr. Thomas W. Turner also failed in Hampton.[59]

The only other major candidate for city council, Victor Ashe in Norfolk, initially was disqualified because of a technicality. According to the provisions of the War Voters Act of 1945, a candidate had to register his candidacy prior to April 13, 1948. Ashe missed the deadline. He declared he thought the wartime act had become inoperative and said he had intended to register at a later date set by the city charter. Ashe appealed his case to the Court of Law and Chancery, which decided against him.[60] Attorney General J. Lindsay Almond upheld the court's decision, ruling that the wartime act took precedence over the city charter until July 1948. The Attorney General did allow, however, that the Negro might enter the race if voters used rubber stamps bearing Ashe's name. Though defeated, by using more than a hundred such stamps Ashe polled 2,707 out of a total of 10,477 votes.[61]

In 1948 Virginia Negroes turned their attention to the presidential campaign also. In national elections since 1936, their vote had been almost wholly for the Democratic ticket. Now, for the first time since 1932, the Negro vote wavered, turning in large numbers toward a Republican candidate. Despite the stand taken by President Harry S. Truman in favor of a vigorous civil rights

[57] *Journal and Guide*, April 17, 1948; Luther P. Jackson commented that Valentine, who received 980 votes and placed fifth in a seven-man race for three seats, lost because his candidacy was regarded as a threat to white supremacy and therefore whites rounded up their voters.

[58] *Ibid.*, Feb. 14, April 3, Aug. 10, 1948. Mrs. Wheeler lost in a close race to incumbent C. Robie Sturdivant by a 162 to 150 vote. The *Journal and Guide* charged that the loss was due to the gerrymandering of Jackson Ward, which, prior to January 1947, had more Negro votes than white.

[59] *Ibid.*, Feb. 14, March 13, 1948.

[60] *Ibid.*, April 24, May 8, 1948.

[61] *Ibid.*, June 5, 1948.

program and an even stronger civil rights plank adopted by the Democratic National Convention in Philadelphia on July 14, some Negroes looked skeptically at the Democrat from Missouri.[62] To them the issue appeared to be the sincerity of Truman as a civil rights leader.

Both Negro weeklies in Virginia conceded that he had come a long way as President and was obviously sincere in his program for civil rights, but they nevertheless denied that he believed in social equality. According to one Negro reporter, in 1944 Truman had agreed that all citizens were entitled to equality of opportunity, but not to social equality. There would never be social equality.

If colored people sit down and eat at a counter in a downtown drugstore in Independence, Missouri, they will be booted out because the management of these places has a right to refuse to serve anyone it pleases.[63]

Truman was further accused of having voted to retain the poll tax as a Senator in 1942 and now was expediently using a "cheap political trick" for its removal. "When and if it becomes expedient, Mr. Truman could conceivably just as ruthlessly trade away the interests of the Negro for the support of some other group which he felt more important." [64]

It was claimed that Truman did not personally favor the more militant civil rights platform of the National Convention. In the more than two hundred speeches delivered after his nomination, he made little mention of the civil rights plank. Perhaps, the papers speculated, the break from the party by Southern Democrats into a "Dixiecrat" party and the subsequent nomination of J. Strom Thurmond of South Carolina for president caused Truman to think twice before pushing the issue and further alienating Democrats. Whatever his motives, Truman's silence seemed to be a concession to the white South.[65] Finally, Negroes were anxious

[62] Key, *Southern Politics,* 330–34.
[63] Morris Milgram, interview with Truman, Oct. 1944, in *Afro-American,* Oct. 9, 1948.
[64] *Journal and Guide,* Oct. 30, 1948.
[65] For comprehensive coverage of the Dixiecrat movement, see Emile B. Ader, *The Dixiecrat Movement* (Washington, D.C., 1955), *passim;* Key, *Southern Politics,* 329–44.

over the Democratic vice-presidential candidate, Southerner Alben W. Barkley of Kentucky. Should Truman be reelected and die in office, "Can *AFRO* readers imagine what would happen to minority groups if the Senator from Kentucky should thus become President?" [66]

In contrast, the Negro press accorded accolades to Thomas E. Dewey, the Republican candidate from New York. According to the Richmond press, as early as 1937 Dewey had declared, "There is no room for race prejudice in this city [New York]." In 1939, as a gubernatorial candidate, he asserted, "I would rather go down in defeat than be elected by votes based on race or religion." A few years later, at the 1944 Republican National Convention in St. Louis, Dewey informed an *Afro* reporter, "You don't cure people of their prejudices by knocking them on the head and saying—'You have got to like Catholics, Jews, or colored people;' you have got to live with them and convince them there are no differences." [67] Dewey's record as governor of New York convinced many Negroes he was the best choice in 1948. He had advocated and signed into law a state F.E.P.C., had worked to stamp out discrimination in public housing and labor unions, and had put through a state law preventing insurance companies from charging Negroes higher rates than whites. More Negroes had received appointments during Dewey's governorship than during that of any other New York chief executive, including Franklin D. Roosevelt. [68]

But the sentiment of the Negro press was by no means that of all colored people in the Old Dominion. Groups such as the Virginia Organization for the Re-election of Truman were formed, and many prominent Negro political figures actively campaigned for him. Cochairman Dr. Harry T. Penn of Roanoke and educator Dr. Thomas H. Henderson of Richmond planned to raise $35,000 for the Democratic campaign. As its slogan the group adopted "A Dime a Human for the Re-election of Truman." [69] Others

[66] *Afro-American,* Oct. 9, 1948; *Journal and Guide,* Oct. 16, 1948.
[67] *Afro-American,* Oct. 16, 1948; Moon, *Balance of Power,* 208–9.
[68] *Journal and Guide,* Oct. 30, 1948; Heard, *Two Party South,* 232.
[69] *Afro-American,* Oct. 30, 1948.

who came out for Truman included Roscoe C. Jackson, president
of the Richmond Democratic Voters' League, Dr. J. M. Tinsley,
W. Lester Banks, and attorney Spottswood W. Robinson III, all
of the Virginia N.A.A.C.P.[70]

An even wider cleavage in the Negro voting pattern developed
as other Negroes supported former Democratic Vice President and
cabinet member, Henry A. Wallace. As a third-party candidate
on the Progressive ticket, Wallace, noted for his "championship
of the underdog, his demand for an end to racial discrimination,
and his defiance of the South's segregation pattern," threatened
to drain votes away from Truman.[71] In an attempt to counter such
a threat, the Virginia Citizens Committee for Truman and Human
Rights argued that though Negroes recognized Wallace's efforts
as commendable, the campaign should be approached realistically.
Raymond P. Alexander, Philadelphia attorney, speaking on September 12 to a Negro audience at Richmond's Beneficial Hall,
insisted that "Wallace, however sincere he may be, cannot hope
to win and admits it. Therefore a vote for Wallace is a vote
against Truman and a large number of such votes will defeat
Truman and his entire civil rights program." [72]

Amid the divided political loyalties of Virginia Negroes, this
statement made by Executive Secretary of the N.A.A.C.P. Walter
White, seemed applicable in the 1948 presidential campaign: "No
person and organization can deliver the Negro vote; it is an im-
ponderable and independent vote, and the Negro increasingly demands results for his support." [73] The support given in the past to
Franklin D. Roosevelt and the Democrats was in danger as the
Negro closely scrutinized the qualifications of the individual candidates.

With the presidential choices before them and with a sizable

[70] New York *Herald-Tribune,* Sept. 16, 1948, cited in *Times-Dispatch,*
Oct. 16, 1948.

[71] Moon, *Balance of Power,* 204–5. Incidentally, Negro Jerry O. Gilliam
also ran as a Progressive for a House seat in the Second Congressional
District.

[72] *Times-Dispatch,* Sept. 13, 1948.

[73] Moon, *Balance of Power,* 213–14; Heard, *Two Party South,* 227–35
passim; Afro-American, Sept. 18, 1948.

minority in this independent mood, the *Afro-American* estimated that between 30,000 and 40,000 Negroes in the Old Dominion went to the polls. In all likelihood, the majority remained within the Democratic camp, unwilling to forget the benefits "that accrued to the race under the New Deal." [74] Truman carried the state with 200,786 votes to 172,070 for Dewey, 43,393 for Thurmond, and 1,863 for Wallace. If a majority of the 53,035 registered Negroes voted and if, as claimed by the *Journal and Guide*, 75 per cent of that number voted for Truman, then the Democratic victory was attributable at least in part to the Negro vote.[75] In Norfolk, where an estimated 6,118 Negroes were registered, Truman won 9,370 to 7,556. According to the *Afro-American*, over 8,500 colored voters in Richmond pushed Truman past his Republican opponent by a count of 16,446 to 14,549.[76]

Negroes may have remained loyal to the Democratic party on the national level, but a respected Negro weekly maintained that they did not back Byrd-machine candidates. Incumbent Senator A. Willis Robertson easily defeated Republican Robert Woods 253,865 to 119,366, but the Negro vote favored Woods. In the Second District congressional race Negroes cast their lot with Republican Walter H. Hoffman, because they remembered that his Democratic opponent, Representative Porter Hardy, Jr., had opposed Truman's civil rights program. In the same contest the Progressive candidate, Negro Jerry O. Gilliam, pulled only 1,912 votes and ran a distant third. He failed to carry any of Norfolk's 32 precincts.[77]

The next two years proved disappointing politically for Virginia Negroes. Admittedly a number of candidates appeared, doubtless spurred on by Oliver Hill's election to the Richmond council in 1948, but none were elected. In 1949 the four Negro candidates

[74] *Afro-American*, Oct. 30, 1948; *Estimated Number of Voters, April, 1948.*

[75] *Statement of the Vote for President, November 2, 1948; Journal and Guide*, Nov. 13, 1948.

[76] *Estimated Number of Voters, April, 1948; Statement of Vote, 1948; Afro-American*, Dec. 4, 1948.

[77] *Statement of Vote, 1948; Journal and Guide*, Nov. 6, 1948; *Afro-American*, Nov. 13, 1948.

for the House of Delegates in the August primary could poll a combined total of but 13,117 votes. William L. Ransome, Baptist pastor and president of the Richmond Civic Council, made the best showing with 8,355 votes, but it proved good enough only for twelfth position in a 17-man race for seven seats. His total did not approach the 13,187 garnered by the seventh-place winner.[78] In Norfolk, with an estimated 6,390 Negro voters, "very little enthusiasm" was displayed, and attorney Arnett Bibbins polled only 2,777 ballots in the House of Delegates primary. In the neighboring city of Portsmouth, Dr. Harvey N. Johnson, pastor of the Ebenezer Baptist Church, ran last with 1,369 votes in a 5-man race. The victors, Winston Bain and W. H. W. Caswell, polled 2,700 and 2,090 votes respectively.[79] The *Afro-American* commented in dismay that approximately 1,000 registered Negroes had not bothered to vote in the contest. Finally, in the York County Assembly race, Negro Charles S. Franklin with 616 votes, ran well behind white incumbent Paul Crockett and Mrs. Catherine C. Blow at 1,980 and 1,021 respectively. But, unlike other Negro candidates, Franklin apparently received a sizable white vote, since the State Board of Elections recorded only 325 colored votes in the county in 1949.[80] The only victories in 1949 were to the minor office of justice of the peace won in Petersburg by an undertaker, James A. Jackson, and an electrical contractor, Harold Stewart.[81]

Though President of the Virginia Voters' League Luther P. Jackson appeared optimistic about the 66,409 Negroes who had met the three-year poll tax requirement in 1949 and were eligible for registration,[82] apparently white candidates for governor paid the figure little mind. According to the Negro weekly in Richmond, a questionnaire submitted to gubernatorial candidates asking their views on matters of concern to Negroes was virtually

[78] *Times-Dispatch*, Aug. 3, 4, 1949; *Journal and Guide*, Aug. 6, 1949.

[79] *Estimated Number of Voters, April, 1949; Virginian-Pilot*, Aug. 3, 4, 1949; *Journal and Guide* and *Afro-American*, Aug. 13, 1949.

[80] *Journal and Guide*, Aug. 13, 1949; *Estimated Number of Voters, April, 1949*.

[81] *Ninth Annual Report, Voting Status, 1948–1949*, 6.

[82] *Ibid.*, 4.

ignored by the aspirants. Only State Senator John S. Battle submitted a formal reply, but he too avoided answering specific questions.[83] Obviously, Jackson's tabulations had little effect on white candidates in Virginia, who as yet did not consider the Negro vote much of a factor in determining the outcome of elections.

Nevertheless, the decade of the 1940's was more fruitful politically than any other since 1900. Gains made, primarily during the post-World War II years, in poll tax payment and voter registration as well as candidacies for office, were hopeful signs for the future. Though only Oliver Hill was successful in his race for city council in Richmond, his victory provided incentive for others. Whether Negroes would take advantage of the victory remained to be seen.

[83] *Afro-American,* July 23, 1949.

X

Prelude to Massive Resistance

DURING the 1950's the primary role of Negroes in Virginia politics was not one of participation, despite the fact that their voter registration total rose from 69,266 to 100,424 by 1960 or that they ran regularly for elective office and also served on city Democratic and Republican committees. Rather, as a result of the school desegregation issue initiated by the *Brown* v. *Board of Education* decision in 1954, the Negro became the political issue of the day. Race relations suffered, the race bogey again haunted the Commonwealth, and the Democratic party, led by Senator Harry Flood Byrd, fought its campaign against school integration at the polls and through General Assembly legislation. The organization, which had shown signs of weakening since the late 1940's, found in "massive resistance" not only an opportunity to "protect" the Commonwealth's white school children but also a chance to refurbish its faltering machine. Two instances spelled out in the next chapter (the January 9, 1956, referendum and the 1957 gubernatorial election) illustrate how the Virginia Democracy utilized the racial crisis to its advantage and won decisively.

Virginia Negro weeklies reveal that during these years Negro citizens ran for political office regularly. In Richmond, Norfolk, Portsmouth, Roanoke, Newport News, and counties such as Nansemond and Charles City where the Negro vote was high, there were candidates for city council, justice of the peace, county supervisor, the House of Delegates, and the state senate. The majority were professional men of high standing in predominantly

Negro communities: doctors, dentists, lawyers, journalists, under-takers, and clergymen. However, with the exception of gaining an occasional position as justice of the peace, county supervisor, or member of a Democratic or Republican city committee, the office seekers were unsuccessful.

Perhaps the victory by Oliver W. Hill in 1948 and his narrow defeat for reelection in 1950 spurred Negro candidates on during the next few years. Hill had the backing of the Richmond Civic Council, which also sponsored six other biracial candidates. The single-shot method of voting, employed by Negroes so often in the past, was no longer considered necessary since the primary objective of electing one candidate had been accomplished with Hill's victory two years before. "For the first time in this century" Negroes apparently believed they could back a biracial ticket con-sisting of candidates whose records were not inimical to their interests.[1] Twenty-three candidates vied for eight seats in the Richmond city council, and by the narrow margin of 46 votes Hill was edged out of eighth position by Robert A. Wilson, 12,534 votes to 12,488.[2] Though the defeat was disappointing, there was the encouraging sign that approximately 6,000 whites had cast their ballots for Hill. One source, however, could not help express-ing its dismay at the poor showing by Negroes, who should have cast at least 12,000 votes.[3]

Though evidently disappointed in the following year because Hill was not appointed to replace a resigned member of the Rich-mond city council, and because Richmond attorney Roland Ealey lost in the August 1951 Democratic primary for the House of Delegates,[4] Negroes looked hopefully to 1952. In that year, of the seven candidates for city council, C. Thomas Younge of Ports-mouth and Thomas W. Young of Norfolk conducted the most aggressive campaigns. The Portsmouth candidate, proprietor of

[1] *Afro-American,* June 3, 1950.
[2] *Times-Dispatch,* June 15, 16, 1950.
[3] *Afro-American,* June 17, 1950.
[4] *Journal and Guide,* March 3, May 5, Aug. 11, 1951. Ealey ran eighth in a race for seven seats, far behind the last winner, 8,141 to 5,938.

a barber shop (a Negro establishment where politicking was generally rabid), hoped to win in heavily Negro-populated Harrison Ward. Negro registration was about 500 votes, approximately 200 more than the white. According to the Younge forces, his defeat by Charles L. Grimes by the narrow margin of 336 to 329 was pure skulduggery. In at least eight instances servicemen who were exempt from paying the poll tax were prohibited from voting. However, an appeal to the hustings court on these grounds was dismissed.[5]

Showing the most promise of victory was the independent candidate Thomas W. Young. A graduate of Hampton Institute, with degrees in journalism and law from Ohio State University, a member of the Norfolk bar since 1933, and president and general manager of the *Journal and Guide* since 1933, Young campaigned actively from mid-January until election day on June 10. Not only did he keep himself before the Negro reading public, but Young personally campaigned before civic and church groups and made active use of radio and television, the latter an expensive medium hitherto seldom used by Negro candidates. Decrying any single-shot Negro voting, and realizing he could not win without part of the white vote, Young campaigned on a platform beneficial to both races. He advocated continuation of slum clearance, a redevelopment program, improvement of transportation facilities, extension of street lighting, representation for all segments of the population on boards and commissions, continuation of public schooling, an early solution to parking problems, strengthening of the city manager government, and sensible economy in government.[6] Despite his vigorous campaigning and the polling of a record 5,436 votes for a Negro candidate, Young ran behind a four-man slate which swept the field, with its low man, Robert F. Ripley, amassing 9,075 votes. Of Young's total, the *Journal and Guide* estimated that approximately 2,500 were white votes.[7]

Not unusual was the insinuation that the race issue had been

[5] *Ibid.,* April 5, May 10, 1952.
[6] *Ibid.,* May 10, 1952; *Virginian-Pilot,* June 11, 1952.
[7] June 14, 1952.

injected into the campaign. According to the Norfolk weekly, after Young had appeared on television on election eve, attorney Walter Hoffman, a Republican, backing the four-man administration, also via television implied that a Negro in council would handicap the city in its relation with the armed forces. Hoffman added that "the four-man ticket was 'free of any ties to any particular group or RACE.' " While the *Journal and Guide* doubted this statement cost Young any white votes already pledged to him, it doubtless increased the administration's votes among the undecided.[8] Whether or not this allegation was true, Negroes believed it constituted a real handicap to members of their race in running for office.

In two other contests it was a case of "just a few more votes." In Portsmouth, Mrs. Nancy Wheeler, who had lost in 1948 by only twelve votes, was defeated again by incumbent E. Robie Sturdivant, 180 to 151. Attorney W. Hale Thompson of Newport News placed fourth in a field of seven for three seats, behind incumbent I. Leake Wornam, 1,856 to 1,438.[9] During the remainder of the decade, close elections and victories on the lowest local levels were not unusual,[10] but no candidates gained the higher positions of councilman or assemblyman.

Aside from the payment of the poll tax and the general apathy which continued among Negroes, a third deterrent to success by colored candidates was that they campaigned as individuals, without the benefit of party affiliation or backing, even when they ran in Democratic primaries. Only once since post-World War II had a Negro received white organizational support, when Oliver Hill made his unsuccessful attempt for reelection to the Richmond City

[8] June 14, 1952. According to Negro candidates Oliver Hill, Victor Ashe, B. A. Cephas, Jr., John H. Owens, and Dr. William Ferguson Reid, "whisper campaigns" against Negroes, especially over the telephone, are not uncommon. All candidates, however, agreed that this was the work of "lower class" whites.

[9] *Journal and Guide,* April 5, 1952.

[10] Typical of a county position won in a predominantly Negro section was the Board of Supervisor's office won by Samuel W. Crump in St. Peter's Magisterial District, New Kent County, where 59 per cent of the population was Negro. *Afro-American,* Nov. 19, 1955.

Council in 1950.[11] Thus, without white support, many Negro candidates campaigned mainly in colored districts, hoping to gain enough Negro votes to win by the single-shot method.

The single shot was evident in the June 1956 Portsmouth councilmanic election. With thirteen candidates vying for seven seats, Dr. Hugo A. Owens finished eighth behind John E. Scott, 2,453 to 2,391, even though "98% of the colored vote" (which according to the State Board of Elections was 3,444) supported Owens.[12] Another example occurred in the Democratic primary for the House of Delegates from Richmond in July 1957. Campaigning as an independent Democrat, attorney Colston A. Lewis opposed the recent public school segregation legislation passed by the General Assembly, advocated federal aid to education, an interracial commission, and abolition of the poll tax. About a week before the election, "over 100 Richmond leaders," at a meeting sponsored by the *Afro-American,* urged a "single shot" vote for Lewis as the best means to utilize the Negroes' 13,000 votes.[13] Remembering Oliver W. Hill's defeat in 1950 when Negroes had voted for an entire biracial slate, some contended that voting for other candidates would only hinder Lewis. Apparently aware of the Negro sentiment concerning the defeat, the *News Leader* had predicted, "Last Tuesday's lesson will not be lost upon the Negro voters in this region. Unless we miss our guess, they will return at the next election to utilize the 'solid shot' again as they have the legal right to do." [14] Also, because the school segregation issue loomed so large and racial bitterness was so intense during the 1954–60 period, much of the white vote was considered lost anyway; thus, Negroes believed themselves forced to resort to the single shot.

[11] Personal interview with Hill, Sept. 23, 1965, Washington, D.C.

[12] *Journal and Guide,* June 16, 1956; *Estimated Number of Voters, April, 1956.*

[13] *Afro-American,* June 29, 1957.

[14] *News Leader* editorial, June 17, 1950, cited in *Journal and Guide,* March 5, 1957. Hill flatly opposed "single shotting" and insisted he always appealed for the white vote because elections could not be won without it. Personal interview, Sept. 23, 1965.

Employing those tactics on election day, Lewis received 6,239 votes, running eighth in a field of fourteen candidates for seven positions, missing victory by 932 votes. The failure of the Negroes to get out the vote certainly cost him the election, but whites concerned over Negro single shotting also refused to vote for Lewis. Negro voter registration of approximately 13,000 was no match for the white's 53,000.[15]

Led by the *Journal and Guide,* opponents of single shotting contended that not only were feelings between the races worsened by voting only for Negro candidates, but the friendship of whites previously sympathetic toward colored citizens was lost. On the other hand, voting an entire slate might elect white candidates sympathetic to Negroes. Looking ahead briefly to the 1960 councilmanic race in Norfolk, Victor Ashe, chairman of the Norfolk Citizens' Committee, believed it made common sense to vote for whites Sam T. Barfield and William L. Shepheard as well as Negro Joseph A. Jordan, Jr. All three opposed the school segregationist attitudes of the incumbents Lawrence C. Page, Lewis L. Layton, and Paul Schweitzer. Though Jordan lost in his bid, by not single shotting Negroes helped elect Barfield and defeat segregationist Lawrence C. Page. It was estimated that single shotting would have cost Barfield 4,200 votes, lowering his total to less than 6,000 rather than the 10,032 votes he received in victory.[16]

Negro candidates met with some success in election to Democratic and Republican city committees from predominantly Negro precincts, mainly in the larger Tidewater cities. It was not untypical either, especially in the Norfolk–Newport News and Arlington and Roanoke areas, for them to attend statewide party conventions as delegates and alternates.[17] But in no instance did they shape party policy. Individual membership did not neces-

---

[15] *Afro-American,* Nov. 9, 1957.
[16] *Journal and Guide,* June 11, 18, 1960.
[17] Personal interviews with Victor Ashe, Oliver W. Hill, David E. Longley. Prominent Negroes on Democratic city committees included Ashe, Hill, and Dr. Harry T. Penn of Roanoke. Longley, for many years considered by fellow Negroes as "Mr. Republican," was the first of his race to be selected to serve on the Richmond city committee in the twentieth century.

sarily entail political power and almost without exception they could be outvoted by white delegates.

Two instances should illustrate the inability of Negroes to shape policy within party ranks even at the grass roots level. In the first, insurance executive David E. Longley, spokesman for the eight Negro committeemen in the hundred-man Richmond Republican organization, in 1951 requested that Negro attorney Herman T. Benn be nominated for city council. The request was denied on the basis that owing to the school desegregation issue, Benn's nomination would create an unfavorable impression with the remainder of the white G.O.P. As a result, Longley believed he had no recourse but to resign from the committee. Thereafter he declared himself an independent voter.[18] In the second instance, Oliver W. Hill, member of the Richmond Democratic committee in 1957 and 1959, maintained that in order to exclude Negroes, election rules were revised in 1961 and committeemen were no longer elected by precinct but by convention. The reason for the change, according to Hill, was because Negro voters refused to back state and local Democratic candidates.[19]

Not until 1964 when Clarence L. Townes, Jr., of Richmond was made special assistant to the chairman of the Republican party in Virginia, was a Negro appointed by either party to a position of statewide prominence. Analyzing this situation, one observer commented:

In states of the Upper South, Negroes can be conceded political *participation* without a commensurate concession of political *power*. Participation without power makes for hat-in-hand politics. Negroes are to be found in both Virginia parties, and in both factions of the dominant party, but in no party or faction do they have any real power as *Negroes*. . . . It would appear that any improvements of Negro schools, hiring of more Negro public employees, or other gains within the caste system emanate more from whatever sense of paternalistic responsibility there is present than from recognition of Negro rights or political bargaining power.

In a very real sense the Negro is an object of southern politics

[18] Personal interview, Sept. 16, 1965, Richmond.
[19] Personal interview, Sept. 23, 1965, Washington, D.C.

rather than a participant therein, and Virginia is no exception to the rule.[20]

Turning momentarily to national politics, Negroes hoped Truman would seek another term as they once again made civil rights their major issue in the 1952 presidential campaign. No doubt they were in accord with the President's statement to the Howard University graduating class that Negroes had made marked gains in their search for equality. More than 1,000 members of the race had been admitted to graduate and professional schools in ten hitherto-closed state universities. Integration in the armed services, especially in the Korean conflict, was nearly complete. Job opportunity had broadened since 1948 as a result of a Fair Employment Board in the Civil Service Commission. Voting in the South had increased with the abolition of the poll tax in Tennessee and South Carolina and hopefully it would soon be abolished in the five remaining poll tax states. Disappointed that Truman chose not to run for reelection, Negroes leaned toward the Democratic candidate Adlai Stevenson. Walter White of the N.A.A.C.P. explained that he favored the Democrats because they pledged not only to continue their efforts "to eradicate discrimination based on race, religion, or national origin" but also to continue to "favor federal legislation . . . to secure these rights to everyone." The Republicans also acknowledged the need for "supplemental action within its constitutional jurisdiction to oppose discrimination on the grounds of race, religion, or national origin." Nevertheless, disappointed Negro delegates at the G.O.P. convention in Chicago objected to the "watered down" comment that it remained "the primary responsibility of each state to order and control its own domestic institutions, and this power, reserved to the states, is essential to the maintenance of our federal republic." [21]

Some Negro Republican spokesmen, among them the cochair-

[20] Robbins L. Gates, *The Making of Massive Resistance: Virginia's Politics of Public School Desegregation, 1954–1956* (Chapel Hill, N.C.: University of North Carolina Press, 1962), 24; Matthews and Prothro, *Negroes and the New Southern Politics*, 52–53.
[21] *Journal and Guide*, July 19, 26, 1952.

man of the Richmond G.O.P., David Longley, were critical of the Democratic nomination of Southerner John Sparkman of Alabama for Vice President, but based on the past records of Southern Vice Presidents John Nance Garner, Harry S. Truman, and Alben Barkley, Sparkman appeared to others to be a "reasonably safe risk." Most Negroes agreed with Oliver Hill that after twenty years of commendable performance, "the party that has done the most for us" should have the continued support of the colored community.[22]

In addition, many Negroes could not become endeared to the Republican candidate, Dwight D. Eisenhower. While campaigning in the Old Dominion, he made no mention of civil rights but instead appeared to court the "Democrats for Eisenhower" faction. For example, while in Petersburg, he commented that:

I must say that any party that can produce a man like Harry F. Byrd seems to be a top flight sort of outfit. As a matter of fact, not long ago, or some time back, I remember reading a crack that we have too many Byrds in Congress. Well, I disagree; I would like to see more like this one.[23]

Three weeks later, on October 17, Senator Byrd in a radio address from Winchester announced he could not support Stevenson because of the latter's continuation of Trumanism which led to excessive taxes, waste in government, socialism, and the attempted passage of an F.E.P.C. act. To Negroes, Byrd's announcement was tantamount to an endorsement of Eisenhower.[24]

On election day Eisenhower polled 349,037 ballots to 268,677 for Stevenson, with most of the approximately 70,000 eligible Negroes who voted undoubtedly favoring the Democrat. For example, in the four main Negro precincts in Richmond, estimates

[22] Personal interviews with Longley and Hill, Sept. 17, 1965, Richmond, Sept. 23, 1965, Washington, D.C. Political analyst Samuel Lubell also did not envision a return to the G.O.P., mainly because Negroes had gained comparative economic prosperity under the Democrats since the time of Roosevelt. *Times-Dispatch,* Oct. 14, 1962. Both Negro weeklies supported Stevenson.

[23] *Journal and Guide,* Oct. 4, 1952.

[24] "Byrd-Man without a Party," *ibid.,* Oct. 25, 1952; *Times-Dispatch,* Oct. 18, 1952.

showed that from 68 per cent to 89 per cent of the 9,000 Negro voters favored Stevenson. In Norfolk with approximately 3,000 voting, the percentage was gauged at 89 per cent. That city's major Negro precinct, the Twenty-first, polled 866 votes for Stevenson to Eisenhower's 133.[25]

The significance of the election, however, was not in the number who may have voted, but in the growing Republican strength, on the congressional as well as the presidential level. Three of the congressional districts elected Republicans to the House of Representatives; namely, Richard H. Poff in the Sixth, William C. Wampler in the Ninth, and Joel T. Broyhill in the Tenth. To some political observers, this upsurge by the G.O.P. appeared to be an indication of discontent with Virginia's one-party rule. Among Democratic organization men, who sensed a sagging in the "machine" since the late 1940's, it was another possible ill omen for the future.[26] That the machine was ailing was evident in the close Democratic gubernatorial primary in August 1949 between organization candidate John S. Battle and more liberal Colonel Francis Pickens Miller.[27] The 1949 threat and the Republican gains of 1952 unquestionably had their effect, but the major scare thrown into the organization came in the 1953 gubernatorial election. State Senator Theodore ("Ted") Roosevelt Dalton of Radford, "tall, blond jovial extrovert, immensely popular in Virginia," a man of unusual ability whose integrity was not even questioned by Democrats, came "frightening close" to defeating organization candidate Thomas B. Stanley, 182,887 to 225,878. It should be noted that over 17,000 of Stanley's 42,989-vote majority came

[25] Henry J. McGuinn and Tinsley Lee Spraggins, "Negro in Politics in Virginia," *Journal of Negro Education,* XXVI (Summer 1957), 382–83; Henry Lee Moon, "The Negro Break-Away from the Democrats," *New Republic,* CXXXV (Dec. 3, 1956), 17; Donald Strong, *Urban Republicanism in the South* (University, Ala., 1960), Table 9, 26.

[26] *Times-Dispatch,* Nov. 5, 1952; Richard H. Rovere, *Affairs of State: The Eisenhower Years* (N.Y., 1956), 119–200. Alexander Heard foresaw a resurgence of the Republican party as early as 1948, on the strength of the G.O.P. presidential candidate Thomas E. Dewey's showing. *Two Party South,* iii.

[27] See page 139 in this work.

from the Black Belt Fourth Congressional District, the most populous Negro area, but in terms of actual voting the stronghold of
the Democratic organization.[28] In future elections involving racial
issues, that district's vote totals would be of special significance.

According to Dalton, Negroes played a minor role in the election, but at least 75 per cent of those who voted voted for him,
mainly because he favored abolishing the poll tax.[29] Oliver Hill
added that Negroes either voted for Dalton or "went fishing" on
election day.[30] Though their role as participants was minimal once
again, Negroes were shortly to become more important as an issue
in Virginia politics.

This development was triggered by the ruling of the United
States Supreme Court in the *Brown* v. *Board of Education* decision of May 17, 1954, which declared segregated public schools
to be a violation of the Fifteenth Amendment of the United States
Constitution. The unifying issue needed to regroup the Democratic
organization forces had been found: protection of the Old Dominion's schools against racial integration. It now had a genuine
mission as all-out defender of public education segregated by race,
"the same one which brought it into being in the late nineteenth
century; to save Virginia for the white race." [31] Aside from the
crusading spirit, one observer agreed the organization would take
advantage of the issue to regain lost political ground.[32] A Byrd
man, reported to have hailed the Supreme Court after it had handed
down a decree of implementation on May 31, 1955, commented

[28] Benjamin Muse, *Virginia's Massive Resistance* (Bloomington, Ind.,
1961), 42–43; *Votes Cast for Governor, November 3, 1953; Times-
Dispatch,* Nov. 5, 1953.

[29] Ted Dalton to author, Roanoke, Va., Aug. 31, 1965; *Journal and
Guide,* Nov. 7, 1953.

[30] Personal interview, Sept. 23, 1965, Washington, D.C. However, the
Afro-American, Nov. 27, 1954, contended that Richmond Negroes voted
for Stanley on the assumption one of their race, Dr. W. L. Ransome, would
receive a position on the State Board of Education.

[31] Fishwick, *Virginia: A New Look at the Old Dominion,* 253.

[32] Personal interview with James Latimer, Nov. 5, 1965, Richmond. The
Richmond *Times-Dispatch* newspaperman commented that whether this was
done consciously or unconsciously, it was the line of attack employed.

enthusiastically, "This will keep us in the saddle for 25 years. Why, we'll even have organized labor with us." [33] With the support of Tidewater and Southside, especially the Third and Fourth Congressional Districts, and without seriously antagonizing the remainder of the state, the organization could rejuvenate itself as the stalwart opponent of integration, attacking as the culprits the federal government and the Republicans on the state level.

The political picture of the next six years centered on one issue, "massive resistance" against school integration.[34] It should be recalled that prior to 1954 race relations in Virginia had been better than in most of the South. Negroes ran regularly for public office and on occasion were appointed to governing commissions and school boards. The Byrd organization looked askance upon racial agitation, and even N.A.A.C.P. officials agreed Negroes encountered little opposition when attempting to vote. Educationally, desegregation had begun in higher institutions of learning without incident. A few Negroes had been admitted to the University of Virginia in 1950, to the Medical College of Virginia and to Richmond Professional Institute in 1951, and to Virginia Polytechnic Institute in 1953. Even the three years of litigation in the federal courts over Virginia's segregated schools, as well as the culminating *Brown* v. *Board of Education* decision, caused only minor stir. For the next year state officials and newspapers reacted moderately to the decision. On May 17, 1954, Governor Stanley cautioned that the verdict of the Court called for "cool heads, calm study, and sound judgment," and most observers, like Richmond School Superintendent H. I. Willet, agreed that they should simply "Wait and See." [35] The calm reaction was no doubt a result of the Supreme Court's acknowledgment of the many time-consuming problems involved with ending school segregation.

[33] Insight into the organization during this period is offered in Folliard's "The Byrd Machine," Washington *Post,* June 9–19, 1957. Especially pertinent is Sept. 19, "Organization Thrives on Segregation Issues."

[34] Muse, *Virginia's Massive Resistance;* Gates, *Massive Resistance;* Bob Smith, *They Closed Their Schools, Prince Edward County, 1951–1964* (Chapel Hill, N.C., 1965). See also Woodward, *Strange Career of Jim Crow.*

[35] Smith, *They Closed Their Schools,* 84; *Afro-American,* May 22, 1954.

It appeared evident that a gradual transitional period was inevitable and in the meantime delaying tactics might be devised to sidestep the issue. After a year of marking time, and a Supreme Court decree of implementation on May 31, 1955, level heads were still maintained. The Court had failed to indicate a deadline for compliance, leaving the required time in the hands of district judges, who, with "their proximity to local conditions," raised the hopes of segregationists. According to C. Vann Woodward, "The old four-handed American game between the South, the courts, the Negro, and the Constitution has been going on throughout history, and the South knew all the moves." [36]

What provoked action from white Virginian leadership, however, was that Negroes continued to press for school integration through the federal courts. In the summer of 1955 the N.A.A.C.P. filed desegregation petitions signed by Negro citizens from 170 school boards in 17 states. In Virginia, desegregation suits were filed against school systems in Charlottesville, Newport News, and Norfolk as well as in the counties of Arlington, Prince Edward, and Warren. N.A.A.C.P. national headquarters concentrated its legal efforts in this state. The Virginia N.A.A.C.P., with more members than other Southern state organizations, between 25,000 and 30,000 in 107 branches, employed a legal staff of thirteen attorneys headed by the capable Oliver W. Hill and Spottswood Robinson III. To white Virginians these efforts from an outside influence became "something diabolical." Although better informed citizens gave little credence to such charges, thousands of others viewed the N.A.A.C.P. as a rabble-rousing pawn of the federal government, Communist-infiltrated, financed through sinister sources with lawyers seeking high financial reward or political gain.[37] These suspicions and allegations caused race relations to deteriorate and "massive resistance," or the combating of racial integration anywhere by legal means, was about to begin.

Its genesis came innocently enough in September 1954 when

[36] Woodward, *Strange Career of Jim Crow,* 153.

[37] Muse, *Virginia's Massive Resistance,* 48–49; "Unworthy and Inflammatory Talk," Danville *Register,* Sept. 4, 1956; Petersburg *Progress-Index,* Sept. 23, 1956.

Governor Stanley established a commission to study the problems posed by the Supreme Court decision and to submit appropriate recommendations to alleviate them. Under the guidance of State Senator Garland Gray, Fourth District leader and loyal member of the Byrd organization, it labored until mid-December and then recommended that (1) tuition grants be allotted from public funds to children who preferred to attend private rather than integrated schools; (2) a locally administered pupil placement plan be established, though based on criteria other than race, calculated to keep at a minimum Negroes in white schools; and (3) the compulsory attendance law be amended to provide that no child be required to attend an integrated school.[38] To award tuition grants, a legal hurdle first had to be surmounted. Earlier in a test case the Virginia Supreme Court of Appeals had ruled that payment to students attending private institutions violated Section 141 of the state constitution, which prohibited state appropriations to any school or institution not owned by the state. The Gray Commission therefore counseled the Governor to take steps necessary to amend that section. This Stanley did, calling a special session of the General Assembly on November 30. In a hurried four days, "acting with near unanimity," 93 to 5 in the House of Delegates and 38 to 1 in the senate, the Assembly approved a referendum election for January 9, 1956, on the question of calling a constitutional convention to amend Section 141, paving the way for adoption of the tuition grant plan. The lone dissenting senator, Ted Dalton, proposed an amendment stipulating that the Gray Plan should not affect the constitutional guarantee of public schools in Virginia. Dalton argued, "Unless you insert this provision— spelling out the safeguard to the public school system—I have grave doubts that the electorate of Virginia will approve your constitutional amendment." When assured that the Gray Commission's constitutional amendment would not affect the public school guarantee, Dalton then queried, "Pray tell me, then, why it would

[38] Muse, *Virginia's Massive Resistance*, 8. It should be stressed that the "Gray Plan" advocated that local areas decide for themselves about student placement. That this "local option" was discarded later by the more radical segregationists was to cause much controversy.

hurt to put in my provision?"[39] His proposed amendment was defeated.

Coupled with this preliminary General Assembly action, another indication that race relations were worsening in 1955 occurred in the Richmond Democratic primary for the General Assembly. The only Negro candidate, Oliver W. Hill, though highly respected as an office seeker in three earlier contests, failed to gain any appreciable white backing in this contest. While the other candidates were virtually unanimous in opposing integration, Hill, one of the legal staff of the N.A.A.C.P., appealed for compliance with the Supreme Court decisions. He asked for support not only from integrationists, but also from those "who think they agree with racial segregation and particularly those with closed minds. The vast majority of people who believe in segregation," Hill continued, "do so from fear, superstition and ignorance of the issues involved." The Negro candidate believed his election would be a beginning in destroying the barriers of such misconceptions.[40]

In an atmosphere in which the vast majority of candidates pledged segregation even to the point of closing state parks and "taking the State out of the recreation business," as advocated by State Senator G. Edmond Massie, Hill's chances were slim. On election eve when the Negro political organization, the Richmond Civic Council, announced its endorsements, all but one of those selected declared it came as a surprise to them, as if not wishing to be stained by Negro backing.[41] On election day, Hill ran a poor tenth in a field of 12, polling only 6,683 votes, far behind the last winner, E. Tucker Carlton with 10,809. Hill estimated that in 1948 as an independent he had received 4,000 white votes. In 1950, his total reached almost 9,000, but in this election his votes came almost entirely from Negroes.[42] Until the school segregation issue was ultimately resolved in 1959 Negro candidates would suffer a similar fate.

[39] *Journal of the House, Extra Session, 1955,* 35, 50–51, 55; *Times-Dispatch,* Nov. 30, Dec. 4, 1955.
[40] *Journal and Guide,* Feb. 19, 1955; *Times-Dispatch,* July 10–12, 1955.
[41] *Ibid.,* July 12, 1955.
[42] *Ibid.,* July 13, 1955; personal interview with Oliver Hill, Sept. 23, 1965, Washington, D.C.

On the state level, prior to the January 9, 1956, referendum, one of the most heated, and as it turned out, most lopsided campaigns in recent times took place. Not only did the "massive resisters" have leadership, experience, and the money of the state Democratic organization, but most of the newspapers in the Commonwealth also favored calling a constitutional convention. Voices such as those of ex-Governor John S. Battle, Governor Thomas B. Stanley, and the state's United States Senators, A. Willis Robertson and Harry F. Byrd, were bound to have their effect. Spearheading the proconvention drive of the press was the Richmond *News Leader*. Edited by James Jackson Kilpatrick, Jr., an Oklahoman who "had succeeded in becoming somewhat 'more Virginian than Virginia,' " [43] the state's leading evening daily insisted that the people who paid the bulk of the money for local schools should have the right to make their own decisions. If, in the final analysis it meant segregated private schools, "it would be better than nothing; it would be better than education in racially mixed classrooms." [44] During substantially the same period, Kilpatrick's efforts were also directed toward state "interposition" against federal rulings, and the noble Jeffersonian word quickly became once again part of the South's segregationist vocabulary.

Segregationist organizations, of which the Defenders of State Sovereignty and Individual Liberties was most prominent, made concerted efforts to get out the white vote. Formed in October 1954 in Blackstone, the heart of prosegregationist territory, the Defenders had an enrollment of about 8,000 in November 1955 and about 12,000 a year later. With chapters in many sections of the state the organization campaigned mainly through handbills reminding white citizens that "a vote for the convention is a vote against mixed schools." [45]

Aside from the politicos, the news media, and the more avid segregationists, a sizable following of moderates favored a convention. They endorsed the Gray Commission plan of tuition

[43] Muse, *Virginia's Massive Resistance,* 21.
[44] *News Leader,* Dec. 29, 1955.
[45] Muse, *Virginia's Massive Resistance,* 10, 17; Smith, *They Closed Their Schools,* 90–112; Gates, *Massive Resistance,* 36–81 *passim.*

grants and local option pupil placement, which to them seemed a reasonable solution. Members of this group included educators Colgate W. Darden, Jr., former governor, then president of the University of Virginia; Dr. Dabney S. Lancaster, a former state superintendent of public instruction and former president of Longwood College; and Virginius Dabney, editor of the Richmond *Times-Dispatch*.[46]

The opposition to a constitutional convention was described by the *Times-Dispatch* as a poorly organized, statewide force, inadequately financed, undermanned at the fighting fronts, and usually erratic. The brunt of its attack came from the Society for the Preservation of Public Schools, led by Delegate and State Senator-elect Armistead L. Boothe of Alexandria. Boothe had been one of the five delegates who voted on November 30, 1955, against the special session referendum.[47] The only leading newspaper to come to the Society's aid was the Norfolk *Virginian-Pilot*. The port city daily called for a vote against the convention in order that more time might be allowed to consider a program to meet the Supreme Court's decision, rather than to rush headlong into the end of public school education. Despite its warnings and those of church publications, a scattering of white educators, the Negro press, the N.A.A.C.P., and the Negro Virginia Teachers' Association, the anticonvention forces were no match for their adversaries.[48]

Observers commented that both sides were "running scared," with neither confident of victory, but in the waning preelection days reports based on "straw votes" taken by members of county boards of supervisors, city councils, and school boards indicated a definite proconvention leaning. Among cities recorded were Petersburg, Williamsburg, and Suffolk as well as the counties of Caroline, Carroll, Goochland, Hanover, Halifax, James City, Loudoun, and Orange. As the spokesman for moderation, Senator Ted Dalton warned that such a favorable vote could only embark Virginia "on

[46] Muse, *Virginia's Massive Resistance*, 17.
[47] *Times-Dispatch*, Jan. 1, 1956; Gates, *Massive Resistance*, 197–200.
[48] *Virginian-Pilot*, Jan. 5, 6, 1956; personal interview with J. Rupert Picott, president of the Virginia Teachers' Association, Richmond, Nov. 4, 1965.

a futile plan that may not stand the test of legality," but amid the "white heat" of public opinion Governor Stanley perhaps expressed the public's consensus best in a radio address to the Commonwealth when he warned that a vote against the convention was a vote "for mixed schools." [49]

This was borne out on January 9, 1956, by a near-record turnout (exceeded only by the 620,000 votes cast in the 1952 presidential election) and a resounding two-to-one victory for a constitutional convention, 304,154 to 146,164. Sentiment against integration appeared to be statewide with only the northern Tenth Congressional District in opposition. Intensity of feeling on the issue seemed directly proportional to Negro population density, with those areas of highest colored population voting heaviest for the convention. For instance, in the Fourth District the ratio was five to one, 45,989 to 9,016. In Prince Edward County it mounted to as high as nine to one. [50]

Likewise, in the cities (the Norfolk–Newport News area excepted), the correlation between Negro population percentages and "for" convention votes was high. In the heart of the Fourth Congressional District, Blackstone (39.6 per cent Negro) recorded the largest vote in its history with 1,124 of its 1,200 eligible voters going to the polls and voting 1,047 for and 75 against the convention. Only 53 Negroes voted. Five other cities offered similar, if not as impressive, results: [51]

City % Negro	White registration	Negro registration	Vote for	Vote against
Danville (30.2)	9,092	1,345	5,155	1,175
Hopewell (14.2)	3,650	255	1,693	751
Lynchburg (22.0)	19,600	2,710	4,748	1,997
Petersburg (42.2)	4,653	1,121	3,371	1,326
Richmond (31.7)	52,246	9,705	20,296	11,450

[49] Times-Dispatch, Jan. 4, 5, 1956; Gates, Massive Resistance, 74.

[50] Times-Dispatch, Jan. 10, 1956. For a detailed breakdown of the vote, consult Gates, Massive Resistance, Chapter VII, "Who Voted Where and for What."

[51] Times-Dispatch, Jan. 10, 1956; 1950 Census of Population: Virginia (Washington, D.C., 1952), II, 27–28; Estimated Number of Voters, April, 1956.

In another instance, Colonial Heights, a residential suburb of Petersburg with a smaller Negro population (0.2 per cent) than any other city and no Negro voters as of April 1956, voted 1,376 to 142 in favor of the convention. Its proximity to heavily Negro-populated Petersburg, where much of the Colonial Heights population was employed, made it a "black-belt city, but without blacks." [52]

In so vital an issue one would have expected a formidable Negro turnout at the polls. With most Negro voters naturally opposed to the convention, the *Afro-American* warned, "Don't Sign a Blank Check," and called for 100,000 ballots on election day.[53] State-wide, however, a safe approximation of the 72,063 Negro registrants who voted was set at between 40,000 and 50,000.[54] That this number rejected the convention proposal is evident from the tally of the Negro "political weathervane," Charles City County. With the Negro population at 81 per cent of the county's total and a registration of 704 Negroes and 549 whites, this Black Belt county, a singular exception to others in the area, voted in opposition 513 to 344. Richmond and Norfolk Negroes also rejected the proposal; approximately 8,000 of the 11,569 registered Negroes in the capitol city cast dissenting votes and Norfolk's colored precincts were reportedly in opposition, 3,395 to 74.[55] Such returns were scattered and almost totally unnoticed in the white press, a clear sign of insignificance in the election's outcome. To Benjamin Muse, this was but another example in which Negroes were "subjects but not participants" in deciding a political issue.[56]

[52] Gates, *Massive Resistance*, 94. For further explanation of the whites' attitudes in areas with large Negro populations, see Matthews and Prothro, *Negroes and the New Southern Politics*, 115–18.

[53] Jan. 7, 1956.

[54] *Estimated Number of Voters, April, 1956;* personal interview with W. Lester Banks, Nov. 4, 1965, Richmond; Gates, *Massive Resistance*, 145.

[55] *Times-Dispatch*, Jan. 10, 1956; *Estimated Number of Voters, April, 1956; Afro-American*, Jan. 14, 1956.

[56] Personal interview, Sept. 24, 1965, Manassas, Va.

XI

Massive Resistance: The Negro as an Issue in Virginia Politics

AFTER the January 9, 1956, victory there was little stopping Virginia's segregationist drive. On February 1, with only token opposition, the General Assembly adopted a resolution of "interposition" declaring that the Commonwealth retained the right to interpose its sovereignty against the federal government. Until school integration was validated by constitutional amendment, the state pledged itself to take all legal and constitutional measures "to check this and further encroachment by the Supreme Court, through judicial legislation, upon the reserved powers of the states." [1] Shortly thereafter United States Senator Harry F. Byrd formalized his segregationist stand by calling on other states to support interposition and then by leading 101 Southern members of the nation's Congress in the signing of a "Southern Manifesto," openly defying the rulings of the Supreme Court.[2]

Though the declaration of "interposition" was adopted by six Southern states by summer's end, and the Southern Manifesto registered strong protests against integration, as yet Virginia had enacted no specific legislation to curb it. Undeterred by these paper tigers, the N.A.A.C.P. continued to press its suits against segregated schools. Undoubtedly such militancy prodded Virginia's leadership into its next move, the convening of a special legislation session on August 27. Two days before at Berryville, Senator

[1] *Journal of the House, Regular Session, 1956,* 173–76. The vote was 90 to 5 in the house and 36 to 2 in the senate.
[2] *Times-Dispatch,* March 13, 1956.

Byrd had called on Virginia to fight "with every ounce of our energy and capacity" to hold the nonintegration line in public schools.[3]

The Confederate flag-waving by spectators in the crowded galleries set the tone of the special session. Virginia intended to defend its segregationist rights. It was the third time in ten months the General Assembly had gathered, and during this meeting, twenty-three acts opposing school integration and the N.A.A.C.P. were passed. Much of the discussion centered on legislation proposed by Governor Stanley to "cut off the funds" by state regulation from any school district which accepted school integration. The bill passed the House of Delegates easily (61 to 37), but faced stiffer opposition in the senate (21 to 17), especially from those who criticized the measure as a contradiction of the Gray Commission proposal of local option. Senator Ted Dalton, in opposition, advocated allowing districts the choice of deciding for themselves whether they desired school integration. With the Gray plan, he argued, Virginia, at the worst could face token integration similar to that in North Carolina, but it would avert a head-on clash with the federal judiciary.[4] Senator Mills E. Godwin of Nansemond County directed the Stanley proposals opposing local option in the upper house. He urged the acceptance of the Governor's plan as the first step toward carrying out the interposition resolution's aim of contesting the validity of Supreme Court decisions. Until all of Stanley's bills were "knocked down" by the federal judiciary, declared Godwin, there could not be integration, and Virginians "want a basketfull of bills, if need be, to preserve segregation."[5]

The other significant legislation submitted by Governor Stanley was intended to curb the efforts of troublesome organizations, particularly the N.A.A.C.P., agitating for integrated public schools.

[3] *Ibid.*, Aug. 26, 28, 1956; Muse, *Virginia's Massive Resistance*, 28.

[4] *Journal of the House, Extra Session, 1956*, 85–87, 138, 158; *Journal of the Senate, 1956*, 104–13, 147–48; *Times-Dispatch*, Sept. 20–30, 1956, *passim*. A statute was also passed establishing a State Pupil Placement Board which relegated students to various schools, with the unwritten understanding that Negroes would not be assigned to white schools.

[5] *Times-Dispatch*, Sept. 22, 1956.

Easily passed, the measures "to promote interracial harmony and tranquility" provided (a) that persons, corporations, or associations involved in activities designed "to influence public opinion or legislation or encourage certain legislation," must register with the State Corporation Commission; (b) that a joint committee be established to investigate state enforcement of laws relating to barratry (the practice of exciting and maintaining law suits or persistent incitement of litigation) and that barratry be made a criminal offense; (c) that it be a criminal offense for any person other than an attorney to induce another person to institute court proceedings; (d) that any person, group, or association soliciting funds to finance litigation must register with the State Corporation Committee and furnish full information of its finances and activities; and (e) that a joint investigating committee be established to study and report upon the administration and enforcement of "certain statutes" pertaining to the above-mentioned legislation.[6] Though specific reference was not made to the Negro organization, there appeared little doubt that the bitterness harbored by Virginia lawmakers and the white citizenry in general spurred the legislators on to pass the seven "anti-N.A.A.C.P." acts intended "to investigate, embarrass, curb, or cripple the N.A.A.C.P. in this state." [7]

Besides the active opposition of the N.A.A.C.P., the Negro press, and other colored civic and political organizations, groups such as the Spokesmen for the Virginia Council on Human Relations and the Catholic Holy Name Society protested the passage of the "anti-N.A.A.C.P." acts, denouncing them as a departure from the Virginia tradition of free speech. To these denunciations, perhaps the Petersburg *Progress-Index* best replied for an aroused white Virginia, commenting that as a result of the General Assembly's majority action, "quite the contrary, free speech seems to be in a particularly thriving condition right now." [8]

---

[6] *Journal of the Senate, Extra Session, 1956,* 47–51; *Journal of the House, Extra Session, 1956,* 31–160, *passim.*

[7] Muse, *Virginia's Massive Resistance,* 32; McGuinn and Spraggins, "The Negro in Politics in Virginia," 385; Ralph McGill, "The Angry South," *Atlantic Monthly,* CXCVII (April 1, 1956), 31–34.

[8] Sept. 26, 1956.

To what extent the anti-N.A.A.C.P. legislation curbed the organization politically is difficult to determine. According to one researcher for the Southern Regional Council, this attack on the N.A.A.C.P. was the greatest threat to the increase of Negro suffrage. Negro voter registration in Virginia dropped from 107,152 in 1957 to 91,757 in 1958, and not until 1960 did the figure again climb over 100,000.[9] The decrease, however, may have been owing to a lull after the active gubernatorial campaign in 1957 as much as to pressure against N.A.A.C.P. voter registration efforts. Benjamin Muse calculated that because of the probing tactics of General Assembly investigatory committees, particularly those headed by Delegates John B. Boatwright, Jr., and James M. Thomson, and their demands that N.A.A.C.P. officials appear before them with the organization's records, Negroes shied away from the N.A.A.C.P. resulting in approximately a one-third membership reduction by 1958.[10] Though officials would not submit records and on many occasions refused even to appear before committees which they regarded as "inquisitions," at the Twenty-second Annual Convention of the Virginia State Conference of Branches in Suffolk it was conceded that anti-N.A.A.C.P. laws, investigatory committees, and fear of economic reprisal had forced a drop in enrollment.[11] W. Lester Banks and David E. Longley, respectively its executive secretary and treasurer, while in agreement that the N.A.A.C.P. had been caught off-balance temporarily, believed the long-lasting effect of the legislation was to unify the Negroes against "massive resistance." But, because of the ensuing struggle, which dragged on for five years, Banks conceded that voter registration and politics were secondary to the education issue.[12]

In the midst of the school controversy and the anti-N.A.A.C.P. legislation, the Negroes' only political friends appeared to be the federal judiciary and the Eisenhower administration. The *Brown*

[9] Margaret Price, *The Negro Voter in the South* (Atlanta, 1957), 4–5; *Estimated Number of Voters, April, 1957—April, 1960.*

[10] *Virginia's Massive Resistance,* 48; *Journal and Guide,* Feb. 23, March 9, 1957.

[11] Statement by former treasurer of the Virginia N.A.A.C.P., S. F. Coppage. *Journal and Guide,* April 7, 1957.

[12] Personal interviews, Sept. 17, 1965, Richmond.

v. *Board of Education* decision in 1954 was largely attributed to the Eisenhower appointee to the Supreme Court, Chief Justice Earl Warren. Negroes credited the President with the appointment of 316 members of their race to high government positions in addition to 6,000 jobs ranging from laborers and clerks to attorneys in the legal divisions of the federal government. To Eisenhower went the credit for establishing the Committee on Government Contracts under the chairmanship of Vice President Richard Nixon, as well as for completing integration of the armed services and maintaining economic prosperity.[13]

Most sources agreed that the major attraction of the G.O.P. for Negroes in the 1956 presidential election was not the candidate or the party platform, but hostility against the Byrdites' stand on the school issue. They were incensed at the recommendation for state interposition and riled by the Southern Manifesto, as well as the Democratic State Convention's denunciation of the civil rights bill passed in the United States House of Representatives.[14] Samuel Lubell emphasized the increasing unrest reflected in the Southern Negro vote, recognizing it as "a militant, not a satisfied vote; white Southerners should realize it reflects not contentment but anger." [15] The Norfolk Negro weekly added that though it bore no malice toward the Democrats on the national level, to support them in this election was to vote "for the EASTLANDS, TALMADGES, ELLENDERS, and other White Supremacy boys" who were Ku Klux Klansmen and members of white citizens' councils stifling civil rights legislation in Congress.[16]

[13] *Journal and Guide,* Sept. 12, 1953—Oct. 13, 1956, *passim;* "Why the Negro Should Support the Republican Party," *Crisis,* LXIII (Oct. 1956), 454–59, 509; Henry Lee Moon, "The Negro Vote in the Presidential Election of 1956," *Journal of Negro Education,* XXVI (Summer 1957), 225–26.

[14] Personal interviews with Oliver W. Hill, David E. Longley, W. Lester Banks, and Roscoe C. Jackson; "Can the Negro Afford to Vote Democratic?" *Journal and Guide,* Oct. 13, 1956.

[15] "The Future of the Negro Voter in the United States," *Journal of Negro Education,* XXVI (Summer 1957), 410.

[16] *Journal and Guide,* Oct. 13, 1956. The *Afro-American* perched on the political fence, commenting that though neither candidate would harm the nation if elected, Eisenhower's "record is reasonably good. We think he should be re-elected." Oct. 2, 1956.

Among the white citizenry, a strong "Democrats for Eisenhower" faction carried over from the 1952 presidential race. On the other hand, because of his stand favoring civil rights during the past four years, the Republican candidate underwent severe criticism, especially from Southside newspapers. In Danville *The Register* charged that to gain Negro votes in the North federal government contract allotments were issued according to "the N.A.A.C.P. line as laid down by the Supreme Court and the White House." [17] A Petersburg daily agreed that the civil rights program was but a tool to maintain N.A.A.C.P. support in the North and added that Adlai Stevenson as well as Eisenhower courted the Negroes.[18] This censure was a clear indication that the G.O.P. in Virginia would face rough sledding over the racial issue.

Eisenhower easily defeated Stevenson 386,459 to 267,760, and the Negro electorate with a potential of 82,989 votes, for the first time since 1936, aligned itself with the G.O.P. Charles City County, which had four years earlier voted Democratic, 492 to 342, backed Eisenhower in the present election, 661 to 174. According to an N.A.A.C.P. State Conference survey, Richmond Negroes who had voted 68 per cent for Stevenson in 1952 cast well over 7,000 of their 11,000 vote potential against him in 1956. Negro precincts in Norfolk claimed a 2,604 majority for the G.O.P., and in Portsmouth's Jackson, Jefferson, Lee, and Harrison Wards it was reported that 5,684 Republican votes came from Negroes.[19]

While Negro citizens had a clear choice for the presidency, they were in a quandary concerning whom they should support for the House of Representatives. Because of the school desegregation crisis, candidates for both parties were of like minds opposing integration. Resignedly, one Negro weekly queried, "Why Vote Anyway?" Citing the Tenth Congressional District as an example, the newspaper remarked that if Negroes voted for Repub-

[17] Sept. 22, 26, 1956.

[18] Petersburg *Progress-Index*, Sept. 23, 24, 1956.

[19] *Statement of the Vote for President, November 6, 1956; Estimated Number of Voters, April, 1956; Times-Dispatch, Nov. 7, 1956; Journal and Guide*, Nov. 10, 1956.

lican incumbent Joel T. Broyhill, they cast their lot with one who had signed the Southern Manifesto. If, on the other hand, they voted Democratic for Warren D. Quenstedt, it meant rubber-stamping the Byrd organization and continued support of Southern leadership in Congress, "helping racists get committee chairmanships they need." [20]

In other contests, Democratic Representative J. Vaughan Gary defeated Roy E. Cabell, Jr., in the Third District. Negro voters backed Cabell, a professed state-rights conservative, simply because Gary bore down more heavily against civil rights. In the Fourth District loyal Byrdite Watkins M. Abbitt was so strong that he ran unopposed. Former governor and present incumbent William M. Tuck, who had flirted with the Dixiecrats in 1948, easily defeated Jackson L. Kiser in the Fifth District, 39,771 to 19,263. Both candidates in the Sixth District supported the Southern Manifesto against integration, and there Republican Richard H. Poff turned back John L. Whitehead, 51,279 to 31,043. Though his opponent, Horace B. Clay, was as staunchly opposed to integration as himself, incumbent Howard W. Smith, who as chairman of the House Rules Committee had recently prevented a proposed civil rights bill from reaching the floor of Congress, won easily in the Eighth District, 38,648 to 18,813.[21] Small wonder that with this lack of choice for Negroes, the *Afro* advised colored citizens on election day to "go fishing." [22]

In spite of Republican success in the 1956 presidential contest, that party met with overwhelming defeat in the following year's gubernatorial election. This proved to be another of the many campaigns which centered on the Negro, but in which his role as an active participant was minimal. All other issues between the respective candidates were secondary to the controversy over continued segregation in Virginia's public schools. The Democrats,

[20] *Afro-American,* Sept. 22, 1956; Donald R. Matthews and James W. Prothro, "Political Factors and Negro Voter Registration in the South," *American Political Science Review,* LVII (June 1963), 362–63.

[21] *Times-Dispatch,* Nov. 7, 8, 1956; *Statement of the Vote, 1956;* George S. Schuyler, "The Negro Voter Comes of Age," *American Mercury,* CXXXIV (May 1957), 102–3.

[22] Sept. 22, 1956.

undoubtedly sincere in their pledge of massive resistance against integration, also ably utilized the campaign as a means of revitalizing the Byrd organization. Reporter James Latimer, covering the election for the *Times-Dispatch,* recalled that party members as a whole supported massive resistance, "because they believed it was the best way to win elections, because it represented what many of them really believed in, and because it was the policy laid down by Harry Byrd et al." [23] The G.O.P. could do little but wage a defensive battle.

One of the state's staunchest defenders of segregation, former Attorney General J. Lindsay Almond, who had represented the state in the Prince Edward County case prior to the 1954 Supreme Court decision, received the Democratic nomination. He promised to "oppose with every faculty at our command, and with every ounce of our energy, the attempt to mix white and Negro races in our classrooms. Let there be no misunderstanding, no weasel words on this point. . . . We will not yield as long as a single avenue of resistance remains unexplored." [24]

Almond's opponent, Senator Ted Dalton, by no means an integrationist, opposed the closing of schools through massive resistance. In its stead he advocated local option, as in North Carolina, whereby a locally administered pupil assignment plan offered "a trickle" of integration which could then be defended in the courts. From the outset the campaign went badly for Dalton. In September, the same month that Congress passed the 1957 Civil Rights Bill, President Eisenhower ordered the National Guard into strife-ridden Little Rock, Arkansas, in an attempt to enforce school integration and to preserve order. Southern news media compared Little Rock to a second Fort Sumter, the federal action to a renewal of radical Reconstruction, and the *Times-Dispatch* rightly forecast that the Democrats would not allow the public to forget the Arkansas crisis.[25] Democratic leaders in Virginia, among them Attorney General Albertus S. Harrison, Jr., opened their attacks

[23] Letter to author, Richmond, Va., Sept. 20, 1965.

[24] *Times-Dispatch,* Oct. 2, 1957; Muse, *Virginia's Massive Resistance,* 42–47 *passim.*

[25] Harry S. Ashmore, *An Epitaph for Dixie* (N.Y., 1958), 38–39; *Times-Dispatch,* Oct. 13, 1957.

on Dalton, especially in the pro-organization Third and Fourth Districts. The G.O.P. candidate was castigated for procrastination in protesting Eisenhower's show of force; for though the Radford Republican had made public a telegram he sent to the President protesting against the use of federal troops in a local matter, Harrison maintained the message had been sent long after the incident occurred.[26] On October 3 in Rustburg, United States Representative Watkins Abbitt queried Dalton as to why he had not yet resigned from the National Republican Committee, especially since its chairman praised Eisenhower's Little Rock actions.[27] Congressman William M. Tuck issued a vigorous warning to "those hungry, trigger-happy musketeers in Washington" that Virginia did not intend to submit to a Little Rock.[28]

Since Dalton had been one of the few state senators opposed to massive resistance, the opposition labeled him an integrationist. In Bedford on October 15 Almond reminded his audience that Dalton had voted against Virginia's interposition resolution. Because most of his fellow Republicans had favored the resolution, this appeared a clear indication that Dalton did not even lead his own party in the state.[29] On a second occasion, in Glasgow on October 18, Almond insisted that if his opponent truly stood for segregated schools and the preservation of constitutional rights in the Old Dominion, he would long since have repudiated the enforced integrationist policy of the national G.O.P.[30]

How actively the Democrats campaigned can be judged by the fact that even the organization head, Senator Byrd, who rarely participated in the political hustings, took a lively part in the electioneering. In what one Virginia daily described as his most active campaign since running for governor in 1925, Byrd spoke in Leesburg, Hampton, Richmond, Staunton, and Norfolk, in all places describing his stand as "four-square for massive resistance by all peaceful means." [31]

[26] *Times-Dispatch,* Oct. 2, 1957.
[27] *Ibid.,* Oct. 4, 1957.
[28] *Ibid.,* Oct. 29, 1957.
[29] *Ibid.,* Oct. 16, 1957.   [30] *Ibid.,* Oct. 20, 1957.
[31] *Ibid.,* Oct. 8, 15, 27, 1957; Folliard, "Organization Thrives on Segregationist Issue," Washington *Post,* June 19, 1957.

Electioneering was carried on effectively by the press also, especially in the Southside. The Farmville *Herald* envisioned the state as "At the Crossroads," with its protector, Almond, standing for the principles of "the vast majority of the people, white and Negro" in Prince Edward County, against Dalton the compromiser. The newspaper expressed its gratitude that "the State was not founded on appeasement, but on law and order." It continued: "Praise be, we have still an opportunity to put in executive positions men who will protect freedom, liberty, law and the sovereignty of the Commonwealth," namely, leaders of the Democratic party.[32] The Danville *Register* more caustically implied a connection between the N.A.A.C.P. to the Republican candidates:

Let's be honest. Do you know any Virginians for DALTON-HENDERSON-DILLOW who are not members of the N.A.A.C.P.? There may be some. We do not say there are not. We do say, in all sincerity, that we *do not* know any Danville area voters for D-H-D who are neither Republicans or Negroes. We do know many Republicans and some Negroes who are for DALTON-HENDERSON-DILLOW.[33]

Employing the same approach as the *Register,* Almond in Heathville on October 25 referred to Horace E. Henderson, G.O.P. candidate for lieutenant governor, and Dr. E. B. Henderson, a director of the Virginia N.A.A.C.P., as "the Henderson boys." He charged that the former had almost echoed the Negro's statement that Eisenhower had no alternative but to send troops into Little Rock. Although he did not believe that Dalton was responsible for the "Henderson boys," Almond did hold him responsible for the candidates of his party.[34] Byrd himself engaged in the blacklisting, charging in Halifax on October 30, "It appears that the Justice Department has in mind making the N.A.A.C.P. a fourth branch of the government." [35] On the same day President Eisenhower en-

---

[32] Farmville *Herald*, Nov. 1, 1957.

[33] Danville *Register*, Oct. 25, 1957. See also Emporia *Independent-Messenger*, Oct. 31, 1957, "He [Almond] Stands for Southside Virginia's Democratic Principles." [34] *Times-Dispatch*, Oct. 26, 1957.

[35] *News Leader*, Oct. 31, 1957. Though a staunch advocate for massive resistance, the *News Leader* showed more moderation during the campaign than did many Southside newspapers.

dorsed Dalton, stimulating an additional Democratic barrage against the Radford state senator.

The massive resistance issue brought more than a half million voters to the polls and the majority overwhelmingly favored Almond, 326,921 to 188,628. The victor carried nine of the ten congressional districts, while Dalton, whose percentage in 1953 had reached 43 per cent of the total vote, sank to a lowly 36.5 per cent. Although it was a statewide victory, Almond's major strength came from Southside Virginia. As expected, his majorities in the Southside ranged as high as ten to one. In the Third and Fourth Congressional Districts alone he won by 23,000 votes (39,441 to 16,964) and 29,000 votes (39,906 to 10,316) respectively.[36] Prince Edward County returned 73 per cent of its ballots for Almond, 2,344 to 463; Amelia, 1,098 to 366; Buckingham, 1,190 to 276; Sussex, 1,618 to 341; and Greenville, 1,935 to 433. In the Southside cities Farmville voted six to one for the Democrat, 1,285 to 208, while Petersburg voted three to one, 3,141 to 1,861.[37]

Though unsolicited by the Republicans, the Negro majority voted for Dalton. Scattered returns showed that Charles City County, which had gone Democratic in 1953, returned to the G.O.P., 512 to 295. In Nansemond County, almost totally Negro-populated Pleasant Hill Precinct voted 94 to 4 for Dalton. Reports indicated that Norfolk Negroes strongly favored Dalton, while the predominantly colored Sixth Ward in Petersburg registered a Republican majority, 284 to 234.[38]

Once again, in a campaign centering on the Negro, the Norfolk *Journal and Guide* complained that both parties ignored the interests of Virginia's 750,000 colored citizens, "confining their appeals for support to the white people along with racial discrimination as the only issue." While it chastised the G.O.P. for not actively seeking out Negro votes, it condemned the Democrats for their

[36] *Votes Cast for Governor, Nov. 5, 1957; Times-Dispatch,* Nov. 6, 1957.
[37] Petersburg *Progress-Index,* Nov. 6, 1957; Emporia *Independent-Messenger,* Nov. 7, 1957; Farmville *Herald,* Nov. 8, 1957.
[38] Dalton to author, Roanoke, Va., Sept. 9, 1965; *Times-Dispatch,* Nov. 6, 1957; Emporia *Independent-Messenger,* Nov. 7, 1957; Danville *Register,* Nov. 6, 1957.

racist tactics, including filling mailboxes with scurrilous literature published by the Defenders of State Sovereignty and Individual Liberties entitled *Defenders News and Views*.[39] Judging from previous elections in which the race issue predominated, such tactics were not uncommon.

Displaying the same massive resistance sentiment on the local level, seven Democratic candidates for the House of Delegates in Richmond who promised a determined fight to maintain school segregation won a crushing three-to-one victory over Republican opponents who had advocated local pupil placement. The seventh-place Democrat, Harold H. Dervishian, polled 20,755 votes, while a leading Republican candidate Charles A. Blanton II mustered only 7,444. Described by the *Times-Dispatch* as a capable and highly regarded lawyer, Blanton in preelection speculation had been considered the strongest Republican candidate. Under different circumstances he might easily have won an Assembly seat, but feeling ran too high against any proposal smacking of school integration for him even to approach victory on a local option platform.[40]

In the same contest, Edward D. McCreary, Jr., a Negro independent candidate, polled 9,522 ballots, of which approximately 8,000 were from Negroes.[41] This was but another instance showing that Negro candidates needed white votes to win elections. Similarly, Negro attorney Edward A. Dawley, Jr., running as an independent for the General Assembly in Norfolk, urged race citizens to support him in a single-shot effort. He gained 4,457 votes, mostly cast by Negroes. The tail-end winner, John H. Harper, received 11,590.[42]

One can agree with Dalton's evaluation of the campaign that objectivity had been sidelined in favor of emotional appeals to the electorate. As a result, he commented, "Little Rock knocked me down to nothing." [43] To the victors, however, it was a case of justice prevailing. The Petersburg *Progress-Index,* entitling an editorial

[39] "Race-Baiters and Using the Mails to Spread Hate," *Journal and Guide,* Nov. 2, 1957.

[40] *Times-Dispatch,* Nov. 6, 7, 1957.   [41] *Ibid.,* Nov. 7, 1957.

[42] *Virginian-Pilot,* Nov. 6, 1957; *Journal and Guide,* Nov. 2, 9, 1957.

[43] *Virginian-Pilot,* Nov. 6, 1957; Dalton to author, Roanoke, Va., Sept. 9, 1965.

"Virginia Answers the General [Eisenhower]," characterized the election as a clear indication that Virginians did not intend to lose their rights because of federal encroachments.[44] Senator Byrd hailed it as a victory for massive resistance, to be "recognized through the South and the nation as showing Virginia's determination to resist integration. . . . The result was so outstanding and decisive, it is bound to have great effect."[45] Without question, until massive resistance was struck down by the courts three years later, it did.

The Negro vote, slight though it may have been in 1957, apparently worried some members of the General Assembly. In January 1958, Delegate John B. Boatwright, Jr., introduced a bill to deny the right to vote in the party's next primary to any precinct which had not cast 50 per cent of its votes in the preceding year's general election for Democratic candidates. There could be little doubt of the legislator's intent to cut down the vote in Negro districts even further, since they voted solidly Republican in both the presidential election of 1956 and the 1957 gubernatorial contest.[46]

The measure failed, but a second bill, sponsored by Senator Garland Gray and endorsed by the Defenders of State Sovereignty, passed 21 to 14 in the senate and 50 to 46 in the house. It reinstituted what was commonly referred to as "blank paper" or "white paper" registration.[47] Prior to 1958, according to Sections 24–68 and 24–71 of the state code, county and city registration boards could decide whether a blank or standard registration form should be issued, but most boards offered the latter. With the passage of this bill revising those sections, however, a registrant was required to fill in all necessary information "on a sheet of paper containing no written or printed data, information, questions or words."[48]

W. Lester Banks of the N.A.A.C.P. conjectured that in actual practice the blank paper provision hurt the white vote more than the Negro.[49] While Negroes, through the efforts of voter clinics

[44] Nov. 7, 1957. [45] *Times-Dispatch*, Nov. 7, 1957.

[46] *Journal and Guide*, Jan. 18, 25, 1958.

[47] *Journal of the House, 1958*, 473–74, 1049; *Journal of the Senate, 1958*, 182, 184, 782–83, 977.

[48] *Code of Virginia, 1964 Replacement Volume*, 223–24.

[49] Personal interviews with W. Lester Banks, Sept. 17, 1965, Richmond;

conducted primarily by the N.A.A.C.P. and other civic groups, were able to raise their registration total from 92,757 in 1958 to 94,255 in 1959 and 100,424 in 1960,[50] the whites had no organized programs to educate registrants. This situation perhaps was a factor in an alteration of the 1958 blank paper registration form made in 1960, which merely requested the necessary registration information on a form provided by the registrar, once again implying that the option remained with the local communities. Thereafter, according to Levin Nock Davis, Secretary of the State Board of Elections, the blank paper was replaced by either a standard application or a modified pink form. Though blank where information had to be supplied by the voter, the pink form contained the specific paragraph of the Virginia Constitution at the top of the paper informing the registrant what information was required.[51] After further modification in 1962 and 1965, even this form gave way to a standardized printed application issued by the State Board of Elections.

Aside from the blank paper registration form, it was a credit to Old Dominion officials that during this period voter intimidation was negligible.[52] Nevertheless, Executive Secretary Banks of the Virginia N.A.A.C.P. protested that it still existed, particularly in the Black Belt counties. Admittedly, with an occasional exception, Virginians did not resort to the Alabama-Mississippi type of violence.[53] But, according to Banks, registrars found it difficult to be available during times allotted for registration and often embarrassed Negroes by requiring them to come to the back door

Oliver Hill, Sept. 23, 1965, Washington, D.C.; and Benjamin Muse, Sept. 24, 1965, Manassas, Va.

[50] *Estimated Number of Voters, April, 1958—April, 1960.*

[51] Personal interviews with Levin Nock Davis, Sept. 8, 1965, Richmond, and W. Lester Banks, Sept. 17, 1965, Richmond, Va.

[52] *Report of the United States Civil Rights Commission on Civil Rights, 1959* (Washington, D.C., 1959), and *1961* (Washington, D.C., 1961).

[53] In April 1957, a cross was burned in front of the home of a Mecklenburg County N.A.A.C.P. official. In the following year bomb scares were reported in Richmond and Norfolk Negro high schools serving as polling places. *Journal and Guide,* April 17, 1957, Oct. 25, 1958. The shooting at political leader Moses Riddick, Jr., of Suffolk occurred on the weekend prior to primary elections while he was out soliciting votes. *Ibid.,* July 18, 1959. But Riddick, himself, in a personal interview on Nov. 7, 1965, did not consider intimidation in the 1950's as a major deterrent to Negroes' voting.

of the registrar's home. In Southside areas, where the standard of living was low and most Negroes depended on white landowners for their livelihood, Negro voting was frowned upon by employers. Colored workers who attempted to vote or voice an opinion on an issue such as school desegregation might very well face the loss of their source of income. As an example of the effect of economic coercion, Banks cited Yale Precinct in Sussex County, where, as a result of subtle pressure by white employers, only six Negroes had registered since 1903.[54]

Concurring with Banks, C. G. Gordon Moss, professor of history at Longwood College, and the Reverend L. Francis Griffin, pastor of the First Baptist Church and state president of the N.A.A.C.P., added that in Farmville registrars by various means attempted to slow down registration. As late as 1959 only one day a month was provided to register, and by asking lengthy and obscure questions the local official could hold down the number of registrants to 20 or 25. The Reverend Mr. Griffin also contended that since most Negroes in the Southside city were employed as domestics, they were fearful of being seen registering or voting. The fear may have been unwarranted, but the possibility of loss of employment was sufficient in many instances to make Negroes stay away from polling booths on election day.[55]

Whether or not the anti-N.A.A.C.P. laws, the blank paper registration, and other forms of intimidation were actually restrictive, Negro politics moved sluggishly through the remainder of the decade. Negro candidates continued to run for office, and on occasion were elected as justices of the peace or as county supervisors. However, until the school issue simmered down, Negro leaders for the most part recommended that voters abandon single-shot voting in favor of backing white "moderates" of either party whose views on racial issues were not die-hard and who, if they were segregationist, at least preferred local option to massive resistance in schooling.

[54] Personal interview with Banks, Nov. 4, 1965, Richmond; Price, *Negro Voter in the South*, 4–5; *Journal and Guide*, Aug. 10, 1957.

[55] Personal interviews with Moss, May 28, 1966, Fredericksburg, Va., and Griffin, July 16, 1966, Farmville, Va.

This type of backing was evident in the July 1957 Norfolk primary for the House of Delegates. With the city's schools facing a possible shutdown, the campaign was marred by "hate literature," reportedly issued by the Defenders of State Sovereignty, urging white voters: "If you love your children, go to the polls on Tuesday, July 9th, and vote against mixing of the races in public schools." [56] According to the *Journal and Guide,* the Defenders' candidates, running an independent slate against six incumbents who favored the local option Gray Plan, would have won but for 2,000 "not-wanted-by-either-side" Negro voters favoring the incumbents.[57]

In a second case, the colored community of Richmond, led by the Negro political organization, the Crusade for Voters, backed Edward E. Haddock for state senator in the July 1959 Democratic primary. Earlier in the House of Delegates he had opposed massive resistance and had voted against the blank paper registration form. Reportedly with approximately 9,500 of the 13,000 registered Negroes voting for him, he was able to lead the ticket with 13,711 votes.[58]

Again in Norfolk, it was claimed that a balance of power of 4,000 to 5,000 Negro votes spelled defeat for an entire slate of Defenders of State Sovereignty candidates in the 1959 House of Delegates primary.[59] A similar election occurred in Portsmouth where House of Delegates incumbent Mrs. Inez D. Baker, a massive resistance advocate, lost in the Democratic primary to "moderate" William J. Moody, 7,206 to 2,499. Negroes attributed the victory to the "quiet but extremely effective 'grass roots' Campaign" to muster 4,000 votes.[60]

While the school integration controversy persisted, race rela-

[56] *Journal and Guide,* June 8, 1957; also see Muse, *Virginia's Massive Resistance,* 92–93.

[57] "Forgotten Negro Vote Wins Norfolk Election," *Journal and Guide,* July 13, 1957.

[58] *N.A.A.C.P. Annual Report for 1959* (N.Y., July 1959), 76; *Times-Dispatch,* July 15, 1959.

[59] *Journal and Guide,* July 11, 18, 1959. Racially moderate Edward Breeden, Jr., received the lowest total win count, 11,518, defeating the closest losing State Sovereignty candidate, Reid M. Spencer, with 9,936.

[60] *Ibid.,* July 18, 1959.

tions remained strained and Negroes could expect little political recognition or gain. For two years after the adoption of the Stanley Plan legislation the situation remained unchanged, with the state taking no formal action to enforce segregation but insisting it would be maintained if the need arose. As an aftermath to the Little Rock crisis, supplementary legislation had been passed by the General Assembly in February and March 1958 authorizing the closing of schools patrolled by federal troops or other enforcement personnel. The statutes further empowered the governor to close any school in a district where other schools were already shut down because of the presence of federal forces.[61]

The showdown did not finally come until September 1958, when federal courts ordered schools in Charlottesville, Norfolk, and Warren County to integrate. Governor Almond, employing the authority granted him by the General Assembly, ordered those schools closed. In some instances makeshift private schools were hastily established, and for the next four months they limped along, at best only partially continuing the education of some 12,700 displaced students. Whether the shutting down of schools on a broader base would occur was resolved quickly on January 19, 1959, by two court decisions. In the first the Virginia Supreme Court of Appeals held that the cutting off of funds from schools according to the 1956 legislation violated Section 129 of the Virginia constitution, which stipulated that the General Assembly "shall establish and maintain an efficient system of public free schools throughout the State." On the same day the United States District Court for the Eastern District of Virginia asserted that the fund cut-off statute violated the rights of citizens under the equal protection clause of the Fourteenth Amendment of the United States Consitution. With these decisions, massive resistance legally ended in Virginia.[62]

[61] For material pertaining to House Bills 145 and 631 and Senate Bills 120–225 and 337, see indexes of *Senate* and *House Journals, Regular Session, 1958.*

[62] *Times-Dispatch*, Jan. 20, 1959. In Prince Edward County, however, school closings were just beginning. For full information starting with the June 2, 1959, shutdown, see Smith, *They Closed Their Schools, passim.*

Some die-hard legislators refused to accept the decisions as final and looked forward to enacting further delaying segregationist legislation at the coming session of the General Assembly. In the heat of the moment Governor Almond on January 20 in a radio and television broadcast to the people of the Commonwealth pledged himself to a vigorous continuation of the fight. Upon reconsideration of the matter, the chief executive realized the battle was lost. On January 29 he urged compliance with the court decisions, calling for a cessation to further attempts to revitalize massive resistance. He requested only that compulsory school attendance laws be repealed, that tuition grant legislation be amended so as to exclude any mention of race, and that a law against bomb threats be enacted. For his realistic approach to a losing cause, Almond subsequently suffered heavy censure, particularly from organization Democrats who advocated continued resistance.[63] Nevertheless, in the Assembly the Governor had his way and no legislation of the type enacted between 1956 and 1958 was passed.

A combination of factors had ended massive resistance in Virginia. One of the major factors was the continued pressure by the N.A.A.C.P. legal staff, led by Oliver Hill, Spottswood Robinson III, and W. Lester Banks. Equally important was the sudden awareness by hitherto acquiescent white "moderates" of what the actual closing of schools entailed. It can safely be surmised that white Virginians advocated massive resistance until it became a reality and their own children faced the possibility of a makeshift education or none at all. Those previously unwilling to speak out for fear of being looked at askance by their neighbors now became vocal.

Prior to the September school closings, the Norfolk *Virginian-Pilot* had crusaded virtually alone against massive resistance, while the remainder of the state's newspapers appeared "loath to oppose any policy firmly laid down by Senator Byrd." [64] After the shutdowns such papers as the Lynchburg *News,* the Roanoke *Times,*

---

[63] *Times-Dispatch,* Jan. 21, 30, 1959; Muse, *Virginia's Massive Resistance,* Chapter 31, "What They Did to Almond."

[64] Muse, *Virginia's Massive Resistance,* 96.

the Norfolk *Ledger-Dispatch,* and the Charlottesville *Daily Progress* called for the preservation of public schools. Communities expressed concern through such organizations as Committees for Public Schools, Parent-Teacher Associations, the League of Women Voters, and the American Association of University Women. An experienced journalist maintains that public schooling received a further boost when businessmen, who had previously let the politicians call the tune, spoke up. They finally realized that closed schools endangered their communities' welfare, not only educationally but financially as well, and began to exert pressure on their political leaders. In contrast to North Carolina, which had quietly token-integrated its schools and was now enjoying an industrial boom, Virginia was following a course that could well cause new industry to shy away from troubled areas. Local inhabitants would move to where their children could be educated properly. Anxiety over the formulation of a separate tax structure to provide for a separate educational system bestirred others. Among the many expenses already incurred, in Norfolk the state was paying $172,000 monthly to support idle teachers and to maintain closed schools. Furthermore, abandonment of public schools on a grander scale raised questions about how to deal with school properties and several hundred million dollars' worth of school bonds.[65]

The demise of massive resistance, voluntary or not, held promise for improved race relations. Inasmuch as Negroes were accepted into the hitherto closed school systems of Richmond, Roanoke, Charlottesville, and Norfolk without incident, perhaps such acceptance might also occur in politics. As B. A. Cephas, Jr., a Negro member of the Richmond city planning commission since 1960 and city councilman since 1964, asked in a 1965 interview, with colored citizens serving capably in lesser positions without repercussion, why could they not be entrusted with membership on school boards, city planning commissions, city councils, and in

[65] *Ibid.,* 106–10; Benjamin Muse, *Ten Years of Prelude: The Story of Integration Since the Supreme Court's 1954 Decision* (N.Y., 1964), 178–80.

the General Assembly? [66] In 1959 attorney and civil engineer Lutrelle F. Parker of Arlington was named to the city's planning commission. In 1962 he became its chairman. Cephas expressed the hope that the defeat of segregated schooling had convinced whites that Negroes were here to stay and probably were not so bad after all, and that whites would adopt the attitude of "Why don't we live and let live?" In educational circles this appears to have been the case; Richmond, Lynchburg, Portsmouth, Hampton, and Norfolk were among the major cities which by 1963 had Negroes on their school boards. Biracial commissions, organized mainly since 1959, in which Negroes could voice their opinions and grievances, have also been helpful.[67]

Cephas concluded, however, that amicable relations between races were not enough. Negroes themselves must take the initiative, especially through the ballot, if they are to expect their share of political reward. This is especially true in counties where Negroes are in the majority or provide a political balance of power. The 1960 Census revealed that while Negroes formed a majority of the inhabitants in fourteen counties and approximately 25 per cent to 49 per cent in twenty others, only in Charles City County did they have a majority of registered voters.[68]

A lesson in the power of the ballot could be learned from that Black Belt county. With a population in 1960 of 4,145 Negroes and 917 whites, of which 780 and 558 respectively were registered voters, the Negroes have consistently outvoted the whites.[69]

[66] Personal interview with Cephas, Sept. 8, 1965, Richmond. Specifically, as officeholders in Suffolk and Nansemond County, Negro political leader Moses Riddick, Jr., listed election officials, justices of the peace, deputy sheriffs, assistant jailers, auxiliary jailers, auxiliary deputies, collectors of delinquent taxes, a school board member, a planning board commissioner, and welfare department workers. In 1965 the number of positions totaled 36. Personal interview, Nov. 7, 1965, Suffolk, Va.

[67] Personal interview with Cephas, Sept. 8, 1965, Richmond, Va.; *Journal and Guide*, July 22, Dec. 16, 1961, Aug. 3, 1963. See also Matthews and Prothro, *Negroes and New Southern Politics*, 75–95.

[68] *Census of the Population, 1960: Part 48, Virginia* (Washington, D.C., 1963), 118–25; *Estimated Number of Voters, April, 1960*. See Appendix B below.

[69] *Voting, 1961 United States Commission on Civil Rights Report* (Washington, D.C., 1961), 160–69; *Estimated Number of Voters, April, 1960*.

Political activity has been generated to a large degree by a non-partisan organization, the Charles City Civic Club, which, according to one source, has more influence than the local branch of the N.A.A.C.P. The county has employed a Negro woman as a registrar, as well as Negro clerks and voting judges. In 1952 a Negro, E. T. Banks, was elected county supervisor, a position he held until his death in 1959. Another Negro, Floyd E. Carter, replaced him and has been regularly reelected since.[70]

Awareness by white office seekers of the strength of the Negro vote in Charles City probably explains why even during the massive resistance period little mention was made there of the race issue. Benjamin Muse, observing the obvious Negro voter registration majority in 1957, asked colored citizens why they did not run more Negro candidates. The usual reply he received was that so long as officials were honest and had the interest of their constituents at heart, what difference did the color of the candidate's skin make? Not only could this be offered as a reminder to whites that they need not fear Negro control, but to Negroes as well that with the use of the vote, they could elect white candidates who would represent them fairly.[71] Commenting upon this further, the Reverend S. L. Massie, active in Charles City politics in the 1950's, added that

This is a new colored man they're [the whites] talking to. He doesn't want your wife; he doesn't even want your daughter. He doesn't even want your living room. All he wants is to be in the regular go-along of things, to have first-class citizenship. Give him something else, and he'll let you know he doesn't want it. The colored man wants an honest deal, nothing less.[72]

According to the 1961 Civil Rights Commission report, though many shortcomings remained within Charles City's governmental structure, in the administration of justice it was far ahead of twenty-one other counties studied by the Commission. The county had two Negro justices of the peace, and a substantial number of Negro jurors served on trial juries in civil and criminal cases. There

[70] *Voting, 1961, Civil Rights Report,* 165–66; personal interview with Carter, July 25, 1966, Charles City County, Va.

[71] Personal interview with Carter, July 25, 1966; and Benjamin Muse, Sept. 24, 1965, Manassas, Va.

[72] Gates, *Massive Resistance,* 195.

were also no reports of illegal police practices or mistreatment of prisoners. Much to its advantage, and unlike other Black Belt counties, where Negroes depended primarily on white employers for an agricultural livelihood as sharecroppers, farm day laborers, and domestic workers, Charles City had a more diverse economy. There were few tenant farmers but a sizable number of farm owners, a full-time employee group in the lumber industry, and employment for many others either in Richmond or Williamsburg or in the Norfolk shipyards. The yearly income was also higher than the median $1,100 listed for the other 21 counties in the survey.[73]

One observer noted that economic independence, even though limited as in Charles City County, is needed before Negroes can become politically active. As it becomes available to them, they will become more conscious of their stake in society. Such economic gain appears to be presently underway in Virginia. Much of it can be credited to the expansion of business and industry in urban Virginia, which as it increases leads to a population decrease in rural areas. This expansion, coupled with farm mechanization, sends Negro tenants and sharecroppers migrating, not only northward, but also to Virginia's cities for employment in developing industry.[74] For example, in 1950 there were 737,125 Negroes in Virginia; 337,142 urban and 399,983 rural. Ten years later the total figure rose to 824,506—437,000 uban and 386,799 rural, an approximate decrease of 13,000 rural Negro inhabitants but an urban increase of about 100,000.[75] The voting power of this population increase, if implemented, could be formidable. The

[73] *Voting, 1961, Civil Rights Report,* 152–55, 181; personal interview with Muse, Sept. 25, 1965, Manassas, Va.

[74] Virginius Dabney, "What the G.O.P. Is Doing in the South," *Harper's Magazine,* CCXXVI (May 1963), 86. Also, Everett C. Ladd, Jr., *Negro Political Leadership in the South* (Ithaca, N.Y., 1966), 22–47 *passim;* Donald R. Matthews and James W. Prothro, "Social and Economic Factors and Negro Voter Registration in the South," *American Political Science Review,* LVII (March 1963) 24–44 *passim,* believe urbanization and industrialization are factors for increased political participation, but caution that these factors may be overrated.

[75] *United States Census of Population, 1960: Virginia, General Population Characteristics* (Washington, D.C., 1960), 48; T. Lynn Smith, "The Redistribution of the Negro Population in the United States, 1910–1960," *Journal of Negro History,* LI (July 1966), 167–71.

registration of Negro voters during the same decade rose from 40,116 to 100,424. In 1950, 18,559 registrants were urban and 21,557 rural, while in 1960 the figures stood respectively at 56,871 and 43,553. Table I further reveals the increase in Negroes of voting age and of Negro registrants in major cities.

TABLE I. Increase in Negro population and registration

City	Negro population (over 21)		Negro voter registration	
	1950	1960	1951	1960
Alexandria	6,025	10,635	N.f.a.*	N.f.a.
Danville	6,688	11,473	1,648	1,781
Hampton	10,825	19,095	N.f.a.	2,941
Lynchburg	6,475	11,125	1,752	2,496
Martinsville	2,972	5,692	538	371
Newport News	20,974	39,060	2,431	5,094
Norfolk	45,376	80,621	6,919	11,486
Petersburg	9,821	17,378	1,054	2,316
Portsmouth	21,055	39,681	2,000	5,290
Richmond	53,719	92,331	8,737	15,641
Roanoke	9,519	16,542	1,887	2,698
Suffolk	2,769	4,710	427	600†

* No figures available.

† *United States Census of Population, 1960: Virginia, General Population Characteristics* (Washington, D.C., 1960), 42–49; *Estimated Number of Voters, April, 1951—April, 1960.* Because 1950 figures were incomplete, the following year was referred to. Richmond's total of 8,737 is a 1952 figure.

The easing of racial tension through the ending of massive resistance, a rising urban population, and the opportunity for a modicum of economic gain in the cities by 1960 offered Negroes an opportunity unlike any other in over half a century. An examination of how it was implemented during the next few years follows.

XII

Political Breakthrough, 1960–1964

THE 1960's brought Negroes in the Old Dominion their first real political activity since the 1880's. Most sources acknowledge that between 1963 and 1964 Negroes finally became vote conscious, aware of the importance of the ballot. The remaining pages of this work will investigate how, after over half a century of exclusion from and voluntary non-participation in Virginia politics, Negroes once again became politically active.

The decade began hopefully for Negroes, as both candidates in the 1960 presidential election, Vice President Richard Nixon for the Republicans and Senator John F. Kennedy of Massachusetts for the Democrats, pledged themselves to a strong civil rights program. Undoubtedly the campaign promises were made mainly to woo Northern Negro voters, for as yet, according to one political observer, "the struggle of the Southern Negro seemed peripheral to national politics." [1] Nevertheless, approximately one-half of Virginia's 100,000 registered Negroes made ready to cast their ballots in November.[2]

Negroes initially leaned toward Nixon because he stood for a continuation of the Eisenhower civil rights policy and economic prosperity. While campaigning in Virginia he was lauded by the *Journal and Guide* for refusing to address a Roanoke audience unless it was integrated.[3] On another occasion his running mate,

[1] Theodore H. White, *The Making of the President, 1964* (N.Y., 1965) 164–65.
[2] *Journal and Guide*, Nov. 21, 1960.   [3] *Ibid.*, Sept. 24, 1960.

Henry Cabot Lodge, even intimated in Albany, New York, that if elected Nixon would appoint a Negro to his cabinet.[4]

Senator Kennedy, who also took a strong stand on civil rights, was at a disadvantage among Negroes because of the selection of Senator Lyndon B. Johnson of Texas as his running mate. Though Johnson had played a key role as Senate majority leader in shaping the 1957 and 1960 civil rights bills, Negroes expressed concern over his earlier record which totaled 39 out of 50 roll call votes against civil rights legislation, six of which opposed the elimination of the poll tax. According to Theodore H. White, after twelve years of the give-and-take in the Senate, Johnson's politics appeared to be those of "the cute operator" who knew all the tricks.[5]

Despite this initial disadvantage, Virginia Negroes soon veered toward the Kennedy camp, mainly because Nixon did not follow up early attempts to capture their vote. Facing the choice of making an all-out effort for Southern white votes or for Negro support, primarily in the North, the Republican candidate chose the former. Nixon later regretfully admitted that he had erred.[6] His strategy seemed sound in Virginia, where Democratic leaders including Senator Byrd and Representatives Smith and Tuck kept silent and made no effort to endorse Kennedy. Negroes considered their "golden silence" a Nixon endorsement.[7] They also interpreted Senator Byrd's introduction of President Eisenhower, when the latter was campaigning for Nixon in Staunton, as another indication that the Republicans were not trying to aid Negroes.[8] Colored citizens were further alientated by the race baiting of the Virginia Democrats for Nixon. For example, the Nixonites insinuated that Representative Adam Clayton Powell of New York endorsed Kennedy because the latter's "punitive civil rights program" was

[4] *Times-Dispatch,* Oct. 19, 1960.

[5] *The Making of the President, 1960* (N.Y., 1961), 132–33, 172–77; Gloster B. Current, "Why Nixon Lost the Negro Vote," *Crisis,* LXVIII (Jan. 1961), 5–14 *passim; Afro-American,* May 7, 1960.

[6] Simeon Booker, "What Republicans Must Do to Regain Negro Votes," *Ebony,* XVII (April 1962), 47–55 *passim;* Eli Ginzberg and Alfred E. Eichner, *The Troublesome Presence: American Democracy and the Negro* (N.Y., 1964), 317.

[7] *Journal and Guide,* Nov. 9, 1960.   [8] *Ibid.,* Oct. 29, Nov. 5, 1960.

directed against the South and because Kennedy planned to humiliate the South by appointing Negro judges there.[9] Pertaining to the second allegation, E. Blackburn Moore, Speaker of the House of Delegates, in a letter to William C. Battle, director of the Kennedy campaign in the state, inquired into the authenticity of an article in the Washington *Post* saying that Kennedy might select for the Virginia bench a Negro judge from the 4,000 in the nation.[10] Though national Democratic campaign manager Robert Kennedy attempted to reassure a Richmond audience on November 1, asserting that before any judicial appointment was made state leaders would be consulted, Moore's letter was widely distributed among Southside whites.[11]

A stroke of good fortune occurring late in October accidentally won praise for Kennedy from Negroes. When the civil rights leader Reverend Martin Luther King was arrested for refusing to leave the restaurant of an Atlanta department store, only casual notice was paid to it in white newspapers. Among Negroes, though, word spread rapidly that Kennedy had telephoned the anxious Mrs. King expressing his sympathy. "Reliable sources" also had it that the Kennedy influence obtained King's release shortly thereafter. Whether or not this service was actually performed, Democrats played it up as fact by the distribution in Negro neighborhoods of pamphlets describing the episode. One Virginia Negro weekly headlined the rescue on its front page.[12] A close observer of the campaign surmised that it was because of his eagerness to retain white Southern votes that Nixon took no action in King's behalf. For Kennedy, the incident nationally proved valuable in obtaining his narrow victory.[13]

[9] Petersburg *Progress-Index,* Nov. 4, 5, 1960; Danville *Register,* Nov. 6, 1960.   [10] *Times-Dispatch,* Oct. 27–29, 1960.

[11] *Ibid.,* Nov. 3, 9, 1960; *Journal and Guide,* Nov. 5, 1960.

[12] White, *Making of the President, 1960,* 321–23; Arthur M. Schlesinger, Jr., *A Thousand Days: John F. Kennedy in the White House* (Boston, 1965), 929–30; *Journal and Guide,* Oct. 29, 1960.

[13] White, *Making of the President, 1960,* 323. According to another source, Nixon's comment on the incident was that "the Democrats whipped up a fury in Negro areas. I was painted a villain, and my entire record was erased within weeks." Booker, "What Republicans Must do to Regain Negro Votes," 47–48.

Virginia citizens favored Nixon by a vote of 404,521 to 362,-
327. But the Negroes of the state, after their temporary switch to
the G.O.P. in 1956, returned to the Democratic fold. Judging
from scattered results, their influence was slight.[14] They could
boast that the Negro vote was the decisive factor in Kennedy's
triumph in Illinois, Maryland, Michigan, New Jersey, New York,
and Pennsylvania; and the optimistic *Afro-American* commented
that the incoming President would be mindful of the Negroes' con-
tribution.[15]

If the 1960 election generally held promise for Negroes, so too
did the 1961 gubernatorial contest, even though as usual the organization was victorious. The general election, devoid of the
political excitement of the past two campaigns and described as
"Low-Key" by newsman James Latimer, saw Attorney General
Albertus S. Harrison, Jr., easily defeat Republican H. Clyde Pearson, 251,861 to 142,561.[16] The real contest, indeed, had been in
the earlier Democratic primary in July. Running in the primary
against the organization ticket of Harrison for governor, Mills E.
Godwin for lieutenant governor, and Robert Y. Button for attorney general were A. E. S. Stephens (lieutenant governor during
the Almond administration), Armistead L. Boothe, and T. Mum-
ford Boyd respectively. Throughout the month of June, the
Stephens forces assailed their opposition as massive resistance
school closers, primarily with references to the closed schools of
Prince Edward County. The Harrison team retaliated by charac-
terizing their adversaries as "ultra-liberals" working hand-in-hand

[14] *Statement of the Vote for President, November 8, 1960.* Norfolk
Negroes maintained that Kennedy's 22,037 to 17,174 victory was provided
by their 6,000 votes. Though Kennedy only carried 21 of Richmond's 68
precincts, 17 of the former contained 10,579 voting Negroes. Petersburg
press reports indicated a Negro preference for Kennedy, and Charles City
County favored the Democrat, 623 to 337. *Virginian-Pilot,* Nov. 8, 10,
1960; *Times-Dispatch,* Nov. 9, 1960; Petersburg *Progress-Index,* Nov. 9,
1960.

[15] Nov. 12, 19, 1960.

[16] *Votes Cast for Governor, November 7, 1961;* impressive margins were
registered once again in the Third and Fourth Districts, 31,377 to 15,581
and 29,026 to 6,582 respectively.

with the N.A.A.C.P. and the A.F.L.–C.I.O. Stephens argued that the state could operate a Negro school in Prince Edward.[17] Harrison retorted that the state lacked the statutory power and that to open such a school would only disrupt the racial calm which had been restored in the county. Furthermore, Harrison scolded, "If the N.A.A.C.P., the federal government, the Stephenses and the Boothes would leave Prince Edward alone, the responsible people of the county—white and colored—would soon resolve the problem."[18]

A Richmond daily predicted that approximately 50,000 Negroes would go to the polls on July 11.[19] Perhaps sensing the closeness, the *Journal and Guide* as early as mid-March had conducted an antiorganization campaign stressing Byrd's endorsement of Harrison. Clearly in support of Stephens, the newspaper regularly printed the following admonitory slogan: "You cannot vote for or against the Byrd machine in the July primary if you don't register."[20]

Whatever the number of Negro voters on election day, it was not sufficient to prevent a Harrison triumph, 199,519 to 152,639. Examination of the returns reveals that the margin of victory was not as wide as the totals seem to indicate. Stephens fared well in the cities, being edged out 67,460 to 76,733. In the counties Harrison won handily, 122,786 to 85,179, but most of that 37,607-vote majority could be credited to the ever-reliable Third and Fourth Congressional Districts. There he won 31,895 to 12,728 and 33,556 to 17,045, respectively, for a 36,678 majority.[21] Harrison's pledge to continue the segregation fight and his support of the closed schools of Prince Edward County undoubtedly aided him. Nevertheless, the victory was not of the 1957 runaway variety in which virtually the entire electorate subscribed to massive resistance. Perhaps after seven years of controversy over school

---

[17] *Times-Dispatch,* June 19, 24, 28, 1961.
[18] *Ibid.,* June 14, 17, 1961.   [19] *Ibid.,* July 9, 1961.
[20] March 18—July 11, 1961, *passim.*
[21] *Statement of the Vote for Governor, Democratic Primary Election, July 11, 1961; Times-Dispatch,* July 12, 13, 1961.

integration, the issue was wearying Virginia citizens. Should white moderates combine with an active Negro electorate in future primaries and general elections, they might very well offset the conservative Southside majority.

Rising political awareness of Negroes, however, came from causes other than the elections just mentioned. From 1954 through 1959 the school segregation crisis had centered the nation's attention on Virginia, and the state's Negroes had been at the heart of that agitation. But, beginning in 1960, an unprecedented political consciousness arose as the nation's attention shifted to events in the lower South and the major Northern cities. The impetus was largely furnished by "the movement," an almost spontaneous Negro crusade so greatly accelerated by 1964 that it arrested the attention of the entire nation.

According to C. Vann Woodward, the year 1960 marked a turning point for the Southern Negro in several ways. Previously Negroes had not realized their potential nor made extensive use of nonviolent protests. Further, the national conscience was not awakened until then to the injustices suffered by colored Americans in other sections as well as in the South. At no other time had Negroes throughout the nation more actively protested against racial inequality nor had they received the sympathy of such a large segment of the nation's citizens. The standard Negro organizations, among them the N.A.A.C.P. and the Urban League, which had previously moved measuredly for reform, had to make room for other groups who challenged their leadership—from the moderate Southern Christian Leadership Conference and Congress for Racial Equality to the militant Black Muslims. From the initial "sit-in" protest by four Negro students at a lunch counter in Greensboro, North Carolina, in February 1960 to the signing of the Civil Rights Bill of 1965, the resolute efforts of the crusaders were allotted extensive coverage in the news media. Americans were shocked by the violence in Mississippi over the admission of James Meredith to the state university in 1962, and again by the eruption in Birmingham, Alabama, in April 1963 when mass arrests, club-brandishing policemen, police dogs, and high-powered fire hoses were used against the demonstrators led by the Reverend Martin Luther King. In June, the death at the hands of an unknown assailant of Medgar Evars, a Negro official of the Greenwood, Mississippi, N.A.A.C.P., along with that of four children in a Negro Sunday School in Alabama in September, only spurred "the movement" onward, winning more white sympathy. Amid cries of "THE TIME IS NOW," nationwide Negro civil rights leaders planned a march of protest and appeal in Washington on August 28, 1963.

In response to the swelling movement, as well as to personal concern over the Negroes' plight, President Kennedy in June presented to Congress a new civil rights bill greatly strengthened from the one which he had originally proposed. The measure provided for equal access to all public accommodations; prohibited discrimination in any state project receiving federal finances; outlawed racial barriers in employment, in labor unions, or in voting; and authorized the Justice Department to bring suits in cases of school segregation.[22] Though a year was to pass before a civil right bill weathered its way through an intensive Southern filibuster and other congressional snags, it was passed and signed by President Lyndon B. Johnson on July 2, 1964. The fact that Johnson had pledged to continue the program begun by the late President Kennedy and had supported the measure wholeheartedly gave him on the eve of the 1964 presidential election an initial advantage among Negroes that any Republican nominee would have found difficult to overcome.

Although Virginia's Negro community did not undergo the extensive violence or publicity of other areas, hardly a week passed without the Negro newspapers carrying feature articles pertaining to the struggle outside the state. Nor were the Commonwealth's Negroes wholly inactive during these years. Along with the N.A.A.C.P., a branch of the Southern Christian Leadership Conference established in Petersburg in 1960 spearheaded the drive. Herbert V. Coulton of the Petersburg division of the S.C.L.C. con-

[22] Woodward, *Strange Career of Jim Crow*, 191; Schlesinger, *A Thousand Days*, 968–73; Theodore C. Sorenson, *Kennedy* (N.Y., 1965), 493–506.

tended that Negroes could not have received a more beneficial boost than that of the recent violence in the South. "Thank God for ignorance," he commented, for at long last not only the United States, but most of the world was becoming aware of the brutality of the white South and the trials Negroes were enduring in pursuit of their rights.[23]

Not infrequent were sit-ins and picketing against segregated lunch counters in Lynchburg drugstores, against seating by race in Richmond's Mosque, and against segregation in the theaters of Charlottesville and Hampton. Protests were also lodged against the segregated courtroom seating in Petersburg.[24] Complaints arose from city council candidate George W. Newsome in May 1962 of discrimination in Richmond's municipal hiring policy, especially at city hall and on the Department of Welfare clerical staff.[25] Negroes pointed out in 1962 that the Seashore State Park at Cape Henry, shut down in 1959 for fear of integration, had not been reopened.[26] And the ever-present dilemma of the Prince Edward schools, closed since September 1959, remained in the forefront of the news.

Mercifully physical violence was minimal against protesting Negroes in the Old Dominion. On occasion arrests were made, such as that of the executive secretary of the N.A.A.C.P., W. Lester Banks, when he tried to get service at a lunch counter in the Norfolk and Western Railroad terminal at Lynchburg,[27] but until 1963 such incidents were rare.

In the summer of that year, just prior to the March on Washington and in the midst of racial conflict in Cambridge, Maryland, Virginia underwent a period of increased racial unrest. Beginning late in June and continuing through the month of August, the Southside areas of Danville and Farmville were subjected to a series

[23] Personal interview, Sept. 20, 1965, Petersburg, Va. See also White, *Making of the President, 1964,* 170; *Afro-American,* May 8, 1963.

[24] *Afro-American,* Feb. 25, March 11, 25, 1961.

[25] *Ibid.,* May 12, 26, 1962.

[26] *Journal and Guide,* July 28, 1962.

[27] *Ibid.,* Oct. 23, 1962.

of sit-ins, picketings, marches, and other demonstrations against segregated eating places and churches, discriminatory employment practices, and the closed schools of Prince Edward County. On July 10 the Reverend Martin Luther King journeyed to Danville and before an overflowing crowd of more than 1,000 in the High Street Baptist Church warned that "Danville [could] easily become another Birmingham" if whites did not soon accept the necessity for desegregation.[28] When King offered the continued support of the Southern Christian Leadership Conference and urged further protests in the city, forty demonstrators had been arrested. By August 1 over 300 persons were jailed.[29]

Meanwhile, in Farmville on July 27 Negroes attempted to attend Sunday services at a number of white churches, and twenty-three demonstrators were arrested. Three days before the Prince Edward Youth Council of the N.A.A.C.P. had begun similar protests against the closed schools and continued segregation of white businesses. The state president of the N.A.A.C.P., Reverend L. Francis Griffin of Farmville, vowed a continuance of protest as well as "selective buying" by Negroes from white merchants favorable to their cause.[30] Shortly thereafter, seventy-six marchers, mainly students from Virginia Union University, were arrested as they attempted a "D-Day" sit-in at the Holiday Inn and Charcoal House Restaurants. Included among the protesters were white sympathizers such as Professor C. G. Gordon Moss of Longwood College, members of the Student Non-Violent Coordinating Committee, and outsiders from the states of New York, Connecticut, and New Jersey.[31] Protest marches continued sporadically in Farmville during the first ten days of August, even as the forthcoming Washington march was being publicized in the Negro press.

Simultaneously front-page coverage aired further objections by Richmond Negroes to employment inequalities in that city. The N.A.A.C.P. and the Crusade for Voters complained to Mayor

[28] *Times-Dispatch,* July 11, 1963.
[29] *Ibid.,* Aug. 1, 1963.
[30] *Journal and Guide,* Aug. 3, 1963; *Times-Dispatch,* July 28, 1963.
[31] Personal interview with Griffin, July 16, 1966, Farmville, Va.

Eleanor P. Sheppard that only one-fourth of the city's 4,400 employees were Negroes. In a petition to the Mayor the president of the Richmond Branch of the N.A.A.C.P., E. L. Slade, Jr., requested that (1) city hall hire more Negro employees; (2) a law be enacted forbidding discrimination on the basis of race, color, or religion in public accommodations; and (3) a law be enacted prohibiting private companies and school boards from discriminating because of race.[32]

This period of protest, typical of that in the rest of the nation, came to its climax with the mammoth gathering in Washington on August 28. Among the 200,000 participants were over 2,500 Virginians. The Reverend L. J. Campbell, journeying with three busloads of demonstrators from Danville, described the event as similar to leaving East Berlin and entering the Western sector. According to Campbell, "We can't even assemble in Danville." [33]

With so many Negroes in such an aroused state, even the most politically apathetic would find it difficult not to become aroused. The drive was sustained and even accelerated as a result of the 1964 presidential campaign, which posed a direct challenge to Negroes. The choice of candidates was obvious. In their eyes President Johnson represented all that they were striving for, while Barry Goldwater's election could only constitute a setback in the struggle for equal rights. For the first time in the twentieth century there was a strong likelihood that practically all 117,031 Negro registrants in Virginia would vote.

Glancing backward momentarily, in the 1962 congressional elections one finds what appears to be a concrete example of the Negro vote potential in action. In the Third District incumbent J. Vaughan Gary, an advocate of massive resistance in the past, came within a hair's breath (28,914 to 28,566) of being defeated by Dr. Louis H. Williams, "a young Republican obstetrician without a trace of political 'oomph.' " [34] Williams, a Richmond resident for only eight years, polled 14,030 to Gary's 13,829 in the capital city. Endorsed by the Negro organization, the Crusade for Voters,

---

[32] *Times-Dispatch,* Aug. 8, 10, 1963.   [33] *Ibid.,* Aug. 29, 1963.
[34] Dabney, "What the G.O.P. Is Doing in the South," 86; *Statement of the Vote for Members of Congress, Nov. 6, 1962.*

the Republican candidate polled over 70 per cent of the colored vote and carried every predominantly Negro precinct. Only by carrying Colonial Heights and Henrico and Chesterfield counties did Gary gain reelection.[35]

The June 1964 councilmanic elections offer a second such example. Negro candidates were offered in at least ten cities, among them Danville, Hopewell, Lynchburg, Norfolk, Portsmouth, Petersburg, and Richmond. As in past elections, some of them were close also-rans. In Norfolk, Robert D. Robertson placed sixth in a race for three seats, with 6,307 votes, the highest number polled by a Negro there thus far. Solomon Carey placed seventh with 3,268 votes in Portsmouth, not far behind fourth-place winner Wilber T. Leary with 3,879.[36] What was surprising, however, were Negro victories in both Richmond and Petersburg, where B. A. Cephas, Jr., and John H. Owens were elected.

In Richmond, first-time candidate Cephas ran as one of an otherwise all-white team, the Richmond Forward. He also had the backing of the Negro political organization, Crusade for Voters. Campaigning against the incumbent Independent Citizens Ticket of seven whites and two Negroes (Ronald K. Charity and N. A. Eggleston, Jr.), the Richmond Forward charged the opposition had retarded the city's growth and promised a change to accelerate Richmond's progress.[37]

With three Negroes running on two opposing slates, the Crusade split its endorsement by backing five R.F.'s and four I.C.T.'s. Matters were further complicated when for the first time since it was organized in 1956 the Crusade for Voters' political judgment was challenged. A second Negro organization, the Voter's Voice, advocating industrial development and neighborhood improvement programs, backed Charity and Eggleston as well as part of the I.C.T. ticket. Because of this division, and the unpredictability of the city's 13,000 Negro votes, the *Times-Dispatch* commented on election eve that neither side could predict victory.[38]

The Richmond Forward group captured six of the nine seats on

[35] Dabney, "What the G.O.P. Is Doing in the South," 91–92.
[36] *Times-Dispatch*, June 10, 1964.
[37] *Ibid.; Afro-American*, April 25, 1964.
[38] *Times-Dispatch*, June 9, 1964.

election day and Cephas ran second only to Mayor Eleanor P. Sheppard, polling an impressive 16,512 votes to her 18,042. Cephas credited the victory to his campaigning not as a Negro but as a member of a team, with integrated working staffs visiting homes and attending political rallies of both races. An estimated 6,000 to 7,000 whites voted for him, enough to make it evident that a sizable part of the white community was impressed by his sincerity and sense of responsibility.[39] A Norfolk daily depicted his win as one over single-shotting, with Negro and white precinct workers laboring side by side to get out the vote.[40]

Meanwhile, in Petersburg on June 9 a run-off election was called for after none of the five candidates received a majority to win three city council seats. The highest contestant, Lester T. Bowman, had polled 2,009 of the 4,175 votes cast. Negro John H. Owens, proprietor of a cleaning business and a member of the city Democratic central committee, ran fourth with 1,426 votes. In the run-off, with 4,492 whites and 1,775 Negroes qualified to vote, Owens gained a seat on the council, placing third with 1,718 votes. He was the first Negro to do so in Petersburg since Reconstruction.[41]

Owens, like Cephas in Richmond, said he campaigned among both races and estimated that between 450 and 500 whites voted for him. The *Times-Dispatch* argued that Negroes resorted to the single shot for most of Owens' count. In the heavily Negro-populated Third and Sixth Wards, Owens gained 790 votes of a possible 825, while the leading white candidate, Bowman, polled only 35.[42] If single-shotting did occur, it could be attributed in part to the fact that Bowman, a member of Petersburg's biracial committee, had cast the lone dissenting vote against a resolution adopted

[39] *Ibid.*, June 10, 1964; personal interview with B. A. Cephas, Jr., Sept. 8, 1965, Richmond. Eggleston and Charity ran 20th and 21st, polling 6,398 and 6,121 votes respectively.

[40] Undated editorial from *Virginian-Pilot* in *Times-Dispatch*, June 15, 1964.

[41] *Estimated Number of Voters, April, 1964; Times-Dispatch*, June 24, 1964.

[42] Personal interview with John H. Owens, Sept. 30, 1965, Petersburg, Va.; *Times-Dispatch*, June 24, 1964.

in May to end segregation of public accommodations. Also, campaign "hate" literature, allegedly distributed by Bowman's forces, charging that "outside instigators" were stirring up racial tension in Petersburg, was held against the leading white candidate.[43]

The "outside instigators" referred to were possibly members of the Southern Christian Leadership Conference, which had its Virginia headquarters in Petersburg. Though in operation there since 1960, little was heard of its efforts to arouse Negroes politically. According to one of its directors, until 1963 Negroes were not vote conscious, and consequently the organization had stressed equality of employment or of public accommodations. Most of its efforts were concentrated in Danville, Lynchburg, Newport News, Petersburg, and Suffolk. As the momentum increased in 1963 and 1964, the S.C.L.C. joined in voter registration drives. For Owens' campaign alone it was estimated the organization added between 800 and 1,000 Negro voters to the rolls.[44] Campaigns to get out the vote continued throughout the summer. Such soliciting of the vote, not only by S.C.L.C. but by numerous other organizations throughout the Old Dominion, enlarged the number of Negro registrants as the presidential campaign got under way.

For Virginia Negroes, the Republican National Convention in San Francisco held little hope. Senator Barry Goldwater, who had voted against the 1964 Civil Rights Bill, was nominated on the first ballot. Though his past civil rights record was creditable and he promised to uphold the law, Negroes looked upon him as against civil rights. Clarence Townes, Jr., a Richmond Negro representing the Virginia G.O.P. as an alternate delegate (a history-making precedent, as it is believed he was the first of his race to do so in either party since the turn of the century), openly stated he could not follow his fellow delegates as they voted for Goldwater, 20 to 1.[45] The fact that the Arizona Senator, during the same month, voted against the antipoverty bill, which he termed "politically inspired," also lost him Negro support. Further, it was charged

[43] *Ibid.,* June 10, 1964.

[44] Personal interviews with Herbert V. Coulton and John H. Owens, Sept. 30, 1965, Petersburg, Va.

[45] *Times-Dispatch,* July 14, 1964; personal interview with Townes, Sept. 8, 1965, Richmond.

that he wanted to end social security as well as abolish the Tennessee Valley Authority, which had provided aid for so many Negroes, to say nothing about the belief that he was so trigger-happy that he might blunder into a nuclear war. Most important, however, was the criticism stressed by the Negro press that Goldwater, "locked in the unholy embrace of racists, segregationists, and bitter-enders," accepted the support of the white supremacy South and the endorsement of the Ku Klux Klan and Alabama's Governor George Wallace.[46]

The Negro support of President Lyndon B. Johnson, on the other hand, was almost unanimous. So sharply did the line appear to be drawn between the two candidates that even the N.A.A.C.P., which formerly had not committed itself on presidential candidates, openly endorsed the Democratic incumbent.[47] Not only did he represent a continuation of former President Kennedy's program, but he also pledged one of his own, the Great Society. His signing of the 1964 Civil Rights Bill on July 2 and of the Anti-Poverty Bill on August 20 was clear indication to the Negro citizenry of his intentions. Another favorable indication was the adoption by the Democratic National Convention in Atlantic City of the strongest civil rights plank in its history, as well as its unanimous approval for vice-presidential candidate Senator Hubert H. Humphrey of Minnesota, a champion of civil rights legislation since his bold stand for a strong plank at the 1948 national convention. Much of the credit for the passage of the 1964 legislation, the Negroes felt, belonged to Humphrey.[48]

That the Negroes favored Johnson solidly was clear; that they would back him as solidly at the polls was uncertain. Their political participation in the past was erratic and unimpressive, but here

[46] *Journal and Guide,* Sept. 19, 1964; *Afro-American,* Aug. 1, 8, Oct. 24, 1964; *Times-Dispatch,* July 19, 1964; Henry Lee Moon, "How We Voted and Why?" *Crisis,* CXXII (Jan. 1965), 26–31.

[47] "Official N.A.A.C.P. Position on the Presidential Election," *Crisis,* LXXI (Oct. 1964), 500–504; also Matthews and Prothro, *Negroes and the New Southern Politics,* 266–71, 384–88.

[48] *Journal and Guide,* Feb. 13, Oct. 17, 1964; *Afro-American,* Aug. 15, 1964.

was an administration running in high gear to increase Negro opportunities. As of April 1964, 117,031 of the 473,507 Virginia Negroes over twenty-one years of age were qualified voters [49] and, hopefully carrying with them the spirit of the "Negro Revolution," they were beginning to develop a political awareness of the power of the ballot.

Another decisive factor for the increase of Negro registrants was the abolition of the poll tax as a prerequisite for voting in federal elections through the adoption of the Twenty-fourth Amendment on January 23, 1964. Thus, the spirit of the "movement," the removal of the financial burden and inconvenience of the poll tax, and a desire to support the Johnson administration were instrumental in markedly increasing the Negro vote.

Voter campaign projects throughout the state led by the N.A.A.C.P., the Crusade for Voters, the Tidewater Voters' League, the Southern Christian Leadership Conference, and other organizations brought forth Negroes in such large numbers that Richmond, Henrico County, Norfolk, Petersburg, and Portsmouth not only opened more offices to register applicants by the October 2 deadline but in many instances operated them on a night schedule as well.[50] The Voter Registration Education Project, a program of the Southern Regional Council, canvassed the Fourth, Fifth, Sixth, Seventh, Eighth, and Tenth Districts, with its goal the registration of 100,000 additional Negro voters. Special attention was given to the Black Belt Fourth, which in 1960 had a population of 112,-400 whites and 84,900 Negroes but by 1963 a voter registration of 61,100 whites and only 16,100 Negroes.[51] In one part-time project sponsored by the Student Y.M.C.A., college students from eight campuses devoted their Easter vacation to aiding voter registration in Richmond.[52]

---

[49] *United States Census of Population, 1960: Virginia* (Washington, D.C., 1961), 48; *Estimated Number of Registered Voters, April, 1964.*

[50] *Times-Dispatch,* Sept. 12, Oct. 2, 4, 1964; *Afro-American,* Sept. 26, Oct. 3, 1964.

[51] *Times-Dispatch,* Sept. 12, 14, 1964; *Journal and Guide,* Sept. 19, 1964.

[52] *Afro-American,* April 4, 1964.

Whether or not it was the intention of the Virginia General Assembly to prevent a rapid increase of Negro voter strength, at a special session in the previous year on November 19 and 20 it had overwhelmingly approved a certificate of residence plan submitted by Governor Harrison for persons who chose not to pay a poll tax to vote in federal elections. In the event of the ratification of the Twenty-fourth Amendment, such applicants would be required to file certificates of residence not later than six months prior to an election, the same deadline imposed by the poll tax.[53] The certificate requirement went into effect in January 1964. However, as a result of suits filed by Republican State Chairman Horace E. Henderson and Lars Forsenius, vice chairman of the Virginia Young Republican Federation, a federal district court on May 29, 1964, nullified the certificate of residence act on the grounds that it did not provide "equal eligibility" for Virginia residents voting in federal elections. This decision was upheld shortly thereafter when the United States Supreme Court refused to stay the lower court's decree.[54]

Aside from this legislative act which Negroes believed was directed at them as a group, Negroes complained of other discriminatory practices during voter registrations. It was charged that in Halifax County, with a Negro-white population of 26,000 to 32,-000 respectively, registrars devised slowdown methods to curb Negro enrollment.[55] Under the new Civil Rights Act the Richmond office of the Federal Bureau of Investigation probed racial discrimination charges at the city's places of registration, but concluded that the accusation was groundless.[56]

Further difficulty occurred in Petersburg and in Greensville and Brunswick counties, where Negroes filed suits in federal district court against the employment of blank paper registration forms. They charged such applications were literacy tests and therefore a violation of the Fourteenth and Fifteenth Amendments. As mentioned earlier, the blank paper application had been modified since

[53] *Acts of the General Assembly, Extra Session, 1963,* 1–5.
[54] Washington *Post,* May 31, 1964; *Times-Dispatch,* June 25, Aug. 10, 1964.
[55] *Journal and Guide,* May 16, 1964.
[56] *Ibid.,* Oct. 3, 1964; *Times-Dispatch,* Sept. 16, 1964.

1958 until by state constitutional amendment in 1962 it was virtually eliminated. The amendment, passed by a referendum vote of 291,880 to 91,586, stipulated that each locality provide its own form, and if a blank paper was preferred, then a short paragraph specifying the information to be supplied could be inserted at the top of such an application.[57] Miss Ann Jackson, a student at Virginia State College, aided by the Southern Christian Leadership Conference, complained that on August 12 she had been refused registration because registrar Robert Gilliam would not accept her typewritten application. Calling her method contrary to Section 20 of the state constitution, Gilliam insisted instead upon a blank paper form. Federal District Judge John D. Butzner, Jr., upheld Miss Jackson, however, in a temporary injunction for this particular case, asserting that she could indeed substitute her own fill-in form for the blank type provided by the registrar.[58]

Aside from these incidents registration moved along smoothly, and by October the number of registered Negroes had increased from April's total of 117,031 to 173,031. Levin Nock Davis and W. Lester Banks estimated that the total might even be closer to 200,000. While the number of white registrants rose from 940,811 to 1,131,474 during the same period,[59] an essential point to bear in mind was that in a close election the solidly Democratic Negro voters could hold the balance of power and mean a victory for the candidate they supported.

Virginia promised to provide a close race. Johnson's civil rights program met with general disapproval in the white Southside,

[57] *Statement of the Whole Number of Votes Cast for and against Certain Proposed Amendments to the Constitution of Virginia, Nov. 6, 1962;* personal interview with Levin Nock Davis, Sept. 8, 1965, Richmond.

[58] *Times-Dispatch,* Oct. 15, 1964. Along with these complaints, W. Lester Banks threatened legal action by the N.A.A.C.P. because so many unregistered Negroes were turned away by registrars on the final day, Oct 2. Banks claimed 600 such cases occurred in Richmond alone, as well as hundreds of others in Petersburg and Prince George County. *Times-Dispatch,* Oct. 6–31, 1964.

[59] *Estimated Number of Voters, April, 1964, Oct., 1964;* Personal interview with W. Lester Banks, Sept. 17, 1965, Richmond; *Times-Dispatch,* Oct. 30, 1964. See Appendix C below for a breakdown of Negro registration gains.

where the vote was generally heavy. Senator Byrd again maintained his "golden silence," and though Governor Harrison, Lieutenant Governor Mills E. Godwin, and other Democrats supported the party ticket, the Democrats for Goldwater and Byrd had a sizable following.[60] The phrase, "white backlash," became commonplace, suggesting that because Johnson had befriended the Negro otherwise loyal white Democrats would retaliate by voting for Goldwater. For example, the Danville *Register* cautioned white voters that unless they turned out in large numbers on election day, registration figures in counties such as Nansemond and Brunswick indicated a Negro majority there, "and they can and will take over control." [61] The injection of the racial issue into the campaign could be seen more clearly in the *Register's* opposition to the independent candidacy of Negro Samuel W. Tucker of Emporia for the House of Representatives in the Fourth District. Although no one believed that Tucker, an N.A.A.C.P. attorney, could defeat incumbent Watkins M. Abbitt, the Danville paper described the contest as a "Dilemma for Southside." It maintained that Tucker could garner enough votes to become a Negro leader there, making inroads into courthouse politics and eventually threatening white control in ten of the seventeen counties in the district. The *Register* cited as an example of Negro take-over the Petersburg Democratic Committee, which accepted the State Committee's endorsement of President Johnson over the objections of organization Democrats.[62]

The race issue was employed also by the Johnsonites during the campaign. In an attempt to discredit Goldwater as an integrationist and to curb the backlash against Johnson, especially in the Third, Fourth, Fifth, and Sixth Districts, Democrats supplied to those areas over 50,000 pamphlets which Republican forces had originally intended for distribution in heavily Negro-populated

[60] It was believed the Byrd organization suffered a setback when state Democrats in Richmond voted to back Johnson, 633½ to 596½. Though in the city at the time, Byrd did not attend the meeting. *Times-Dispatch,* July 19, 20, Sept. 2, 4, 1964.

[61] Oct. 27, 1964.

[62] Undated Danville *Register* editorial in *Journal and Guide,* Oct. 31, 1964.

Washington, D.C. The circulars revealed Goldwater as a longtime supporter of civil rights legislation. Johnson Democrats calculated that this might convince enough Southside whites to remain within the fold, and their vote combined with 20,000 or more Negro ballots would win the area for Johnson.[63] Obviously displeased by such "racism in its simplest form," the *Journal and Guide* saw little to be gained by labeling Goldwater "a card-carrying member of the N.A.A.C.P." [64]

On November 3 the state polled a record 1,042,267 votes, and Virginia favored a Democrat for the first time since 1948 as Johnson defeated Goldwater 558,038 to 481,879. Indubitably, the incumbent's margin was owing in large measure to the almost unanimous support of the Negro vote, which was estimated at between 100,000 and 160,000.[65] With Negro city registration as of October 1964 at 100,428, Johnson carried twenty-eight cities to Goldwater's seven by 226,359 to 172,455. In Richmond, which had over 29,000 registered Negroes, Johnson won 35,662 to 27,-196. Pro-Johnson returns from the heavily Negro-populated First and Fourth precincts of 649 to 4 and 1,257 to 4 were indicative of the sentiments of colored citizens. Likewise in Petersburg with 3,900 registered Negroes, the Democratic victory of 4,521 to 3,253 appeared dependent upon Negro votes.[66] Even in the cities which Goldwater carried (four of which—Colonial Heights, Danville, Hopewell, and South Boston—were in the area where the racial

[63] *Times-Dispatch*, Oct. 4, 9, 1964.

[64] Oct. 10, 1964.

[65] *Statement of the Vote for President, November 3, 1964;* analysis of vote by the Southern Regional Council in *Journal and Guide*, Nov. 21, 1964; Moon, "How We Voted and Why?" 30; Ralph Eisenberg, "The 1964 Presidential Election in Virginia: A Political Omen?" *University of Virginia News Letter*, XLI (April 15, 1965), 1–4.

[66] *Estimated Number of Voters*, Oct., *1964; Statement of the Vote, 1964; Times-Dispatch*, Nov. 4, 1964. The votes in other pro-Johnson cities follow; the Negro registration totals are given in parentheses after the city: *Charlottesville* (2,181), Johnson, 5,205; Goldwater, 4,415; *Chesapeake* (3,672), J., 9,532; G., 9,038; *Hampton* (5,789), J., 13,542; G., 8,731; *Newport News* (8,307), J., 15,296; G., 10,584; *Norfolk* (15,801), J., 32,388; G., 18,429; *Portsmouth* (6,725), J., 16,073; G., 8,402; *Roanoke* (3,037), J., 15,314; G., 13,164; *Virginia Beach* (2,961), J., 1,579; G., 1,463.

question was a heated one), Negro precincts registered Democratic majorities. In Danville's First, Third, and Ninth precincts, respectively, the votes were 333 to 270, 600 to 171, and 671 to 532.[67]

Johnson carried fifty-nine counties to Goldwater's forty-one, by a count of 331,679 to 308,879. According to the State Board of Elections, Negro county registration totaled more than 73,000.[68] Twenty-seven of Goldwater's counties were located in Southside and lower Tidewater, and for the first time in a century, the Fourth Congressional District voted Republican. Johnson captured eleven heavily Negro-populated counties perhaps by the margin of their votes. For example, in Greensville, where he won 2,262 to 2,245, it was reported that although 85 per cent of all registered voters had gone to the polls, 94 per cent of the total Negroes eligible had done so. Goldwater received the white vote three to one; Johnson received 1,500 Negro votes, enough to win.[69]

Another indication that political awareness had begun among Negroes appeared in the Third and Fourth Congressional District elections. In the Third, the conservative organization Democrat, David E. Satterfield III, opposed Republican Richard D. Obenshain, whose political views did not differ appreciably from Satterfield's, and independent Democrat Dr. Edward E. Haddock. Considered a liberal, Haddock as state senator had consistently supported the cause of the Negroes and of organized labor. In 1964 he supported the Johnson ticket, asserting he would be proud to serve as a member of a presidential commission to help implement a civil rights program.[70] Because of his stand the Crusade

[67] Danville *Register,* Nov. 4, 1964; Petersburg *Progress-Index,* Nov. 4, 1964; Farmville *Herald,* Nov. 6, 1964.

[68] *Estimated Number of Voters, Oct., 1964; Statement of the Vote, 1964.*

[69] Emporia *Independent-Messenger,* Nov. 5, 1964. The votes in other pro-Johnson Southside counties follows; the Negro registration totals are given in parentheses after the county: *Charles City* (793), Johnson, 1,023; Goldwater, 323; *Dinwiddie* (749), J., 2,182; G., 2,096; *Gloucester* (769), J., 1,949; G., 1,631; *Isle of Wight* (1,245), J., 2,656; G., 1,737; *James City* (375), J., 1,744; G., 1,092; *King and Queen* (425), J., 786; G., 699; *Nansemond* (1,953), J., 4,804; G., 2,590; *New Kent* (439), J., 684; G., 677; *Southampton* (1,245), J., 2,556; G., 1,520; *York* (789), J., 3,385; G., 2,992.

[70] *Times-Dispatch,* July 15, Sept. 16, 1964.

for Voters, which generally did not announce its preferences until near the election day, endorsed Haddock on October 22.[71]

Though Haddock ran third in the race, polling 39,223 to Satterfield's 43,880 and Obenshain's 43,226, the results were more significant than the tally indicates. Thanks in large measure to the Negro vote, Haddock carried Richmond with 26,433 votes to 19,-057 for Satterfield and 13,527 for Obenshain. In the outlying and more conservative areas of Colonial Heights and Henrico and Chesterfield counties he fell well behind his opponents.[72] Despite his loss, the show of Negro strength was evident.

In the Fourth District, though incumbent Watkins M. Abbitt easily defeated Samuel W. Tucker, 53,857 to 23,682, the significant factor appeared to be that Negroes could amass a sizable vote in Southside areas. Tucker polled over a thousand votes in each of seven of the district's nineteen counties, while in Petersburg, though losing 3,935 to 2,806, his total was impressive.[73] Should a white candidate with the necessary support from members of both races run in the future, perhaps the combination could provide the necessary margin for victory.

It had been well over half a century since Negroes displayed a semblance of voting strength in Virginia politics. Their impressive showing in 1964 caused observers to take notice. Apparently the "Second Reconstruction" for Negroes in the Old Dominion was beginning to take hold, and 100,000 votes was no mean figure to be used as a balance of power in future elections.

[71] *Ibid.,* Oct. 23, 1964.

[72] *Statement of the Vote, 1964; Times-Dispatch,* Nov. 4, 1964. The vote in the outlying areas was as follows: *Colonial Heights,* Satterfield, 1,350, Obenshain, 1,526, Haddock, 316; *Chesterfield,* Satterfield, 7,863, Obenshain, 11,283, Haddock, 5,217; *Henrico,* Satterfield, 15,610, Obenshain, 16,890, Haddock, 7,257. The total votes in these outlying areas were: Satterfield, 24,823; Obenshain, 29,699; Haddock, 12,787.

[73] *Statement of the Vote, 1964;* Petersburg *Progress-Index,* Nov. 4, 1964.

XIII

The Gubernatorial Election
of 1965

THERE was little doubt that Negroes had played a vital role in Lyndon Johnson's 1964 victory. It remained to be seen whether they could repeat this performance in the gubernatorial election of 1965. More than likely the campaign would be less dramatic than the presidential contest and Negro interest would not be so keen. Secondly, with the poll tax still in effect on the state and local level, the number of Negro registrants might decrease noticeably. One factor in their favor was the passage of the Civil Rights Bill on August 6, 1965—the fourth such bill in eight years and the strongest legislation since Reconstruction. It provided that federal registrars be sent to states which had fewer than 50 per cent of their citizens of voting age registered or voting in the 1964 presidential election and which employed literacy tests, if those states refused to comply with the new law. Virginia at 41 per cent fell into this category, and the Commonwealth's requirement that prospective voters register in their own hand providing necessary information (name, age, place of birth, employment, when last voted, etc.) was considered a literacy test. The law further directed that suits be initiated by the Justice Department against the poll tax as a voting requirement within a state on the ground that its exclusive purpose was to disfranchise Negroes.[1]

Though the Virginia attorney general's office contested the act in the State Supreme Court of Appeals, the State Board of Elec-

[1] *United States Commission on Civil Rights: The Voting Rights Acts of 1965* (Washington, D.C., Aug. 1965); *Times-Dispatch,* Aug. 7, 1965.

tions promptly agreed to comply with the "literacy test" provision of the act.[2] Secretary Levin Nock Davis instructed registrars to continue using standard registration forms supplied by the state, but they were to give assistance to those applicants who could not read or write and allow them to place their mark on the designated line. Though abiding by the law, the disgruntled State Secretary insisted that because of this provision white as well as Negro illiterates who were not capable or qualified to make even their mark properly would be given the vote.[3] To date, while federal referees have been required in Louisiana, Mississippi, South Carolina, and Alabama, Virginia has complied with the letter of the law and has avoided the federal registrars.

Suits were filed against the poll tax on August 7 in Mississippi, Alabama, Texas, and Virginia. Though the capitation requirement remained in effect for Virginia's 1965 gubernatorial election, on March 26, 1966, the United States Supreme Court declared by a six to three majority that the tax was unconstitutional on the state and local level.[4]

Negroes appeared quick to take advantage of the aid being offered them. Voter registration drives were conducted by dozens of civic and political organizations, led by the N.A.A.C.P., the S.C.L.C., and the newly founded Virginia Independent Voters' League.[5] In addition the S.C.L.C. conducted a ten-week door-to-door registration effort by thirty-two out-of-state college students

[2] *Times-Dispatch*, Sept. 30, Oct. 5, 1965. No decision had been rendered by year's end.

[3] Personal interview with Davis, Sept. 8, 1965, Richmond, Va.; *Times-Dispatch*, Aug. 12, 1965. In Virginia, the illiteracy rate in 1960 of individuals 14 years or older was approximately 3.4 per cent of the total population, or 94,000. *School Life, Official Journal of the . . . Office of Education* (Washington, D.C., April 1963), 18.

[4] Washington *Post,* Aug. 8, 1965; *Times-Dispatch,* March 25, 1966.

[5] The Virginia Independent Voters' League, founded in May 1965, was an amalgamation of three organizations: The Virginia Voters League, The Virginia Freedom Democrats, and the Independent Voters League of Suffolk and Nansemond County. Its officers included J. Rupert Picott of Richmond, executive secretary of the Virginia Teachers' Association as president; Milton Reid, regional director of S.C.L.C., in Petersburg, Va., as vice president; and Moses Riddick, Jr., of the Independent Voters League of Suffolk and Nansemond County as executive secretary.

in a project entitled Summer Community Organization for Political Education (S.C.O.P.E.). S.C.O.P.E., with its headquarters in Petersburg, directed its forces at the heavily Negro-populated Southside area in which approximately only 23,000 of the 85,000 Negroes of voting age were registered. Though no official tabulation was made of the increase in Negro registrants by the program, the following figures [6] offered some encouragement:

	Old total	New total	Registration days
Amelia	888	1,119	2
Hopewell	789	1,026	3
Lunenburg	660	1,039	5
Southampton	2,045	2,567	6
Surry	1,140	1,402	When you can catch her
Sussex	1,354	1,866	2

According to H. V. Coulton, except for the unavailability of registrars, as indicated above, field workers encountered little opposition in the registration drive. In Amelia, for example, the registrar refused to grant the request for two additional registration days, while in Sussex only after the S.C.O.P.E.-staged protest demonstrations were two more days added to the existing two. Other timeworn reasons for not registering were that workers did not wish to lose a half-day's pay in order to meet the registrar on one of his few designated dates or that they did not care to face the embarrassment of having to go to the back door of "white folks' homes" to register. Coulton mentioned that at the end of the summer project a number of its workers, encouraged by the S.C.O.P.E.'s initial attempt, planned to delay for another year their return to college in order to continue their work with the S.C.L.C.

---

[6] Personal interview with Herbert V. Coulton, Sept. 30, 1965, and report submitted by Petersburg office of S.C.L.C. to national headquarters, *Voter Registration in Virginia, Report to Atlanta*. Areas included were the cities of Franklin, Hopewell, Petersburg, and Suffolk and the counties of Amelia, Brunswick, Buchanan, Greensville, Isle of Wight, Lunenburg, Mecklenburg, Nansemond, Nottoway, Powhatan, Prince Edward, Prince George, Southampton, Surry, and Sussex.

With this nucleus and thirty additional paid workers, the organization continued voter registration campaigns through the fall of 1965.[7]

Akin to S.C.O.P.E. in its summer program was the Virginia Student Civil Rights Committee, manned by fifteen white and five Negro students from seven colleges in Virginia. Establishing its headquarters at Blackstone, this group centered its voter registration drive in six Black Belt counties in the Fourth Congressional District, where, even though Negroes comprised 47.9 per cent of the total population and were in a numerical majority in ten of the District's eighteen counties, only 18.6 per cent of them were eligible to vote.[8] Benjamin Montgomery, a student at Hampton Institute and chairman of the V.S.C.R.C., believed that if Negroes could become politically active, eventually their economic bargaining power in this predominantly rural area would increase also. As of June 1965 the V.S.C.R.C. reported that the Fourth District ranked 405th of the 435 congressional districts throughout the nation in median income, at $3,532. Nearly one-third of the Negro families there earned less than $1,000 yearly. Chairman Montgomery, after evaluating the situation, concluded, "We decided we didn't need to go to Mississippi to find work that needed doing. We had problems right here."[9] Though no registration figures are available, apparently the organization met with a modicum of success as it maintained a staff of five in Blackstone to continue the work during the fall.

Longtime politically active Moses Riddick, Jr., executive secretary of the Virginia Independent Voters' League, estimated that during the first six weeks of activity by all the above-mentioned

[7] Personal interview with Coulton, Sept. 30, 1965, Petersburg, Va.; *Times-Dispatch*, Aug. 28, 1965.

[8] *Ibid.*, May 3, 1965; *The New Virginia, V.S.C.R. Committee Newsletter,* III (Sept. 1965). The six counties worked were Amelia, Brunswick, Dinwiddie, Lunenburg, Nottoway, and Powhatan.

[9] *Ibid.* For a statistical breakdown consult *Handbook for V.S.C.R.C.: Project in Virginia's Black Belt* (Blackstone, Va., 1965). The V.S.C.R.C. also issued similar handbooks pertaining to each individual county. Benjamin Montgomery to author, Williamsburg, Va., Nov. 23, 1965.

organizations, Negro registration had increased by about 7 per cent, or about 10,000 votes. By election day he predicted 100,000 would be eligible to vote, and looking forward to the 1966 congressional elections Riddick added that the target was for an additional 50,000 to 100,000 new registrants.[10]

Whether or not the total might approach 100,000 by November 1965, both political parties in the gubernatorial race appeared to recognize the significance of the Negro vote. That the G.O.P. did was borne out at its state convention in Norfolk on May 15. According to the *Times-Dispatch,* a sense of uneasiness pervaded the first session as white Republicans made efforts to convince Negroes, after the Goldwater campaign, that they had a place in the party.

At the beginning of this gathering, there was some tentative fumbling among the signal-givers, but then the whole matter was settled gracefully in symbol and substance in two speeches by Clarence Townes, Jr., a Negro, of Richmond, the assistant to the State Chairman. Two modest, plainly-spoken speeches, two standing ovations and everyone felt better about everything.[11]

When Delegate I. Randolph Lovel of Luray proposed that two Negro vice-chairmen be selected, one for the eastern and the other for the western sector of the state, the measure was defeated on the grounds of setting a bad precedent by placing Negroes in a special category. Clarence Townes agreed that the plan would encourage rather than eradicate racism. After consulting Negro leaders, Townes stated that it was wisest that all citizens participate equally within the G.O.P. Delegate John Dalton of Radford then concluded the discussion, declaring that no mention of race should be made and Negroes should be welcomed as Republicans with no barriers.[12]

The nomination for governor went to Roanoke attorney Linwood Holton, who though active in Republican politics had been

[10] Washington *Post,* Aug. 28, Sept. 18, 1965. Because of a United States Supreme Court decision in October 1964, separate voting, property, and tax records by race were struck down; therefore any registration figures subsequently mentioned will be estimates. [11] *Times-Dispatch,* May 16, 1965. [12] *Ibid.*

unsuccessful in two previous attempts to enter the House of Delegates, in 1955 and 1957. With the campaign slogan "Make Virginia First Again," the G.O.P. pledged industrial, educational, and mental health reform programs, elimination of the personal property tax, reform of state election laws, and repeal of the poll tax as a prerequisite for voting. The Democratic nominee for governor, Lieutenant Governor Mills E. Godwin, Jr., was to be portrayed as the massive resistance stalwart of the 1950's and a "quick-change political opportunist," while the Republicans remained the "unswerving champions of steadfast principles."

Holton, in a brisk speech-making campaign, lost no time in attacking Godwin's past record. In Roanoke on September 10 he characterized the Democratic candidate as a champion of massive resistance, who in 1957 had led the senate in enacting legislation which closed schools to 13,000 children. According to Holton, his opponent, who now favored educational advancement for Virginia, was the prime mover in 1960 for an amendment to cut $25,000,000 from the estimate submitted to the Assembly for education.[13] In Arlington, deriding Godwin for his "fast footwork" and political expediency, Holton borrowed a quip once made by the Representative from the Ninth District, W. Pat Jennings, and jokingly inquired, "Will the real Mills Godwin please stand up?" [14]

The Republican candidate continued in this vein as he swung about the state. In Chester on October 4 he decried the fact that Godwin had not committed himself to the elimination of the poll tax.[15] A week later in Falls Church, professing shame because Virginia fell under the terms of the new civil rights act since less than 50 per cent of its eligible voters cast ballots in 1964, Holton promised legislative action to simplify the state's electoral machinery.[16]

Aiming directly for the Negro vote, Holton's campaign literature included a full-page advertisement in the N.A.A.C.P. pro-

[13] *Ibid.*, Sept. 11, 1965.
[14] Washington *Post*, Sept. 16, 1965.
[15] *Times-Dispatch*, Oct. 5, 1965.
[16] *Ibid.*, Oct. 13, 1965.

gram for its meeting in Roanoke from October 29 through 31. Godwin was attacked as follows:

ABOUT MY OPPONENT: "He has apparently forgotten that, just last week, he was boasting of his role as a school closer . . . claiming that massive resistance helped race relations in Virginia. . . ." LET'S END VOTING RESTRICTION, POLL TAXES and ONE-PARTY DOMINATION! [17]

As little as four years before, campaign statements such as these would have brought forth a rain of verbiage from the Democrats. Denunciation of candidates who proposed election reform or poll tax elimination in order to give the Negro the vote had decided many elections for that party over the last half century. That, however, had occurred when the Negro vote averaged between 20,000 and 50,000. Now with the possibility of over 100,000 colored citizens voting, the Democrats also needed their ballots. Indicative of this fact, on February 20 the Democrats held their first integrated Jefferson-Jackson Day dinner dance. Fifteen prominent Negro men and women attended. The presence also of former massive resistance leaders who would have torn off "their right arms to preserve segregation" prompted the *Times-Dispatch* to pose the following question: "Is the conservative old Virginia Democratic organization preparing to woo seriously the growing Negro vote, and will the Negro vote serve to prolong the organization's record of political successes?" [18] On another occasion in Charlottesville candidate Godwin spoke at an integrated fund-raising dinner, promising for all Virginians "full equality under the law." [19]

Besides the Negroes, another faction Godwin could not afford to alienate was the liberal wing of the Democrats, concentrated mainly in the Washington suburbs of the Tenth District and in the Norfolk–Hampton Roads area. If Godwin ran on a conservative ticket as had his predecessors, Holton might capture not only the rapidly growing Negro vote but that of the liberals as well.

[17] *Virginia State Conference of Branches, N.A.A.C.P.* (Roanoke, Va., Oct. 29–31, 1965).
[18] Feb. 22, 1965.
[19] Washington *Post,* April 12, 1965.

Godwin therefore chose to run safely on the platform of "progress in Virginia": for improved education, industry, agriculture, and tourism. For education, as an example, he spoke in figures of a $200,000,000 budget in 1966, almost 23 per cent above the current $155,000,000 and more than four times the outlay ten years before.[20] Addressing the Virginia Teachers' Association, the Negro teachers' organization, in Richmond, he advocated a pay boost for teachers from $3,700 to $5,000 annually. He told of the possibility of a governor's conference being called to institute new programs to solve educational problems. No specific reference in his speech before the Negro educators was made to race relations, but Godwin drew his loudest applause when he briefly alluded to it, stating, "I seek to be the Governor of all the people of Virginia . . . who will share the concern of all the people of Virginia." [21] Though he did not elaborate on the financing of such endeavors or openly sponsor a statewide sales tax, he seemed favorable toward a proposal made during the campaign for this type of levy. Concerning mental health, when Holton stressed the fact that none of the state's four mental institutions were nationally accredited, Godwin promised that Virginia would strive to achieve accreditation within four years.[22]

As Holton criticized Godwin for his conservative past, and the Democratic candidate attempted to make the electorate forget that past, the Virginia Conservative Party, organized in protest against the liberalization of the Democrats, attacked Godwin from the right. Its candidate, a staunch segregationist and John Birchite, William J. Story of Chesapeake, "preaching a gospel considerably to the right of Barry Goldwater," raised the cry of sell-out by Godwin to President Johnson's "Great Sucker Society." Opposed to federal civil rights legislation and the Supreme Court decisions of the past decade, creeping socialism in local affairs, and federal aid to Virginia, the Conservatives intimated that by accepting these measures, Godwin was hoping for a federal judge-

[20] *Times-Dispatch,* Oct. 28, 1965; Washington *Post,* Oct. 21, 1965.
[21] *Times-Dispatch,* Oct. 29, 1965.
[22] Washington *Post,* Oct. 29, 1965.

ship after his term as governor.[23] The Conservatives, stressing their segregationist beliefs, particularly their opposition to the 1965 Civil Rights Act, hoped to make inroads especially in the hitherto strongly Democratic Southside.

The Ku Klux Klan also backed the Conservative ticket. The organization had maintained itself in areas from Fairfax to Bluefield since the 1920's, but its success was ambivalently described by one source as "neither powerful nor absent from the state of Thomas Jefferson.[24] Already enjoying a resurgence in the lower South during the early 1960's, the Invisible Empire spread into heavily Negro-populated Southside Virginia in late summer 1965. Earlier this area had been the scene of Negro voter registration drives. By the November election over thirty weekend Klan rallies before crowds ranging from 250 to 1,000 had been held, usually in recently harvested cornfields on the outskirts of such towns as Victoria, Lawrenceville, South Hill, Blackstone, and Suffolk. Standard for all meetings was race-baiting, featuring such inflammatory remarks as "Now let's have some nigger talk; that is nigger spelled with a small 'n' and two 'g's." It then descended into off-color stories one might hear behind closed doors, tales pertaining to the Negroes' virility or kinship to apes.[25] At these meetings Virginia's Grand Dragon of the KKK, Marshall Robert Kornegay, from Raleigh, North Carolina, pleaded for the preservation of America for God-fearing white Christians. According to the Grand Dragon, our nation was in danger because of encroachment by the federal government on individual and state rights. His critical barbs were wide-ranging—from "the Supreme Court, beards, National Coun-

---

[23] *Ibid.*, Oct. 30, 1965; *Times-Dispatch,* Oct. 31, 1965. Its platform advocated the gradual abolition of all federal aid to Virginia, including approximately $64,000,000 in school subsidies, putting all able-bodied welfare recipients to work, and making sterilization a prerequisite to welfare payments for unmarried mothers who gave birth to a second illegitimate child. A head tax was to be enacted for new revenue as needed, all Virginia officials pledged to accept no federal jobs for ten years after leaving state service, and localities "besieged by lawlessness" were to be loaned aid to unearth all "subversive influences within the state, including [those in] educational and religious institutions."

[24] Chalmers, *Hooded Americanism,* 234.

[25] Personal visit to Klan rally, Nov. 7, 1965, Holland, Va.

cil of Churches, newspapers, 'goatniks,' the F.B.I., Dr. King [whom Kornegay called 'Martin Luther Coon'']," to the "entire Democratic Administration and the Republican Party as well." [26]

Disgruntled that both Godwin and Holton denounced the hooded organization and appeared to be vying for the rapidly increasing Negro vote, Kornegay noted in South Hill on September 18 that there was a third candidate running for governor, the conservative right-wing Story. The Klan leader's statement, thinly veiled, "If you see a white man among them, you'd better vote for the white man," had obvious reference to Story as the Klan's preference.[27] In Governor Harrison's home town of Lawrenceville on September 26, before an audience estimated at 1,000 and in reply to Harrison's statement that the people of Virginia were too intelligent and law-abiding to be drawn into the hooded organization, Kornegay retorted that the Klan "is not dead, Mr. Governor. You will find out." Denouncing violence, the Grand Dragon asserted that victory for white supremacy lay in the democratic process. "What we must do is to get out the vote. The ballot is the answer." [28]

Fortunately there was rarely any intimation of intimidation or violence. On one of these infrequent occasions the Klan scheduled a rally for October 2 near Suffolk close by to the site where the local Independent Voters' League had planned to meet on the same night. Spokesman Moses Riddick, Jr., believed that since the Klan meeting was scheduled on the spur of the moment, it was intended to intimidate the Negroes and possibly disrupt the gathering by a show of force. Insisting that the League would not cancel its meeting, Riddick commented, "We don't want people to think we're running away from anyone. If we changed the place or date, then the same sort of thing would happen again and again. We'd be running all the time." [29]

In anticipation of trouble Suffolk Mayor Kermit R. Kelley issued a statement warning the Klan that any infraction of the law would

[26] Washington *Post*, Sept. 21, 1965.
[27] *Ibid.*, Sept. 20, 1965.
[28] *Ibid.*, Sept. 27, 1965; *Journal and Guide*, Oct. 2, 1965.
[29] *Journal and Guide*, Oct. 2, 1965; Washington *Post*, Oct. 24, 1965.

be severely dealt with. Neither that organization, added Kelley, nor any other "ultra-conservative" group had any place in Suffolk and Nansemond County, inasmuch as it could only create disorder and blemish the community's reputation. Apparently the Klan heeded the decree, for not only was there no clash but, according to one source, Negroes distributed civil rights literature to whites entering the Klan meeting.[30]

Otherwise, aside from minor complaints of a beating of a white civil rights worker at a Klan rally at Victoria or of a cross burning in Richmond, not until October 31 in Suffolk was there violence. Two Negro political leaders at a rally in behalf of Godwin were shot by assailants from a passing car. Independent Voters' League President Eli Ricks considered it an attempt to frighten Negroes away from the polls in Nansemond County, but upon police investigation the shooting was charged to a feud among a group of acquaintances, with one of the parties aiming his rifle at someone in another car and the shot going astray.[31]

Opinions vary as to whether or not the Klan "caught on" in the Southside. Columnist Helen DeWar, covering the Virginia election for the Washington *Post,* and Moses Riddick considered the organization a minor irritant, moving "From Cow Pasture to Cow Pasture." [32] James Latimer, on the other hand, was surprised that there had been so many rallies and more people in attendance than he would have guessed, even though they might be just curiosity-seekers. The Klan had not been popular in Virginia in the past, and this appeared to be the most concerted effort to date to establish it firmly.[33]

Attendance decreased, however, as the novelty wore off. At one of the last preelection meetings on October 29, near Brunswick, it was reported that fewer than 250 attended. Perhaps it could be charged to the chilly autumn evening air or to the fact that the concurrent investigations of the Klan by the House Un-American

[30] *Times-Dispatch,* Oct. 2, 1965; personal interview with Riddick, Nov. 7, 1965, Suffolk, Va.

[31] *Times-Dispatch,* Sept. 6, Nov. 2, 1965; *Afro-American,* Nov. 6, 1965.

[32] Washington *Post,* Sept. 21, 1965. See also Danville *Register,* Oct. 22, 23, 1965, and *Virginian-Pilot,* Nov. 7, 1965.

[33] Personal interview with Latimer, Nov. 4, 1965, Richmond, Va.

Activities Committee promoted caution. Probably the open denunciations of the organization by the candidates of both major parties caused interest to decline. A waitress in a roadside restaurant, when told by this writer that he planned to attend the Sunday afternoon meeting in Holland, acknowledged that recent gatherings had been disappointing and hoped for some spark to add life to them. Thus, though testimony gathered by the House investigations revealed that there were Klaverns in Lunenburg, Mecklenburg, and Nansemond counties as well as in Portsmouth and Newport News, perhaps in the long run the Klan was but a minor threat. Undoubtedly, though, in the 1965 election many voters took it seriously and followed Kornegay's suggestion made at Kenbridge on October 31 urging Southsiders to vote "for a white man and you know who that is." [34]

To offset the apparent gains of the Conservatives, Democratic party leaders attempted to assure Black Belt voters that Godwin had not forsaken them by having such stalwarts as Fifth District Representative William M. Tuck and Fourth District's Watkins N. Abbitt speak on his behalf. In one such instance, at a picnic rally in Buckingham County, Abbitt appeared on the same platform with Godwin and cautioned his audience that a vote for the Conservative Story "would be utterly futile . . . though many of us agree with what has been said by the conservative candidate." Abbitt, in in-

[34] Washington *Post*, Oct. 21, 1965; *Times-Dispatch*, Nov. 1, 1965. One other group, the American Nazis, who ran George Lincoln Rockwell for governor on the White Constitutional Party ticket, is worthy of note. Mouthing the same white supremacy jargon as the Ku Klux Klan, the party and its display booth were banned from the Atlantic Rural Exposition at the State Fair Grounds in Richmond at the request of the N.A.A.C.P. because of the anti-Negro literature it attempted to distribute there. *Ibid.*, Nov. 1–2, 1965. On another occasion one of the organization's "storm troopers" was arrested for causing a disturbance by interrupting a speech made by Wiley A. Granton, special assistant to the United States Attorney General, at the N.A.A.C.P. State Convention in Roanoke. After he threw mock tickets offering free passage back to Africa into a Negro crowd, a near riot was avoided by his quick arrest. According to one source, the Negroes had the last laugh, since he was arrested by two Negro policemen, issued his warrant of arrest by a Negro magistrate, and prosecuted and found guilty through the efforts of three Negro N.A.A.C.P. attorneys. Personal interview with W. Lester Banks, Nov. 4, 1965, Richmond; *Afro-American*, Nov. 6, 1965.

troducing Godwin, recalled that the candidate had led the massive resistance forces in the state senate, "and we are not going to forget those hectic days." [35]

Holton, speaking in Arlington on the following day, denounced Godwin as " a political opportunist who stands for one thing in northern Virginia and another in conservative Southside." He made specific reference to Abbitt's praise of the fight Godwin had waged for massive resistance and then contrasted the situation in the Tenth District, where the Democratic Chairman Armistead Boothe welcomed Godwin as a "reformed man." To Holton it boiled down to some of Godwin's people making promises of progress to northern Virginians while trying to convince Southside voters "that what is said up here doesn't mean anything." [36]

Whether or not this was true, Godwin received the backing of the majority of the Democrats in the Second and Tenth Districts. The liberal Norfolk *Virginian-Pilot,* usually skeptical of organization Democrats, commented in its endorsement of Godwin that his plan for educational needs was "the most progressive program ever devised for Virginia." [37] Even the A.F.L.–C.I.O., which Virginia Democrats rated frequently little higher than Communists and which in turn had not backed a Democrat since 1937, endorsed Godwin.[38] According to the *Times-Dispatch,* much of Godwin's liberal backing came because he pledged to move Virginia forward, not recklessly, "but [by assuring] continuation of sound government." [39] Another newspaper similarly commented, "Although the transformation is far from total, this much seems clear: the Virginia Democratic Party, in its present campaign image, is more in line with the national Democratic position than it has been since Senator Byrd's break with Franklin D. Roosevelt three decades ago." It concluded that Godwin was still a good organization man, however, and would not lose the support of most of the state's conservative leaders.[40]

[35] *Times-Dispatch,* Oct. 28, 1965.　　[36] *Ibid.,* Oct. 29, 1965.
[37] Oct. 26, 1965.　　[38] Washington *Post,* Oct. 15, 1965.
[39] Oct. 27, 1965.
[40] Helen DeWar, "Virginia's Bulging Its Byrd Cage," Washington *Post,* Oct. 24, 1965.

Regarding Negro support, colored spokesmen initially appeared to face a dilemma. Their obvious choice should have been Holton, who said he supported everything for which the Negroes had worked. But to cast ballots for the Republican, who stood a slim chance of winning, might mean wasted votes. Furthermore, even if he was victorious, Holton's reform program faced a hostile Democratic legislature. On the other hand, a vote for Godwin meant backing a past foe—a leader of massive resistance. Despite his present campaign pledges, could Negroes rely upon the word of this Democrat and his party, which had done little for them in the past? The remaining alternative for Negro citizens was to vote for neither candidate and "go fishing" on election day, but it was conceded that this already had been done too often with undesirable results. In view of the enlarged registration during the past two years and the apparent need by both factions for their vote, Negro voters appeared to be holding a balance of power and would be courted.[41]

Amid these alternatives, Negroes for the first time in many years appeared to turn toward the Democrats. The Virginia Independent Voters' League, supposedly the spokesman for 200,000 voters, received unaccustomed front-page newspaper coverage when it announced its support of Godwin on October 24. The League reasoned that Godwin of necessity had revised his segregationist stand since the mid-1950's. It also accused the Republicans of being equally guilty with the Democrats in the attempt at massive resistance. While Godwin had supported President Johnson in the past election, Holton had been a postconvention Goldwaterite. In the present contest, despite Holton's appealing civil rights stand, Godwin had the "power structure." Negroes, therefore, must be realistic and pragmatic, just as was the Democratic candidate. Commented one Negro official, "The Byrd Democrats are actively wooing us, so they must think they need us." [42]

The V.I.V.L. endorsement was followed by that of the Crusade for Voters Committee of Virginia, which optimistically claimed to represent 200 Negro organizations. In a poll of its members, it

---

[41] Personal interview with Moses Riddick, Jr., Nov. 7, 1965, Suffolk, Va.
[42] *Virginian-Pilot,* Oct. 26, 1965; Washington *Post,* Oct. 25, 1965.

was reported that 70 per cent were for Godwin, 15 per cent for Holton, and 15 per cent undecided.[43]

These claims were quickly challenged by other Negroes, who argued that those two organizations did not represent the majority of Virginia's Negroes. Though he did not mention the groups by name, Jewell Carrington, president of the Halifax Countyside Voters' League, contended that more Negro organizations affiliated with the Independent Voters' League supported Holton than Godwin. In Roanoke, George Lawrence, Negro member of the Republican city committee, expressed his astonishment "at their [Virginia Independent Voters' League and Crusade for Voters] audacity in trying to foster off their personal sell-out as the wishes of the majority of the Negro voters in the state." [44] Dr. L. C. Johnson, president of the Petersburg N.A.A.C.P., also believed the city's voters leaned toward Holton, despite the fact that three days later, on October 28, approximately 200 persons reportedly representing a majority of the Petersburg voting population met at Mount Olivet Baptist Church and endorsed Godwin.[45] In Richmond, Wilfred Mundle, vice chairman of the city's G.O.P., called the Virginia Independent Voters' League "a paper tiger" with fewer than 200 members, instead of 200,000, and asserted that it was "in fact, an instrumentality of the Democratic party created by Sidney Kellam [Democratic national committeeman for Virginia]." [46] This was seconded by David E. Longley, state treasurer of the N.A.A.C.P., who in decrying the endorsement by the Crusade for Voters Committee of Virginia stated that "they call it practical politics. We call it betrayal." [47] At the state N.A.A.C.P. convention in Roanoke on October 29, the state president of the N.A.A.C.P., the Reverend L. Francis Griffin of Farmville, commenting on the Longley statement, backed Godwin not only on the basis of practical politics and as the lesser of two evils, but because he believed that the Negro people must at some time make the decision to be solidly behind one party. Griffin added that Negroes would remain unable to

[43] Washington *Post,* Oct. 27, 1965.
[44] *Times-Dispatch,* Oct. 26, 1965.   [45] *Ibid.,* Oct. 26, 29, 1965.
[46] *Journal and Guide,* Oct. 20, 1965; *Times-Dispatch,* Oct. 27, 1965.
[47] *Times-Dispatch,* Oct. 27, 1965.

change the political philosophy or outlook of either party without first "making inroads into the party. . . . If you support a party, sooner or later, you'll have a voice in the party." He admitted he was as much opposed to Byrd as ever, "but a protest vote alone won't help anything." [48]

Some Negroes remained in a quandary and like the state's leading Negro weekly, the *Journal and Guide,* chose not to back either candidate. This Norfolk paper hoped that a close election in which the Democrats narrowly won might awaken them to the value of the Negro vote. On the other hand, if the Republicans won, or even made a show of strength, it was hoped that a true two-party system might develop as a result.[49]

It was obvious from the newspaper coverage that the Negro vote would be influential in determining the outcome of the election. Aiming for that vote, on October 26 in a half-hour radio and television question and answer session Holton made his strongest bid thus far to the colored citizenry. When queried whether he would consider appointing a Negro to the State Board of Education if elected, Holton replied, "Yes, if one is available, and I am sure they [*sic*] are, because it is only fair." [50] Godwin had been noncommittal on the same question.

"Our Vote Makes Godwin Governor" was the election day bulletin of the Richmond *Afro-American*. Gaining approximately 48 per cent of the votes, 269,526, the Democratic candidate won by a margin of 57,319, defeating his opponents Holton and Story whose votes totaled 212,207 and 75,307 respectively. Negroes were ready to claim that their votes, ranging in estimates from 60,000 to 100,000, provided the margin of victory.[51] In a November 4 editorial, "Where the Mandate Is," the Norfolk *Virginian-Pilot* editorially commented that G.O.P. plans for an upset had been shattered by Godwin's "garnering a landslide majority" of

[48] *Ibid.,* Oct. 30, 1965; personal interview with Griffin, July 16, 1966, Farmville, Va.   [49] *Journal and Guide,* Nov. 6, 1965.

[50] *Times-Dispatch,* Oct. 27, 1965.

[51] Washington *Post,* Jan. 14, 1966. The State Board of Elections estimated that between 150,000 and 200,000 Negroes were registered to vote. Rupert Picott of the V.I.V.L. calculated that 61,000 voted. W. Lester Banks, of the N.A.A.C.P., though not offering a specific number, believed Picott's

the state's Negro votes.[52] Initial reports from urban Tidewater areas seemed to substantiate this. Richmond's ten largest Negro precincts, which had voted for the Republican gubernatorial candidate in 1961 by a 3,198 to 424 vote, reversed themselves and favored Godwin, 4,006 to 940. One of these precincts recorded a 250 to 45 vote favoring Godwin over Holton. In Portsmouth's predominantly Negro polling places estimates ranged as high as 83 per cent for Godwin, whereas four years before Negroes had voted Republican by similar lopsided margins and had voted as high as ten to one for Dalton in 1953.[53] In Petersburg the Godwin majority allegedly reached three-to-one and four-to-one proportions.[54] The Roanoke *Times,* while noting that the poll tax had reduced the size of the Negro vote as compared to the 1964 presidential contest, maintained that a majority of the Negroes supported Godwin.[55]

On the day following the election Dr. William S. Thornton, acting chairman of the Virginia Crusade for Voters, a firm proponent of the view that the Negro vote had held the balance of power for Godwin, announced that he and other Negro leaders hoped to confer with the Governor-elect in the near future. Thornton expected to submit requests to Godwin for his consideration, among which would be recommendations for better educational facilities, increased employment of Negroes on the state level, and the abolition of the poll tax as a voting prerequisite.[56]

Not all observers, however, were as willing to concede that the Negro vote had provided Godwin's margin of victory. The Governor-elect, at a news conference in Richmond on November 4, admitted that approximately 50,000 colored citizens had voted, and that apparently he drew heavily from them in Richmond, Nor-

---

figure was too low. Moses Riddick, basing his figure on returns from Richmond, Petersburg, Norfolk, Portsmouth, and the Eastern Shore, estimated upward to 100,000, of which 70 to 80 per cent voted for Godwin. Personal interviews with Picott, Banks, and Riddick, Nov. 4, 7, 1965; *Virginian-Pilot,* Nov. 5, 1965.

[52] Nov. 4, 1965.

[53] *News Leader* and *Virginian-Pilot,* Nov. 3, 1965.

[54] Petersburg *Progress-Index,* Nov. 3, 1965.

[55] Nov. 3, 1965.   [56] *News Leader,* Nov. 4, 1965.

folk, and Portsmouth. On the other hand, it seemed evident that the Negro vote in the Fourth, Fifth, and Sixth Districts went to Holton. A concurring opinion, voiced by an "astute and usually well-informed state Democratic leader," was that few more than 60 per cent or 65 per cent of the 50,000 Negroes who voted backed Godwin. Governor Harrison remarked that "these things have their balances and counter-balances," and while Godwin may have gained new support from Negroes or the A.F.L.–C.I.O., he lost that of many whites who ordinarily would have voted Democratic but instead cast their lot with Story. Because Godwin had given President Johnson a lukewarm endorsement in 1964, he became a victim by association of the sentiment in the Southside against the national administration, civil rights, voting rights programs, and other federal intrusions. Harrison insisted that Godwin had been misjudged as a liberal "New Dealer, Fair Dealer and Great Society man," when he was in truth a "realistic conservative." [57]

Evidence of losses to Story could be found in the results in the Third and Fourth Congressional Districts. Whereas Harrison had carried both in 1961 by comfortable margins of 15,797 and 22,444 respectively, Godwin's majorities were considerably less. In the Third he polled 31,645 to Holton's 22,844 and Story's 17,-937. This last was no mean total for a third-party candidate, especially in view of the fact that Southside politicians including Representatives Tuck and Abbitt had moved into the area to aid Godwin. In Chesterfield County, where the Ku Klux Klan had held voter rallies as late as November 1, the Conservative candidate won by 5,616 to 4,623 for Holton and 4,315 for Godwin. In the Fourth District Godwin's total was 22,510 to Holton's 7,873 and Story's strong 15,597. The latter carried ten of the district's nineteen counties.[58] In Danville, though Godwin polled 2,420 votes to Holton's 245 and Story's 1,647, it was the first time in decades that a Democrat had polled such a low total in victory.[59] And, according to the Conservative candidate for attorney general, John W. Carter, his party had just begun to fight. He foresaw a permanent realign-

[57] *Times-Dispatch,* Nov. 4–5, 1965.

[58] *Ibid.,* Nov. 4, 1965; *Virginian-Pilot,* Nov. 3, 1965.

[59] Danville *Register,* Nov. 3, 1965.

ment of parties, pitting the Conservatives against the combined liberal forces of the Democrats and Republicans. In its plans for the future, the Conservative party intended, first, to act as a watchdog on the General Assembly, drawing up periodic reports and ratings of legislators for its constituents. Carter warned that officeholders "who put their careers on the block to endorse Godwin are going to be held responsible for what Godwin does in Richmond. If he gets up there and plays footsies with Lyndon Johnson's playmates, a lot of his friends in Southside Virginia are going to bite the dust." Secondly, groundwork was already being laid for the running of candidates for the state legislature in 1967.[60] Perhaps the Danville *Register* best echoed Carter's sentiments with the comment that the lesson to be drawn from the 1965 election was that citizens in the "Southside of Virginia, and some other areas as well, will have little to do with a Democratic party led by the elements which [oppose] the conservative posture and action of the party that has led the government for 80 years." [61]

The problem among statewide candidates of pleasing an electorate with such divergent political viewpoints perplexed local candidates as well. White candidates had to consider the advisability of openly seeking the aid of the rapidly increasing number of Negro voters. Despite the fact that these votes might swing the balance of power, the majority of voters were still white. To press too strongly for the increasingly important Negro vote could very well lose a candidate conservative white support.

This dilemma was evident in two campaigns for the House of Delegates, one in the Fredericksburg area and the other in the Richmond section. In the first of these, the legislator represents the city of Fredericksburg and Spotsylvania and Stafford counties. On July 13, 1965, the incumbent, George C. Rawlings, considered a liberal and the antithesis of the "Byrd organization man," narrowly edged out fellow-attorney Kenneth T. Whitescarver in the Democratic primary, 3,408 to 3,128. Rawlings failed to carry five of the six precincts in Fredericksburg and lost his home city

[60] *Times-Dispatch,* Nov. 5, 1965.
[61] Nov. 3, 1965. See also editorial, "State of Flux," in Petersburg *Progress-Index,* Nov. 3, 1965.

by 51 votes but squeaked by in Spotsylvania by 171 votes and in Stafford by 160. His margin of 236 votes in Fredericksburg's Fourth Precinct, where the Negro registration is heaviest, saved him from defeat.[62] Rawlings had the backing of Citizens United for Action, a Negro voter group.

His opponent in the general election was H. Ryland Heflin, a Republican who had lost to Rawlings in 1963 and was running as an independent in this campaign. He criticized Rawling's first-term record as nonproductive and charged that the delegate had made "an unholy alliance" with northern Virginia, Norfolk, and the southwestern part of the state and had nothing in common with his own Sixty-first District people.[63] Some prognosticators predicted that the conservatives who had supported Whitescarver in July would not vote Democratic in November and instead would shift to Heflin. There were rumors of a whisper campaign depicting Rawlings as a "nigger lover" who had forsaken his white constituents. To counteract this charge, said some observers, the Citizens United for Action endorsed no candidate in the general election. The group mentioned only that it would attempt to get out a large vote, undoubtedly expecting that most of it would be for Rawlings. It was safer to keep the endorsement quiet to avoid arousing white conservatives.[64]

In a further development on Friday evening, October 29, at the final campaign dinner for Rawlings, the Democratic Representative for the Eighth Congressional District, Howard W. Smith, endorsed the Democratic ticket. To those in the know this move was intended to assure Democrats that Rawlings was not too liberal to receive the backing of even such arch-conservatives as Judge Smith. Some Negroes, however, characterized the endorsement as a concession to the enemy. Undeniably without their vote Rawlings would have lost the primary and they intended to back him solidly in November. But, according to one Negro political leader at the

[62] Fredericksburg *Free Lance-Star,* July 14, 1965; *Times-Dispatch,* Aug. 29, 31, 1965.

[63] *Times-Dispatch,* Oct. 31, 1965.

[64] Personal interviews with The Reverend Lawrence A. Davies, spokesman of Citizens United for Action, Nov. 9, 1965, and Dr. Philip W. Wyatt, President of the Fredericksburg N.A.A.C.P., Nov. 5, 1965.

dinner, other Negro backers who had originally intended to attend stayed away because of the presence of Smith.[65] Such was Rawlings' predicament. He needed both the Negro and the white vote to win, and like many white candidates throughout the state was walking the political tightrope.

On election day Rawlings won 4,339 to 4,018. Though he lost in Stafford, 1,762 to 1,425, he received comfortable margins in Fredericksburg and Spotsylvania, winning 1,557 to 1,203 and 1,357 to 953 respectively. In the city's heavily Negro-populated Fourth Precinct, Rawlings scored a 364 to 149 victory. Of a possible 500 registered Negroes, one observer estimated between 300 and 350 voted, almost wholly for the incumbent.[66] If so, it was the margin of victory.

In the Richmond contest most candidates sought the Negro vote, estimated at between 20,000 and 30,000, and to add to the campaign excitement, two prominent Negroes were among the candidates for the House of Delegates. The Democratic slate included surgeon Dr. William Ferguson Reid, while the G.O.P., hoping to regain the Negro votes lost in the 1964 presidential election, nominated insurance executive Clarence L. Townes, Jr. The campaign was a hectic one, beginning with the July primary in which Reid, with the backing of the Crusade for Voters and "several prominent white leaders," apparently ran ninth, losing by a hair's breath to incumbent T. Dix Sutton, 14,585 to 14,526. Reid posted fifth in Richmond, polling 12,041 votes, of which he estimated 6,000 were white. But in Henrico County, which had a small Negro population, he received only 2,485 votes.[67] Earlier, Negroes had objected to the General Assembly's combining the county with Richmond and having the new district's eight assemblymen elected at large. They interpreted this redistricting as an

[65] Personal interview with Reverend Mr. Davies and with Mrs. Mildred Brown Queen, Oct. 29, 1965, Fredericksburg, Va. Mrs. Queen, an undertaker, was a key precinct worker getting out the Negro vote.

[66] Fredericksburg *Free Lance-Star,* Nov. 3, 1965; personal interview with Reverend Mr. Davies, Nov. 9, 1965.

[67] Personal interview with Reid, Sept. 8, 1965, Richmond; *Times-Dispatch,* July 14, 1965. Another Negro, Colston A. Lewis, received 9,921 votes with negligible white support.

attempt to offset the growing Negro vote in Richmond by the white vote in Henrico.[68]

In the Negro community it was rumored that Reid failed to receive wholehearted Negro support because the Crusade for Voters had not sponsored racially moderate FitzGerald Bemiss for renomination to the state senate. When some Negroes heard of the slight, they did not vote for Crusade-backed Reid.[69] According to a leading Negro weekly, George A. Pennell, the former president of the Crusade, resigned shortly after the election because of the group's failure to endorse Bemiss. Pennell asserted, however, that his resignation resulted from his disagreement with the policy of withholding Crusade choices until election eve, which gave the group a "sinister and secretive" image. It was also believed that Reid lost white votes because Third District Chairman J. Clifford Miller, who sent out Democratic endorsement of candidates, deliberately omitted Reid when the Crusade slighted Bemiss.[70]

According to the *News Leader,* because of Reid's defeat "local Republicans are spitting in their hands and hungering for November." [71] For the first time since 1951 the Republicans were offering a full slate of candidates for state office. Unless the defeated Reid ran as an independent, most Negroes would vote for Townes and, hopefully, the remainder of the G.O.P. slate. Townes, the first Negro to hold a prominent state position in the Republican party since the 1890's, as special assistant to the chairman of the party in Virginia, vice chairman of the Third District Committee, and vice chairman of the Richmond Committee, appeared to be a promising votegetter. An advocate of a two-party system in the Commonwealth, he criticized the massive resistance Democrats such as Godwin who suddenly had turned liberal and attempted

[68] The reapportionment, though contested, was upheld by the United States Supreme Court on Oct. 25, 1965. *Times-Dispatch,* Oct. 26, 1965.

[69] *Ibid.,* July 14, 1965; personal interview with Roscoe C. Jackson, Sept. 8, 1965, Richmond.

[70] *Journal and Guide,* July 24, 1965. This was also the belief of Oliver Hill and Roscoe C. Jackson in personal interviews. Dr. Thornton, though, justified such secretive eleventh-hour selections, maintaining that earlier notice might tab a candidate as racial, allowing opponents to use this against him.

[71] Undated *News Leader* editorial in *Journal and Guide,* July 31, 1965.

to cash in on civil rights legislation initiated by Republicans during the Eisenhower administration.[72]

Because of the closeness of the primary results Reid petitioned the Richmond hustings court for a recount. During this tabulation an envelope supposed to have contained Skipwith Precinct's ballots from Henrico County (216 for Sutton and 82 for Reid), was found to hold only blank voter forms. As a result, by the ruling of a special three-judge court, Reid was declared the winner by 56 votes.[73] Embarrassed election officials insisted the wrong envelope had been discarded accidentally, but Dr. Milton A. Reid, regional director of S.C.L.C. in Petersburg representing Dr. Reid, charged pro-Sutton political chicanery. After a grand jury investigation, the Virginia Supreme Court of Appeals upheld the decision. It denied Sutton the right to have his name on the November ballot in favor of Dr. William Ferguson Reid, the first Negro ever to be nominated in a Democratic primary for the House of Delegates.[74] Though angry Sutton followers promised a write-in campaign in his behalf, it held little promise of success. The likelihood of Townes corralling most of the Negro voters for the G.O.P. appeared doubtful.

Adding to the interest of the campaign was a flare-up late in August between the Reid and Townes factions when the latter was accused of having worked for the defeat of Reid by urging Negroes not to vote in the July primary. Prior to the primary some Democrats charged that automobile bumper stickers issued by the Republicans advised, "Wait until November, Vote G.O.P." One witness, John T. Carstarphen, "a registered Democrat since 1931," accused Townes and others of actively working to discourage Negroes from voting while hundreds of other Negro Republicans were instructed to cast their votes against Reid. Townes firmly denied the allegations as "a sinister campaign to confuse, distort and split the colored vote by pitting Reid against me." Though he admitted the party had issued bumper stickers, they were only

[72] *Times-Dispatch,* July 14, 1965; Townes campaign literature and personal interview, Sept. 8, 1965, Richmond.

[73] *Times-Dispatch,* July 23, 1965.

[74] *Ibid.,* Sept. 3–23, 1965, *passim.*

to remind registered Republicans not to vote in the Democratic primary. Taking the offensive himself, Townes retaliated with an attack on Reid's campaign techniques. "He [Dr. Reid] tried to tie Goldwater around my neck while praising the likes of Godwin. . . . This is just drum-beating for white folks." [75] After the charge was answered by a countercharge the matter rested.

As election day neared, in the Negro sections of Richmond it was evident an active campaign was in progress. Stickers and placards distributed by the respective parties, advertising the Negro candidates as members of the ticket, were especially evident. (The campaign literature was by no means restricted to Negro areas, as the daily newspapers also presented Townes and Reid as party candidates.) In the waiting room of the office of Dr. William S. Thornton, acting president of the Crusade for Voters, campaign literature sponsored by his organization headlined "We Believe in a Two Party System" and urged Negroes to back both Townes and Reid. Though the *Journal and Guide* commented that such party-splitting strategy in order to back both Negroes might "lift as many eyebrows as it provokes 'amens,'" Dr. Thornton was confident that with 12,000 Negro and 8,000 white votes both men stood a chance of election.[76]

Late in the campaign, as was the Crusade for Voters' custom, the organization issued its endorsements backing the state Democratic ticket, Townes, Reid, and four other Democrats in the Richmond-Henrico race. The following day, October 31, Townes repudiated the endorsement. Hitherto he had known of its backing of Reid and himself, but with the Crusade backing four other Democrats, Republican Townes believed he had been endorsed "only because it would not be politically expedient to leave me off their ticket." [77]

On election day Reid ran well and seemed likely to place seventh or eighth until the late returns from predominantly white Henrico County began trickling in. He finally dropped from seventh to

[75] *Afro-American*, Sept. 4, 1965; personal interview with Townes, Sept. 8, 1965.

[76] *Journal and Guide*, Oct. 23, 1965; personal interview with Dr. Thornton, Oct. 28, 1965, Richmond.

[77] *Times-Dispatch*, Nov. 1, 1965.

tenth, polling 19,489, only 4,245 of which were from recently annexed Henrico. To the astonishment of those who had dismissed attempts by sympathizers of T. Dix Sutton for a write-in vote, he gained the eighth House seat with 20,615 votes. While Sutton garnered only 8,961 votes in Richmond, his total in Henrico of 11,554 spelled the difference.[78]

Townes, never really in the running, placed fifteenth with 13,-937 votes. The hope that he might carry the Negro votes into the G.O.P. was not realized. Two Republican incumbents, Louis S. Jenkins, Jr., and S. Strother Smith, Jr., who had the Crusade for Voters' support in 1963, were defeated. It was evident that the Negro voters, on the local as well as the state level, had shifted their allegiance to the Democratic party. Had they supported the G.O.P. once again, "several Republican candidates apparently would have won." [79]

Looking ahead to Negro influence on future elections, if the Conservative threat, with its approximately 75,000-vote total in the gubernatorial race, is long-lasting, the Democrats have two alternatives for the future: either to regain the Conservative following or strengthen its ties with the moderates and the Negroes. With the 1966 election for the United States Senate fast approaching, of necessity a decision has to be made soon. The Negro vote, estimated at over 100,000 in the 1964 presidential race and between 50,000 and 100,000 in the gubernatorial contest, appears to be here to stay. Judging from the extensive newspaper coverage allotted them during the preceding two years, Negroes have reached a point where their backing is actively sought. The elimination of the poll tax, as well as the ease with which citizens can register to vote as a result of the Civil Rights Act of 1965, will undoubtedly bring more Negroes to the polls in the future.

Furthermore, for the first time since Luther Porter Jackson established the Virginia Voters' League in the 1940's, Negroes are attempting to maintain a statewide political organization, the Virginia Independent Voters' League. Jackson's organization, though

[78] *News Leader*, Nov. 3, 1965.
[79] Observation by James J. Kilpatrick, election night, November 2, 1965, over radio station WRNL, Richmond; *Times-Dispatch*, Nov. 4, 1965.

it had encouraged Negroes to pay the capitation tax and to register, did not take a partisan stand on specific issues or candidates. According to Moses Riddick, executive secretary of the more recent Voters' League, one of its basic purposes is to act as a guide and educator for Negroes, informing them about which candidates and causes would best aid them. Admittedly, political action had been taken before by such groups as the N.A.A.C.P. and S.C.L.C., but their efforts were primarily on a volunteer basis or part-time efforts combined with other causes, such as equal job opportunity or integrated schools. The newly established V.I.V.L. intends to make its political efforts full-time, with one or more paid officials to act as coordinator for the state. Riddick surmises that previously a basic shortcoming among Virginia Negroes has been the lack of such a spokesman for the majority of the colored citizenry.[80] That the organization speaks for 200,000 Negroes, as it boasted in the 1965 election, may be questionable, but it is the closest move by Negroes thus far to statewide action and appears to be off to a strong beginning.

[80] Personal interview, Nov. 7, 1965, Suffolk, Va.; "Moses Riddick, He Has the Votes," *Virginian-Pilot,* Jan. 23, 1966.

XIV

Conclusion

AFTER being involved in Virginia politics for over forty years, Negroes were effectively removed as a political force by the provisions of the state constitution of 1902. A major argument for their political elimination was that with the Negro vote so easily purchasable corruption and fraud would continue in elections as long as they could vote. By removing "the cause" of dishonesty the two parties allegedly would return to honest issues rather than constantly watching whether the other was cheating in elections. Many Democrats and Republicans alike, therefore, expected Negro disfranchisement to open the way to the reestablishment of a two-party system in Virginia. Although the Negro had been all but excluded from political activity and even voting by 1900, it was deemed necessary to formalize his exclusion by law, namely, by framing the constitution of 1902.

The constitution's suffrage provisions to disfranchise Negroes were highly effective. Because of their ignorance of state election laws and their general lack of education, Negroes were unable to meet the first electoral requirement, passing the literacy test or "temporary understanding clause" which remained in effect until January 1, 1904. For those capable of passing a reasonable test, especially difficult questions were asked by local registrars. Thus, it was not surprising that of the 147,000 Negro males over 21 years old only 21,000 were registered in 1904. To complete the process of disfranchisement, an annual capitation tax was levied in 1904 as a prerequisite to voting. For the next fifty years voter participation by the Negro was so slight that in 1950 there were but 40,376 registered Negro voters in Virginia. Moreover, many of those eligible did not vote. A safe estimate of the total number of Negro voters would probably have amounted only to between 20,-000 and 30,000.

In an attempt to regain the suffrage, the Negroes from 1902 through 1908 waged an unsuccessful legal struggle in the courts against the disfranchisement provisions and the practices of state and local officials. Had the colored people of the Old Dominion been able to present a united front against the state, perhaps they might have succeeded; but the more militant faction, led by Negro attorney James Hayes and former Virginian John S. Wise, was in the minority. Realizing disfranchisement was an accomplished fact, Negro leaders such as editor John T. Mitchell, Jr., and lawyer Giles B. Jackson adopted the policy formulated by Booker T. Washington, that the race would first have to prove itself educationally and economically before attempting an active role politically.

Negroes who had been loyal supporters of the Republican party since the Civil War also found little aid or consolation from the Party of Emancipation, for it, too, steadily turned its back on them. Republican leaders who spoke for the party in Virginia, such as Colonel Campbell Slemp and his son C. Bascom, agreed that a cleansing of the ranks would be beneficial to all and would once more restore honest, two-party politics to the state. In an attempt to rid itself of the label "party of the Negro," for the next twenty years the G.O.P. excluded Negroes so effectively from its state and local conventions and from its patronage lists that it became a white man's or lily-white party. Negro voters, nevertheless, clung to a party that disowned them.

Though eliminated as an active participant in Virginia politics, the Negro "participated" indirectly throughout this period. The race issue remained, as it had in the last half of the nineteenth century. White candidates, especially Democratic ones, could raise the race issue against any prospective officeholder believed harboring friendship for Negroes or wishing to return them to active participation in Virginia politics and thereby endanger the election of the suspected "nigger lover." Notable examples of this occurred in the Richmond mayoralty contest of 1936, the gubernatorial elections of 1905, 1921, and 1957, and in the presidential election of 1928.

The political status of the Negro changed little during the 1917–20 period, even though in World War I he loyally supported the war effort both as soldier and civilian, with hopes for a better life in the future. At war's end, despite a brief political revival, the Negroes' situation quickly reverted to that of prewar days. Nevertheless, on two occasions interest and activity were renewed. The passage of the women's suffrage amendment to the United States Constitution raised Negro hopes that it might act as an incentive to the race. The addition of women slightly increased the number of Negro voters, but it failed to improve the political bargaining power of the Negro.

The second example of political rejuvenation occurred during the 1921 gubernatorial campaign. In protest against twenty years of neglect and outright dismissal from the Republican ranks, some Negro Republicans, primarily from the Richmond area, ran an entire slate of race or lily-black candidates against that of the lily-white G.O.P. Never expecting to win, the lily blacks hoped to illustrate to white Republicans that they could not win either without Negro support. After this futile attempt, Negro political activity once again became minimal until 1928, when colored-white relationships in the Republican party were strained almost to the breaking point.

With Virginia Democrats in almost complete control in a one-party system, the Negroes could not become active participants in state or local politics. The only alternative remaining to them arose on the national level, mainly during presidential election years and within the Republican party. In 1928, however, a few Negroes for the first time deserted the Republicans and voted for the Democrat Al Smith. They charged that in an attempt to win the Southern vote, G.O.P. nominee Herbert Hoover had adopted the lily-white policy of the Republican party in most of the South.

The Great Depression, coupled with what the Negroes considered to be Hoover's lily-whitism, turned even more Virginia Negroes toward the Democratic candidate Franklin D. Roosevelt in 1932.

Even so, despite its dislike for Hoover, the Negro majority remained loyal to the party of emancipation.

Not until Roosevelt's second campaign, convinced by New Deal relief that F.D.R. had not relegated him to the position of "the forgotten man," did the Negro support wholeheartedly the Democratic incumbent. Thereafter Negroes did not turn away from that party's national candidate until the 1948 election, when, because of the feeling that Harry S. Truman was insincere in his civil rights program, a strong minority voted for Thomas E. Dewey.

In the crucial year 1928, attempts were also first made by Negroes to enter the Democratic party on the state and local level. Back in 1905 the Democratic party had ruled and the General Assembly subsequently backed the ruling by law that only white Democrats were eligible to vote in party primaries. In Virginia, where victory in the Democratic primary was tantamount to election, citizens who were restricted to voting in general elections could only second the party's earlier choices. In a court battle from 1928 through the mid-1930's, the Negroes finally succeeded in eliminating the white primary. Despite the victory, during the remainder of the 1930's and the war years which followed, participation by Negroes in the primaries and in general elections was so slight that total registration even in a peak year (1945) did not exceed 38,000. Of that number, it was estimated that less than 15,000 actually voted.

The Negro voter's own indifference and apathy were deterrents to his political participation. He had been relegated to the background so long that it was difficult for him to participate actively and he commonly regarded politics as "white folks' work."

For the Negro as well as the white another stumbling block to voting was the annual poll tax. But payment did not guarantee the Negro the right to register. During the 1920's and 1930's he faced a hostile or, at best, unfriendly local registrar who, by asking difficult questions or by unfair grading, justified his refusal to register colored applicants. It was not until the late 1930's that registrars, partially owing to court decisions against them, discontinued what had been ruled illegal questioning.

Despite these obstacles, many of which were self-imposed, a

nucleus of dedicated civic-minded Negroes attempted to awaken their race to its potential political strength. Agencies such as the N.A.A.C.P., the Virginia Voters' League, the Richmond Democratic Voters' League, and the Southern Regional Council labored throughout the 1930–50 period, though usually with only limited success.

In post-World War II days Negroes awakened to an active political role. Gradually voter registration rose, as did election participation. Further, after a dormant period dating back to the late nineteenth century, Negroes again ran for political office, particularly as candidates for city council. In 1948 these efforts were successful in one case when attorney Oliver W. Hill won in Richmond. A few candidates ran, though unsuccessfully, for seats in the General Assembly. As increasing numbers continued to register and vote, the State Democratic Committee also placed Negroes in minor positions in the party.

The anti-poll-tax movement of the 1940's was another attempted breakthrough. Particularly from 1946 through 1949, Negroes fought alongside anti-Byrd Democrats, Republicans, and members of labor unions for abolition by constitutional amendment. This struggle was unsuccessful and thereafter the issue remained virtually dormant until the Twenty-fourth Amendment to the federal Constitution in 1964 made the poll tax unconstitutional in federal elections. Two years later the United States Supreme Court ruled against the tax in state and local elections. Judging from the noticeable increase in registrants since the capitation tax has been abolished it is evident that it had been a significant deterrent.

During the 1950's Negroes continued to seek political office, but except for occasionally winning a few lesser positions such as justice of the peace or county supervisor they were defeated. The Negroes lacked individual and group leadership as well as the necessary financial support to campaign effectively. Moreover, they were forced to run as independents because neither of the major parties were willing to include them on their slates. Not until the 1960's, when it became evident that their vote could provide a balance of power, did Negro candidates become a part of previously all-white slates. In the meantime, the brunt of their support, not nearly enough to gain victory, came from members of their own race.

As so often in the past, the role of the Negro in Virginia politics during most of the 1950's was that of "issue" rather than "active participant." From the time of the *Brown* v. *Board of Education* decision in 1954 until Virginia's school-closing tactics were declared invalid by federal court decisions in 1959, the race issue was emphasized by the Democratic organization led by Harry F. Byrd, Sr., which pledged itself to retain segregated schools. The General Assembly passed laws to implement the "massive resistance" policy and also attempted through restrictive legislation such as the anti-N.A.A.C.P. acts to curb the integrationists. Opposition to mixed schools also proved instrumental in gaining victory for more than one office seeker. This influence was particularly evident in the victory by J. Lindsay Almond, Jr., in the 1957 gubernatorial election.

Not until massive resistance was legally broken did race relations become less strained and Negro citizens make another effort to advance in Virginia politics. What occurred thereafter was remarkable. The 1960's became the time of "the movement," when Negroes, after a half century of seeming indifference, overcame their lethargy and became active participants in state and national politics. The Twenty-fourth Amendment, federal court action, and congressional civil rights voting acts also proved valuable in lessening the remaining restrictions on voter registration and in swelling the number of Negro votes. Not only were Negroes successful in gaining positions on the city councils of Richmond and Petersburg in 1964, but their approximately 100,000 votes cast for President Lyndon S. Johnson in that year apparently provided the margin necessary for his victory in Virginia.

As a result of that impressive showing, both parties openly sought Negro votes in the 1965 gubernatorial race, and for the first time in this century it was done with little fear of being smeared "party of the Negro." Democratic candidate Mills E. Godwin, a leader of the "massive resistance" forces in the previous decade, reversed himself in 1965, campaigning on a platform of continued progress for all Virginia's citizens. His platform appeared to sway even reluctant Negroes into the Democratic camp, so much so that some observers claimed that the Negro support of between 50,000 to 100,000 votes won for Godwin.

As Virginia enters the second half of the 1960's, all indications point to a large Negro vote, some observers predicting it may exceed 200,000. If this occurs and Negroes attain power in future elections, there remains little doubt that both parties will more actively seek their vote. It may not be unreasonable to predict that their ballots will in part spell the beginning of the end of the organization in the Old Dominion. Moreover should the Negroes develop a partisan statewide political organization, their bloc of votes could be equally instrumental in gaining many rights and privileges hitherto denied them in the twentieth century.

Appendixes, Bibliography,
and Index

Appendix A

November 1902
Voter Registration

City registration	1900	1902
Richmond		
Colored	6,427	760
White	12,338	9,093 [a]
Bristol		
Colored	354	27
White	789	1,513 [b]
Petersburg		
Colored	2,400	620
White	4,600	2,040 [c]
Manchester		
Colored	650	67 [d]
White		
Waynesboro		
Colored	149	5
White	317	627 [e]

[a] Reduction was most severe in predominantly Negro-populated Jackson Ward, which registered 2,983 Negro in 1896 and 347 Negro in 1902. Richmond *Dispatch,* Oct. 2, 1902. This was at a time when population was 33,038 Negro and 60,201 white. *Ibid.,* July 6, Oct. 9, 1902; Petersburg *Daily Index-Appeal,* Oct. 8, 1902.

[b] Richmond *Times,* Sept. 28, 1902.

[c] *Ibid.*

[d] *The Nation,* LXXV (Dec. 25, 1902), 496, cited in Martin, *Negro Disfranchisement in Virginia.*

[e] As of Sept. 11, 1902, Richmond *Times.*

City registration (*cont.*)	1900	1902
Norfolk		
Colored	1,826	504
White	6,732	4,698 [f]
Winchester		
Colored	339	29
White		861 [g]
Culpeper		
Colored	1,075	153
White	2,153	1,463 [h]
Alexandria		
Colored	3,152	139–144
	votes cast in	
White	presidential election	1,674–1,677 [i]
Fredericksburg		
Colored	353	65
White	998	681 [j]
Windsor		
Colored	107	7
White	208	114 [k]

County registration	1900	1902
Accomac		
Colored	2,472	495
White	5,473	3,718 [l]
Amelia		
Colored	1,099	128
White	743	671 [m]

[f] *Ibid.,* Oct. 16, 1902; Norfolk *Virginian-Pilot,* Oct. 15, 1902.

[g] Richmond *Times,* Oct. 16, 1902; Petersburg *Daily Index-Appeal,* Oct. 17, 1902.

[h] Richmond *Times,* Oct. 21, 1902.

[i] *Ibid.,* Oct. 11, 1902; Alexandria *Gazette and Virginia Advertiser,* Oct. 11, 1902. The colored registration in 1902 was approximately 1/10 of its potential; the white registration was ½ of its potential.

[j] Fredericksburg *Daily Star,* Oct. 15, 1902.

[k] Richmond *Times,* Sept. 6, 1902.   [l] *Ibid.,* Oct. 23, 1902.

[m] *Ibid.,* Oct. 25, 1902.

County registration (*cont.*)	1900	1902
Appomattox		
Colored	753	41
White	1,313	1,152 [n]
Bath		
Colored	Approx. 150–290	22
White	Approx. 1,100	645 [o]
Brunswick		
Colored	1,876	212
White	1,422	1,644 [p]
Charlotte		
Colored	1,597	132
White	1,657	1,075 [q]
Chesterfield		
Colored	Approx. 1,000–1,700	198 [r]
White	2,860	
Elizabeth City		
Colored	Approx. 1,750	250
White	2,411	1,583 [s]
Frederick		
Colored	182	50
White		2,138 [t]
Gloucester		
Colored	1,480	215
White	1,524	984 [u]
Goochland		
Colored	1,218	285 [v]
White		

[n] *Ibid.*, Oct. 18, 1902.   [o] *Ibid.*
[p] *Ibid.*, Oct. 15, 1902.
[q] *Ibid.*, Nov. 2, 1902.
[r] Richmond *Dispatch*, Nov. 2, 1902.
[s] Richmond *Times*, Oct. 2, 1902.
[t] *Ibid.*, Oct. 6, 1902; Petersburg *Daily Index-Appeal*, Oct. 17, 1902. The 1902 white registration was approximately 80 per cent of the 1900 white registration.
[u] Richmond *Times*, Oct. 17, 1902.
[v] Richmond *Dispatch*, Nov. 2, 1902.

County registration (*cont.*)	1900	1902
King William		
Colored	970	232 [w]
White		
Loudoun		
Colored	1,248	220
White		2,491 [x]
Nansemond		
Colored	2,200	325
White	2,100	1,560 [y]
Prince Edward		
Colored	1,876	173
White	1,280	868 [z]

[w] *Ibid.*

[x] Richmond *Times,* Oct. 23, 1902. The 1902 white registration was approximately 60 per cent of the 1900 white registration.

[y] Norfolk *Virginian-Pilot,* Oct. 8, 1902; Petersburg *Daily Index-Appeal,* Oct. 9, 1902.

[z] Richmond *Dispatch,* Nov. 2, 1902.

Population and Voters
in Selected Counties in 1960

	Population		Registered voters	
	Negro	White	Negro	White
Counties with over 50% Negro population				
Amelia	3,995	3,806	638	1,983
Brunswick	10,428	7,348	765	3,764
Caroline	6,594	6,037	1,055	2,295
Charles City	4,415	917	674	558
Cumberland	3,450	2,910	No figures available	
Dinwiddie	13,678	8,499	879	3,618
Greensville	6,718	3,889	949	3,464
Isle of Wight	9,022	8,133	1,063	3,556
King and Queen	3,066	2,759	445	740
Mecklenburg	12,929	12,718	5,492	529
Nansemond	17,165	11,529	3,311	1,737
New Kent	2,314	2,126	862	432
Northampton	9,174	7,778	2,175	345
Southampton	11,766	8,165	4,645	875
Counties with approximately 25% to 49% Negro population				
Accomack	11,837	18,779	797	5,414
Buckingham	4,845	6,015	465	1,275
Charlotte	5,329	8,037	294	3,062
Essex	3,163	3,509	280	865
Fluvanna	2,722	4,502	127	872
Goochland	4,432	4,773	752	1,920
Halifax	14,812	18,702	477	4,730
James City	4,085	7,439	307	1,105

Counties with approximately 25% to 49% Negro population (*cont.*)

Lancaster	3,635	5,535	(1,800)*
Louisa	5,145	7,793	380	2,090
Lunenburg	5,286	7,233	460	2,495
Middlesex	2,612	3,700	266	1,260
Norfolk	8,092	15,370	1,385	7,337
Northumberland	4,343	5,840	722	2,553
Nottoway	5,011	6,466	515	3,310
Pittsylvania	19,944	38,339	531	8,261
Powhatan	2,674	5,383	505	1,470
Prince Edward	4,443	5,383	1,100	2,775
Richmond	2,213	4,159	270	1,215
Westmoreland	5,166	5,872	378	3,466

Source: *Census of the Population, 1960: Virginia* and *Estimated Number of Voters, April, 1960.*
* Race not specified.

Appendix C

Gains in Negro Voter Registration in Areas with Large Negro Populations, 1964

City	April 1964	October 1964
Alexandria	1,762	2,548
Charlottesville	1,336	2,181
Danville	2,876	3,246
Hampton	4,076	5,789
Hopewell	350	750
Lynchburg	2,162	3,446
Newport News	6,511	8,307
Norfolk	10,071	15,801
Petersburg	2,881	3,919
Virginia Beach	1,480	2,961
County		
Accomack	519	979
Albemarle	855	1,215
Alleghany	170	800
Amelia	734	888
Amherst	805	1,275
Arlington	1,263	2,525
Bedford	895	1,343
Buckingham	480	825
Campbell	876	1,132
Caroline	910	1,601
Charles City	793	943
Charlotte	532	808
Chesterfield	1,464	1,794
Culpeper	490	807

County (*cont.*)		
Dinwiddie	749	1,284
Fairfax	1,124	1,904
Fauquier	725	1,492
Gloucester	769	1,172
Greensville	1,078	1,890
Halifax	1,215	1,700
Hanover	1,017	1,639
Henrico	831	1,527
Henry	642	1,574
Isle of Wight	1,245	1,893
James City	375	960
King and Queen	425	513
Louisa	468	1,279
Mecklenburg	495	620
Nansemond	1,953	2,792
Nelson	607	704
Northampton	330	810
Northumberland	858	1,021
Nottoway	785	1,320
Powhatan	539	867
Prince Edward	725	1,112
Prince George	578	986
Richmond	210	353
Rockbridge	490	950
Southampton	1,245	2,045
Spotsylvania	430	632
Stafford	540	712
Surry	764	1,140
Sussex	1,020	1,354
Tazewell	482	768
York	789	1,623

Source: *Estimated Number of Voters, April, 1964 and Oct., 1964, State Board of Elections.*

Bibliography

I. *Manuscript Papers*

William A. Anderson Papers, Alderman Library, University of Virginia. Valuable material on the disfranchisement cases argued while Anderson was Attorney General from 1902 through 1910.

John W. Daniel Papers, Alderman Library, University of Virginia. Pertinent because of an investigation into the constitutionality of disfranchisement in other states which Daniel made before Virginia adopted disfranchisement.

Henry D. Flood Papers, Manuscripts Division, Library of Congress, Washington, D.C. Primarily routine congressional business, but letters by Flood to political workers in Virginia important for attitude of Democratic leadership toward the Negro during the 1904–21 period.

Luther Porter Jackson Papers, Johnston Memorial Library, Virginia State College. An extensive and rich collection hitherto untapped containing Jackson's personal and political correspondence, records of the Virginia Voters' League, and poll tax records from 1939 through 1950, as well as other materials pertaining to his nonpolitical work, among which is his extensive correspondence with Negro historian Carter G. Woodson. Should be consulted for any work on the Virginia Negro in the 1940's.

Booker T. Washington Papers, Manuscripts Division, Library of Congress, Washington, D.C. Used mainly for Washington's attitude toward the Negro in politics during the years from 1900 through 1910.

John S. Wise Papers, at home of grandson John S. Wise, Farmington, Va. Gives new information about the disfranchising cases during the early 1900's. Valuable speeches and letters of Wise which reveal how the attitude of Republicans rapidly shifted toward a "lily-white" position during those years.

Of limited value were the papers of Carter Glass, Duncan Lawrence Groner, George Jefferson Hundley, Claude A. Swanson, and Thomas Staples Martin, all available in the Alderman Library, University of Virginia, and those of Roscoe E. Lewis in the Hampton Institute Library.

II. *Unpublished Theses, Dissertations, and Special Studies*

Allen, James E., "The Negro in the 1940 Presidential Election," M.A. thesis, Howard University, 1955.

Blackburn, Helen M., "The Populist Party in the South," M.A. thesis, Howard University, 1941.

Brewer, James H., "The Futile Trumpet: The Wars of the Richmond *Planet* against Disfranchisement and Jim Crow, 1900–1904," MS, Virginia State College, 1959.

Bunche, Ralph, "The Political Status of the Negro," MS, Library of Congress, 1940, 7 vols.

Caldwell, Julia E., "The Presidential Election of 1928 in Virginia," M.A. thesis, Howard University, 1953.

Cheek, William Francis, III, "The Forgotten Prophet: The Life of John Mercer Langston," Ph.D. dissertation, University of Virginia, 1961.

Crawford, George Washington, "John Mercer Langston: A Study in Virginia Politics, 1880–1890," M.A. thesis, Virginia State College, 1940.

Doss, Richard Burke, "John Warwick Daniel: A Study in the Virginia Democracy," Ph.D. dissertation, University of Virginia, 1955.

Eckenrode, Hamilton James, "A History of Virginia Since 1865: A Political History," MS, University of Virginia, undated.

Edwards, Rondle E., "A Study of the Virginia Constitutional Convention as Seen Through the Richmond *Times*," M.A. thesis, Virginia State College, 1960.

Ferguson, Henry S., "The Participation of the Lynchburg, Virginia Negro in Politics, 1865–1900," M.A. thesis, Virginia State College, 1955.

Ferrell, Henry Clifton, Jr., "Claude A. Swanson of Virginia," Ph.D. dissertation, University of Virginia, 1964.

Hall, Alvin L., "Virginia Back in the Fold: The Gubernatorial

Campaign and Election of 1929," MS term paper for Edward Younger, University of Virginia, March 4, 1963.

Hathorn, Guy, "The Political Life of C. Bascom Slemp," Ph.D. dissertation, Duke University, 1953.

Higgenbotham, Charmion Woody, "The Danville Riot of 1883," M.A. thesis, Virginia State College, 1955.

Horn, Herman Lionel, "The Growth and Development of the Democratic Party in Virginia Since 1890," Ph.D. dissertation, Duke University, 1949.

Johnston, James Hugo, Jr., "A History of Virginia State College," MS, Virginia State College, June 1963.

Jones, Robert R., "James Lawson Kemper, 1823–1895," Ph.D. dissertation, University of Virginia, 1964.

Kirby, Jack, "Governor Westmoreland Davis and the Molding of Twentieth Century Virginia," M.A. thesis, University of Virginia, 1964.

Larsen, William Edward, "Andrew Jackson Montague," Ph.D. dissertation, University of Virginia, 1961, 2 vols.

Lewis, John Latané III, "The Election in 1896 of William Jennings Bryan in Virginia," MS term paper for Edward Younger, University of Virginia, January 1959.

Mabry, William A., "The Disfranchisement of the Negro in the South," Ph.D. dissertation, Duke University, 1933.

McFarland, George, "Growth of Political Democracy in Virginia, 1865–1900," Ph.D. dissertation, Princeton, N.J., 1935.

Melzer, John T. S., "The Danville Riot, November 3, 1883," M.A. thesis, University of Virginia, 1963.

Moore, Lois Grier, "William Alexander Anderson: Attorney General of Virginia, 1902–1910," M.A. thesis, University of Virginia, 1959.

Quenzel, Carrol H., "Is History Repeating Itself in Virginia?" MS, Mary Washington College, 1964.

Steamer, Robert Julius, "The Supreme Court and Negro Suffrage," M.A. thesis, University of Virginia, 1951.

Weathers, Victor Duvall, "The Political Life of Allen Caperton Braxton," M.A. thesis, University of Virginia, 1956.

Wheatley, Harold Gordon, "The Political Career of William Atkinson Jones," M.A. thesis, University of Virginia, 1953.

Willis, Stanley, "The Gubernatorial Campaign and Election, Virginia, 1921," MS term paper for Edward Younger, University of Virginia, March 4, 1963.

III. *Official Documents and Books*

Acts and Joint Resolutions Passed by the General Assembly of Virginia, Richmond, 1902–63, *passim.*

Annual Report of the Attorney General to the Governor of Virginia, 1905, 1907, 1912, 1930–31.

Annual Report of the Secretary of the Commonwealth to the Governor and General Assembly of Virginia, 1908, 1921.

Cases Decided in the Supreme Court of Appeals in Virginia: September and November Terms, 1931 and January Term, 1932.

Census of the United States, 1900–60.

Code of Virginia, 1924, 1928, 1954, 1964 Supplements and 1960 Replacement Volume.

House Journal and Document, Commonwealth of Virginia, 1904–62.

Report of the Comptroller to the Governor of Virginia, Fiscal Year ending June 30, 1954.

Report of the Estimated Number of Voters in Virginia, State Board of Elections, 1938–64.

Report of the Subcommittee for a Study of Constitutional Provisions Concerning Voting Status in Virginia, 1941 (Gooch Committee).

Report of the United States Civil Rights Commission on Civil Rights, 1959 and 1961.

School Life, Journal of the . . . Office of Education. Washington, 1963.

Statement of the Vote Cast in the Commonwealth of Virginia for President of the United States and Members of Congress, 1924–64.

Statement of the Vote for Governor, Lieutenant Governor and Attorney General, General Elections and Primaries, 1929–61, *passim.*

Statement of the Vote for Members of Congress and Senator, General Elections and Primaries, 1934–62.

Statement of the Whole Number of Votes Cast for and against Certain Proposed Amendments to the Constitution of Virginia, Nov. 8, 1949; Jan. 9, 1956; Nov. 6, 1962.

United States Commission on Civil Rights: The Voting Rights Act of 1965.

IV. *Reports and Documents of Various Organizations*

Annual Report of the National Association for the Advancement of Colored People for the Years 1917 and 1918. New York, 1919.

Annual Report of the Virginia Voters' League, The Voting Status of the Negro. Petersburg, Va., 1941–50.

Handbook for the Virginia Student Civil Rights Committee: Project in Virginia's Black Belt. Blackstone, Va., 1965.

NAACP, Virginia State Conferences of Branches: Twenty-fifth Anniversary Series, 1935–1960. Richmond, Va., 1960.

NAACP Annual Report for 1959. New York, July 1959.

A New Birth of Freedom: NAACP Report for 1964. New York, July 1965.

Official Report of the Proceedings of the Fourteenth Republican National Convention. Columbus, Ohio, 1908.

"The Republican Party in Virginia Platform, Adopted in the State Convention held in Norfolk, Virginia, June 14, 1921," *Rare Virginia Pamphlets.* Richmond, 1921.

Virginia State Conference of Branches, National Association for the Advancement of Colored People Program. Roanoke, Va., October 29–31, 1965.

Voter Registration in Virginia, Report to Atlanta: Southern Christian Leadership Conference. Petersburg, Va., 1965.

V. *Scrapbooks*

Hampton Institute Political Scrapbooks, Collis P. Huntington Library, Hampton Institute. Thirty scrapbooks containing newspaper clippings pertinent to Negroes politically in the state and the nation. Those used for this work were "Negro Women, Negro Suffrage," and "President Harding and the Negro, December, 1921–1923."

John H. Mitchell, Jr., Scrapbook, Collis P. Huntington Library, Hampton Institute. A small collection of newspaper items, but through out-of-state newspapers, one gains insight into Mitchell's shift from active participant in Virginia politics to that of acceptance of disfranchisement after the 1902 constitution went into effect.

C. Bascom Slemp Scrapbooks, Southwestern Museum, Big Stone Gap, Virginia. Apparently the Slemp Papers have either been lost or loaned to a researcher and not returned, but the political scrapbooks dating from 1900 through 1928 offer a good coverage of the political life of Virginia's leading Republican.

VI. *Personal Interviews*

Victor H. Ashe, Norfolk attorney; W. Lester Banks, executive secretary of the Virginia Branch of the N.A.A.C.P.; Floyd E. Carter, member of

Charles City County Board of Supervisors; B. A. Cephas, Jr., Richmond city councilman; Dr. B. A. Coles, Charlottesville dentist; Herbert V. Coulton, voter registration director, SCLC, Petersburg; Reverend Lawrence A. Davies, Fredericksburg city councilman; Levin Nock Davis, secretary of the State Board of Elections; The Reverend L. Francis Griffin of Farmville, state president of the N.A.A.C.P.; Attorney Oliver W. Hill; former Richmond city councilman; Mrs. Luther Porter Jackson; Roscoe C. Jackson, former president of the Richmond Democratic Voters' League; James Hugo Johnston, Jr., former dean of Virginia State College; James Latimer, Richmond *Times-Dispatch* newspaper correspondent; David E. Longley, former member of Richmond Republican Committee; Professor C. G. Gordon Moss, Longwood College; Benjamin Muse, author; John H. Owen, Petersburg city councilman; J. Rupert Picott, President of Virginia Teachers' Association and Virginia Independent Voters' League; Mrs. Mildred Brown Queen, undertaker and precinct worker, Fredericksburg; Dr. William Ferguson Reid, Richmond surgeon and unsuccessful House of Delegates candidate, 1965; Moses Riddick, Jr., president of Suffolk and Nansemond County Independent Voters' League and executive secretary of Virginia Independent Voters' League; Dr. William S. Thornton, director of the Richmond Crusade for Voters and Virginia Crusade for Voters; Dr. J. M. Tinsley, former president of the State Conference of the N.A.A.C.P.; Clarence L. Townes, Jr., special assistant to the Republican State Chairman; Dr. Philip W. Wyatt, former president of the State Branches of the N.A.A.C.P.

VII.   *Correspondence to Author from:*

Theodore R. Dalton, Federal District judge, Roanoke, Va., Aug. 31, Sept. 9, 1965; Mrs. Maurice N. Derbigny, Hampton, Va., June 24, 1964; Mrs. Lottie E. Driver, librarian at Newport News Public Library, June 5, 1964; James Latimer, Richmond *Times-Dispatch* newspaper correspondent, Sept. 20, 1965; Professor Allen W. Moger, Department of History, Washington and Lee University, Lexington, Va., Aug. 17, 1964; Horace Scott, secretary of the Independent Order of St. Luke, Richmond, June 22, 1964; Thomas W. Young, publisher of the Norfolk *Journal and Guide,* June 3, 1964.

VIII.   *Newspapers* (Unless otherwise noted, all are Virginia newspapers.)

Alexandria *Gazette and Virginia Advertiser,* 1902–5.
Big Stone Gap *Post,* 1901–5. Presented political news from Republican

Ninth District viewpoint, the hometown organ of Campbell and C. Bascom Slemp.

Bristol *Herald-Courier,* 1902–28.

Brooklyn, N.Y., *Eagle,* 1903–5.

Charlottesville *Daily Progress,* 1902–6, 1918–21, 1946.

Danville *Register,* 1905–65.

Emporia *Independent-Messenger,* 1956–64.

Farmville *Herald,* 1902–6, 1956–65.

Fredericksburg *Daily Star,* 1902–10.

Fredericksburg *Free Lance-Star,* 1910–66.

Lynchburg *News,* 1902–64. Owned in 1902 by Carter Glass, one of the leaders in the disfranchisement movement, and the subsequent support of white supremacy.

Newport News *Daily Press,* undated clippings.

New York *News,* 1904–22.

New York *Times,* 1902–50.

Norfolk *Journal and Guide,* 1916–65. The major Negro weekly in Virginia, reliable and respected. One of the most valuable sources for this work.

Norfolk *Virginian-Pilot,* 1902–66. Like most Virginia newspapers during the early 1900's, this paper favored disfranchisement of the Negro. Beginning in the 1920's, however, along with the Richmond *Times-Dispatch* and *News Leader,* the *Virginian-Pilot* worked for Negro political rights.

Petersburg *Daily Index-Appeal,* 1902–20. One of the few newspapers in the state which devoted a regular column specifically to Negro news.

Petersburg *Progress-Index,* 1920–65.

Richmond *Afro-American,* 1938–65. Superseded *Planet;* reasonably objective, but inferior in the quality of reporting and writing to the *Journal and Guide.*

Richmond *Evening Journal,* 1900–1905.

Richmond *Dispatch,* 1900–1902. A major advocate of disfranchisement, along with the *Times* it provided the best coverage of the 1900–1902 political picture in the Old Dominion.

Richmond *News,* 1900–1904.

Richmond *News Leader,* 1905–65. See note on Norfolk *Virginian-Pilot.*

Richmond *Planet,* 1898–1938. Held lead among Negro weeklies until coming of *Journal and Guide* in 1916. News tended to be biased.

Richmond *Times,* 1900–1902. See note on Richmond *Dispatch.*

Richmond *Times-Dispatch,* 1902–66. See note on Norfolk *Virginian-Pilot.*

Roanoke *Times,* 1900–1965.

Staunton *Old Dominion Sun,* 1902–6.

Tazewell *Republican,* 1900–1910. Owned and edited by William C. Pendleton, it became one of the severest critics of the Democrats, especially during the early disfranchisement period.

Washington, D.C., *Colored American,* 1896–1905. A Negro weekly, it stressed the economic and educational needs and goals of the race rather than the politics of the period.

Washington, D.C., *Post,* 1900–1966.

IX. *Books*

Ader, Emile B., *The Dixiecrat Movement.* Washington, D.C., 1955.

Bardolph, Randolph, *The Negro Vanguard.* New York, 1959.

Blake, Nelson M., *William Mahone of Virginia: Soldier and Political Insurgent.* Richmond, Va., 1935.

Boris, Joseph E., ed., *Who's Who in Colored America: A Biographical Dictionary of Notable Living Persons of African Descent in America.* New York, 1927.

Brenaman, Jacob Neff, *A History of Virginia Conventions.* Richmond, Va., 1902.

Cappon, Lester Jesse, *A Bibliography of Virginia History since 1865.* Charlottesville, Va., 1930.

Catt, Carrie Chapman, comp., *Woman Suffrage by Federal Constitutional Amendment.* New York, 1917.

Chalmers, David M., *Hooded Americanism: The First Century of the Ku Klux Klan.* New York, 1965.

Dabney, Virginius, *Below the Potomac.* New York, 1942.

——, *Dry Messiah: The Life of Bishop Cannon.* New York, 1949.

——, *Liberalism in the South.* Chapel Hill, N.C., 1932.

De Santis, Vincent P., *Republicans Face the Southern Question—The Departure Years, 1877–1897.* Baltimore, 1959.

Essary, J. F., ed., *Selected Addresses of C. Bascom Slemp.* Washington, D.C., 1938.

Fishwick, Marshall W., *Virginia, A New Look at the Old Dominion.* New York, 1959.

Fleming, James G., and Christian E. Burkell, eds., *Who's Who in Colored America: An Illustrated Biographical Study of Notable Living Persons of African Descent in America.* New York, 1950.

Franklin, John Hope, *From Slavery to Freedom: A History of American Negroes*. New York, 1947.

Fry, Henry P., *The Modern Ku Klux Klan*. Boston, 1922.

Gates, Robbins L., *The Making of Massive Resistance: Virginia's Politics of Public School Desegregation, 1954–1956*. Chapel Hill, N.C., 1962.

Ginsberg, Eli, and Alfred E. Eichner, *The Troublesome Presence: American Democracy and the Negro*. New York, 1964.

Hampton Institute, *Classified Catalog in the Collis Huntington Library, Compiled by the Workers of the Works Projects Administration*. Hampton, Va., 1940.

Hancock, Elizabeth H., ed., *Autobiography of James E. Massey*. New York, 1909.

Heard, Alexander, *A Two Party South?* Chapel Hill, N.C., 1952.

——, and Donald S. Strong, *Southern Primaries and Elections: 1920–1949*. University, Ala., 1950.

Hirshson, Stanley P., *Farewell to the Bloody Shirt: Northern Republicans and the Southern Negro, 1877–1893*. Bloomington, Ind., 1962.

Jackson, Giles B., and D. Webster Davis, *The Industrial History of the Negro Race in the United States*. Richmond, 1908.

Jackson, Luther Porter, *Negro Officeholders in Virginia, 1865–1895*. Norfolk, Va., 1945.

Key, V. O., *Southern Politics in State and Nation*. New York, 1949.

Ladd, Everett C., Jr., *Negro Political Leadership in the South*. Ithaca, N.Y., 1966.

Larsen, William, *Montague of Virginia: The Making of a Southern Progressive*. Baton Rouge, La., 1965.

Lee, Ulysses, *The Employment of Negro Troops: United States Army in World War II*. Washington, D.C., 1966.

Leuchtenburg, William E., *Franklin D. Roosevelt and the New Deal, 1932–1940*. (*The New American Nation Series,* ed. by Henry Steele Commager and Richard B. Morris.) New York, 1963.

Lewinson, Paul, comp., *A Guide to Documents in the National Archives: For Negro Studies*. (Publication Number One of the Committee on Negro Studies.) Washington, D.C., 1947.

——, *Race, Class, and Party; A History of Negro Suffrage and White Politics in the South*. New York, 1932.

Lewis, Roscoe E., supervisor, *The Negro in Virginia: Compiled by the Workers of the Writer's Progress of the Works Projects Administration in the State of Virginia*. New York, 1940.

Link, Arthur S., *Wilson: The New Freedom*. Princeton, N.J., 1956.

——, *Woodrow Wilson and the Progressive Era: 1910–1917 (The New American Nation Series,* edited by Henry Steele Commager and Richard S. Morris.) New York, 1954.

Lipson, Leslie, *The American Governor from Figurehead to Leader*. Chicago, 1939.

Logan, Rayford W., *The Betrayal of the Negro: From Rutherford B. Hayes to Woodrow Wilson*. New York, 1954, 1965.

——, *The Negro in the United States: A Brief History*. New York, 1957.

McDanel, Ralph Clipman, *The Virginia Constitutional Convention of 1901–1902. (Johns Hopkins University Series in Historical and Political Science Series.)* Baltimore, 1928.

Mangum, Charles Staples, *The Legal Status of the Negro*. Chapel Hill, N.C., 1940.

Manning, Joseph, *The Fadeout of Populism*. New York, 1940.

Martin, Robert S., *Negro Disfranchisement in Virginia. (Volume I of the Howard University Studies in the Social Sciences,* edited by Abram L. Harris.) Washington, D.C., 1938.

Matthews, Donald R., and James W. Prothro, *Negroes and the New Southern Politics*. New York, 1966.

Meier, August, *Negro Thought in America, 1880–1915*. Ann Arbor, Mich., 1963.

Moger, Allen Wesley, *The Rebuilding of the Old Dominion*. Ann Arbor, Mich., 1940.

Moon, Henry Lee, *Balance of Power: The Negro Vote*. New York, 1948.

Moos, Malcom, *The Republicans: A History of Their Party*. New York, 1956.

Morton, Richard L., *History of Virginia since 1861*. Chicago, 1924.

——, *The Negro in Virginia Politics, 1865–1902*. Charlottesville, Va., 1919.

Muse, Benjamin, *Ten Years of Prelude: The Story of Integration since the Supreme Court's 1954 Decision*. New York, 1964.

——, *Virginia's Massive Resistance*. Bloomington, Ind., 1961.

Myrdal, Gunnar, *An American Dilemma: The Negro Problem and Modern Democracy*. New York, 1944.

Newby, I. A., *Jim Crow's Defense: Anti-Negro Thought in America, 1900–1930*. Baton Rouge, La., 1965.

New York Public Library, *Dictionary Catalog of the Schomburg Collection of Negro Literature and History.* Boston, 1962, 9 vols.

Ogden, Frederick D., *The Poll Tax in the South.* University, Ala., 1958.

Pearson, Charles C., *The Readjuster Movement in Virginia.* New Haven and London, 1917.

Pendleton, William C., *A Political History of Appalachian Virginia, 1776–1927.* Dayton, Va., 1927.

Peters, William, *The Southern Temper.* New York, 1959.

Porter, Kirk, *National Party Platforms.* New York, 1924.

Price, Margaret, *The Negro Vote in the South.* Atlanta, 1957.

——, *The South and the Ballot.* Atlanta, 1959.

Pringle, Henry, *Life and Times of William Howard Taft.* New York, 1939, 2 vols.

——, *Theodore Roosevelt.* New York, 1950.

Pulliam, David L., *The Constitutional Conventions of Virginia from the Foundation of the Commonwealth to the Present Time.* Richmond, 1901.

Quarles, Benjamin, *The Negro in the Making of America.* New York, 1964.

Rice, Arnold S., *The Ku Klux Klan in American Politics.* Washington, D.C., 1962.

Rovere, Richard H., *Affairs of State: The Eisenhower Years.* New York, 1956.

Schlesinger, Arthur Meier, Jr., *A Thousand Days: John F. Kennedy in the White House.* Boston, 1965.

Scott, Emmet J., *Scott's Official History of the American Negro in the World War.* Washington, D.C., 1919.

Sheldon, William DuBose, *Populism in the Old Dominion: Virginia Farm Politics.* Princeton, N.J., 1935.

Smith, Bob, *They Closed Their Schools, Prince Edward County, 1951–1964.* Chapel Hill, N.C., 1965.

Sorenson, Theodore C., *Kennedy.* New York, 1965.

Spencer, Samuel R., *Booker T. Washington and the Negro's Place in American Life.* (*The Library of American Biography,* ed. by Oscar Handlin.) New York, 1955.

Spicer, George W., *The Supreme Court and Fundamental Freedoms.* New York, 1959.

Storey, Donald, *Urban Republicanism in the South.* University, Ala., 1960.

Tatum, Elbert Lee, *The Changed Political Thought of the Negro, 1915–1940*. New York, 1941.

Thorpe, Francis Newton, ed., *The Federal and State Constitution, Colonial Charters, and Other Organic Laws of the United States, Territories and Colonies Now and Heretofore Forming the United States of America*. Washington, D.C., 1906.

Van Deusen, John G., *The Black Man in White America*. New York, 1944.

The Warrock-Richardson Virginia and North Carolina Almanack. Richmond, Va., 1888–1920.

Wertenbaker, Thomas Jefferson, *Norfolk: Historical Southern Port*. Durham, N.C., 1931, 1962.

White, Theodore H., *The Making of the President, 1960*. New York, 1961.

——, *The Making of the President, 1964*. New York, 1965.

Wise, John S., *The Lion's Skin: A Historical Novel and a Novel History*. New York, 1905.

Woodson, Carter G., *The Negro in Our History*. Washington, D.C., 1922.

Woodward, C. Vann, *Origins of the New South, 1877–1913*. (Vol. IX of *A History of the South* Series, ed. by Wendell Holmes Stephenson and E. Merton Coulter.) Baton Rouge, La., 1951.

——, *The Strange Career of Jim Crow*. 2d ed., New York, 1966.

Work, Monroe N., comp., *A Bibliography of the Negro in Africa and America*. New York, 1928.

——, ed., *Negro Year Book: An Encyclopedia of the Negro*. Tuskegee, Ala., 1918–26.

The World Almanac and Book of Facts. New York, 1917–23, 1925, 1927–28, 1949.

Wynes, Charles E., *Race Relations in Virginia, 1870–1902*. Charlottesville, Va., 1961.

X. *Articles*

Andrews, Norman P., "The Negro in Politics," *Journal of Negro History*, V (Oct. 1920), 420–36.

Booker, Simeon, "What Republicans Must Do to Regain Negro Votes," *Ebony*, XVII (April 1962), 47–55.

Coulter, E. Morton, "The Attempt of William Howard Taft to Break the Solid South," *Georgia Quarterly Review*, XIX (June 1935), 134–44.

Current, Gloster B., "Why Nixon Lost the Negro Vote," *Crisis,* LXVIII (Jan. 1961), 5–14.

Dabney, Virginius, "What the GOP is Doing in the South," *Harper's Magazine,* CCXXVI (May 1963), 86–94.

Davis, Curtis Carroll, "Very Well-Rounded Republican: The Several Lives of John S. Wise," *Virginia Magazine of History and Biography,* LXXI (Oct. 1963), 461–81.

Eisenberg, Ralph, "The 1964 Presidential Election in Virginia: A Political Omen?" *University of Virginia News Letter,* XLI (April 15, 1965), 1–4.

Grantham, Dewey W., Jr., "The Progressive Movement and the Negro," *South Atlantic Quarterly* (Oct. 1955), 461–77.

Hathorn, Guy B., "The Congressional Campaign in the Fighting Ninth: The Contest between C. Bascom Slemp and Henry C. Stuart," *Virginia Magazine of History and Biography,* LXVI (July 1958), 337–44.

"Highlights of Virginia Suffrage History," *Southern Planter,* XC (Feb. 1938), 5.

Jackson, Luther P., "Race and Suffrage in the South since 1940," *New South,* III (June–July, 1948), 3, 25.

Johnston, J. H., Jr., "Luther Porter Jackson, 1892–1950," *Negro History Bulletin,* XIII (June 1950), 195–97.

Key, V. O., "The Future of Our Political Parties: The Democratic Party," *Virginia Quarterly Review,* XXVIII (Spring 1952), 161–75.

Link, Arthur S., ed., "Correspondence Relating to the Progressive Party's 'Lily White' Policy in 1912," *Journal of Southern History,* X (Nov. 1944), 480–90.

——, "The Negro as a Factor in the Campaign of 1912," *Journal of Negro History,* XXXII (Jan. 1947), 81–99.

McGill, Ralph, "The Angry South," *Atlantic Monthly,* CXCVII (April 1, 1956), 31–34.

McGuinn, Henry J., and Tinsley Lee Spraggins, "The Negro in Politics in Virginia," *Journal of Negro Education,* XXVI (Summer 1957), 378–89.

Matthews, Donald R. and James W. Prothro, "Political Factors and Negro Voter Registration in the South," *American Political Science Review,* LVII (June 1963), 355–67.

——, "Social and Economic Factors and Negro Vote Registration in the South," *American Political Science Review,* LVII (March 1963), 24–44.

Meier, August, "Toward a Reinterpretation of Booker T. Washington" *Journal of Southern History*, XXIII (May 1957), 220–27.

Moger, Allen W., "The Origin of the Democratic Machine in Virginia," *Journal of Southern History,* VIII (May 1942), 183–209.

Moon, Henry Lee, "How We Voted and Why?" *Crisis,* CXXII (Jan. 1965), 26–31.

——, "The Negro Break-away from the Democrats," *The New Republic,* CXXXV (Dec. 3, 1956), 17.

——, "The Negro Vote in the Presidential Election of 1956," *Journal of Negro Education,* XXVI (Summer 1957), 219–30.

Moore, John Hammond, "South Carolina's Reaction to the Photoplay, *The Birth of a Nation,*" *Proceedings of the South Carolina Historical Association* (1963), 30–40.

Mowry, George E., "The South and the Progressive Lily White Party in 1912," *Journal of Southern History,* VI (July 1940), 237–47.

Muse, Benjamin, "The Durability of Harry Flood Byrd," *Reporter,* XVII (Oct. 3, 1957), 26–30.

Nation, LXXV (Dec. 25, 1902), 496.

The New Virginia, The Virginia Student Civil Rights Committee News Letter, I, July 1965; III, Sept. 1965.

Noel, Edgar E., "John Lawson Kemper and the Virginia Gubernatorial Election of 1873," in University of Virginia, *Essays in History,* V (1958–59), 33–46.

"Official NAACP Position on the Presidential Election," *Crisis,* LXXI (Oct. 1964), 500–504.

"The Poll Tax, A Burden upon Education," *Southern Planter,* XCIX (Jan. 1938), 5.

Scheiner, Seth M., "President Theodore Roosevelt and the Negro, 1901–1908," *Journal of Negro History,* XLVII (July 1962), 169–82.

Schuyler, George S., "The Negro Voter Comes of Age," *American Mercury,* CXXXIV (May 1957), 102–3.

Sherman, Richard B., "The Harding Administration and the Negro: An Opportunity Lost," *Journal of Negro History,* XLIX (July 1964), 151–68.

Simpson, Josephus, "Are Colored People in Virginia in a Helpless Minority?" *Opportunity,* XII (Dec. 1934), 373–75.

——, "The Best Negroes in the World," *Opportunity,* IX (Sept. 1931), 283.

Smith, T. Lynn, "The Redistribution of the Negro Population in the

United States, 1910–1960," *Journal of Negro History,* LI (July 1966), 155–173.

"Southern Republican Elimination of the Negro," *World's Work,* IV (Oct. 1902), 2491.

Southern Workman, LXV (Dec. 1916), 702.

Taylor, Lloyd C., "Lila Meade Valentine: The FFV Reformer," *Virginia Magazine of History and Biography,* LXX (Oct. 1962), 471–87.

Thornbrough, Emma Lou, "The Brownsville Episode and the Negro Vote," *Mississippi Valley Historical Review,* XLIV (Dec. 1957), 469–83.

Van Deusen, John G., "The Negro in Politics," *Journal of Negro History,* XXI (July 1936), 256–74.

Watson, Richard L., "The Defeat of Judge Parker: A Study in Pressure Groups and Politics," *Mississippi Valley Historical Review,* L (Sept. 1963), 213–34.

Weber, Palmer, "The Negro Vote in the South," *Virginia Spectator,* C (Nov. 1939), 22.

Weeks, O. Douglas, "The White Primary," *Mississippi Law Journal,* VIII (Dec. 1935), 135–53.

"Why the Negro Should Support the Republican Party," *Crisis,* LXIII (Oct. 1956), 454–59.

Woodson, Carter G., "Fifty Years of Negro Citizenship as Qualified by the United States Supreme Court," *Journal of Negro History,* VI (Jan. 1921), 1–53.

Woodward, C. Vann, "From the First Reconstruction to the Second," *Harper's Magazine,* CCXXX (April 1965), 127–34.

Wynes, Charles, "Charles T. O'Ferrall and the Gubernatorial Election of 1893," *Virginia Magazine of History and Biography,* LXIV (Oct. 1956), 437–53.

Index

The Negro in Virginia Politics, 1902–1965

was composed, printed, and bound by
Kingsport Press, Inc., Kingsport, Tennessee.
The types are Perpetua and Times Roman,
and the paper is Warren's Olde Style.
Design is by Edward G. Foss.